ANNE BOLEYN'S FIRST LOVE

Henry Percy, sixth Earl of Northumberland, in a close-up from *The Register of the most noble Order of the Garter* (1724). (Courtesy of Newberry Library Staff, Chicago, LC:16004354)

ANNE BOLEYN'S FIRST LOVE

THE LIFE OF HENRY PERCY

JAN-MARIE KNIGHTS

AMBERLEY

First published 2026

Amberley Publishing
The Hill, Stroud
Gloucestershire, GL5 4EP

www.amberley-books.com

ISBN 978 1 3981 2796 8 (hardback)
ISBN 978 1 3981 2797 5 (ebook)

British Library Cataloguing in Publication Data.
A catalogue record for this book is available from the British Library.

1 2 3 4 5 6 7 8 9 10

Typesetting by SJmagic DESIGN SERVICES, India.
Printed in the UK.

Appointed GPSR EU Representative:
Easy Access System Europe Oü, 16879218
Address: Mustamäe tee 50, 10621, Tallinn, Estonia
Contact Details: gpsr.requests@easproject.com, +358 40 500 3575

CONTENTS

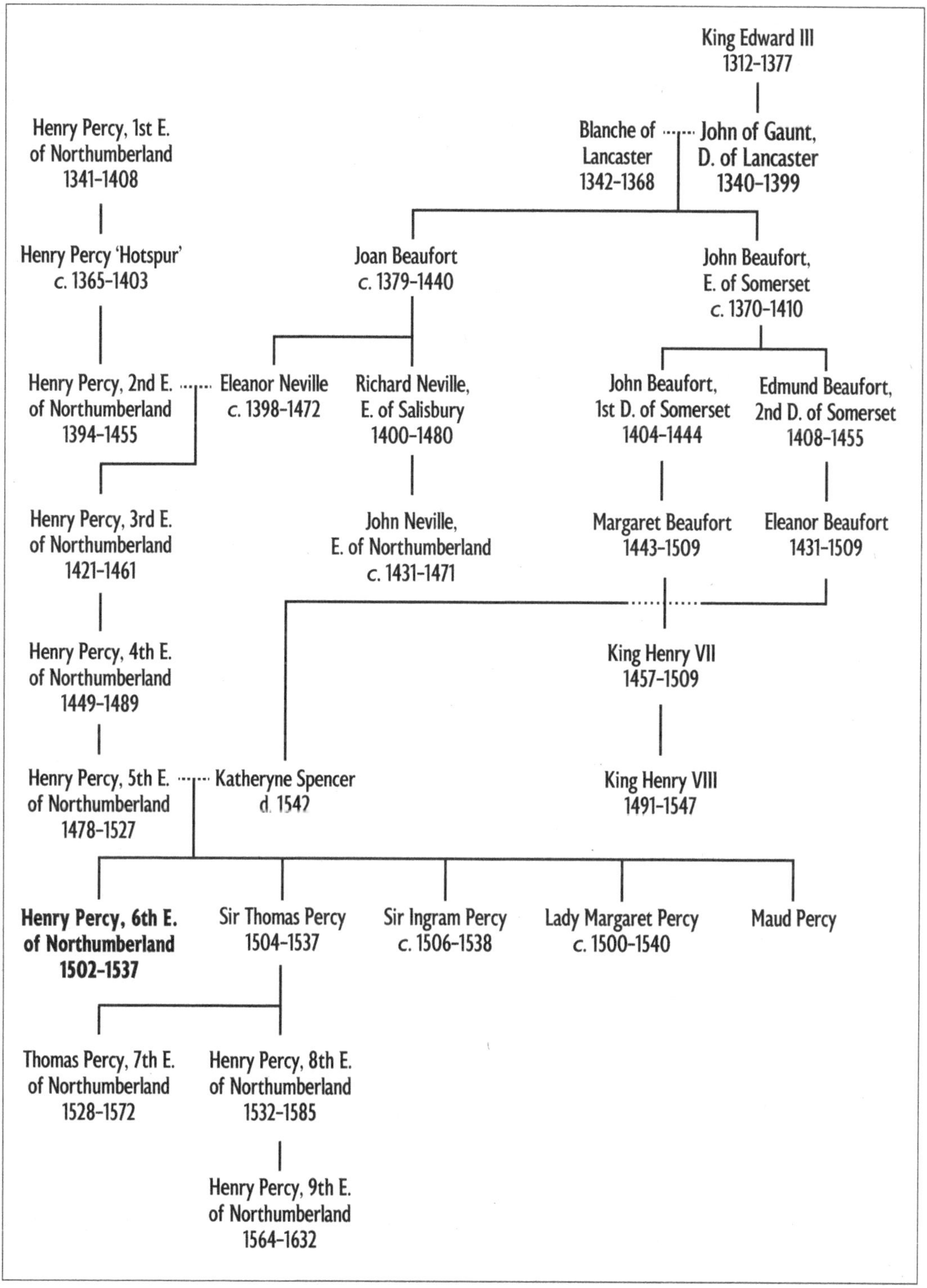

The ancestry of Henry Percy, 6th Earl of Northumberland.

INTRODUCTION

In Henry VIII's court, in the early 1520s, two young people fell in love, but their gentle dreams of marriage were cruelly torn apart by Cardinal Wolsey. Anne Boleyn was 'sent home to her father for a season; whereat she smoked'. Lord Henry Percy, son of the fifth Earl of Northumberland, for fear he might 'tangle and ensure thyself with a foolish girl yonder in the court', was threatened with disinheritance by his father. Mere knight's daughter or not, Anne went on to marry a king and became queen of England; Henry Percy to marry a woman who hated him and accused him of trying to murder her. When last their paths crossed, the woman he had never stopped loving was bravely defending herself while on trial for high treason.

This is a straightforward tale of one man's life, gleaned from contemporary chronicles, records and letters that show there was much more to Henry Percy than the intersection of a few pivotal moments with the woman he loved. Inheriting the title of Earl of Northumberland in 1527, and appointed Warden of the East and Middle Marches to keep order in the borders, he proved to be a strong leader and 'as ready as any man to leap on horseback' to defend England against the Scots. He had a strong sense of justice, was intensely loyal to Henry VIII and was resolute in upholding

Percy family tradition as immortalised in the poetic chronicle written for his father by his secretary, William Peeris. Henry Percy has been called unthrifty and profligate, but the grants of lands and offices he made may reveal another story, while his few surviving letters provide an opportunity to be personally drawn into his world.

BACKGROUND

THE RISE AND FALL OF THE PERCYS

Thirty-two-year-old William de Percy came across the Channel with William the Conqueror, as Peeris' family history tells us: 'Some say they were Normans of Charles blood of France, Came in With William Conqueror which did them advance'. The king was said to love William cordially 'for his merits and manhood' and granted him the hand of his grandniece, Emma de Porte, along with 118 manors in Yorkshire and Lincolnshire. William granted many tenures to his retainers. Purely for himself and his family he kept certain demesnes and built castles at Topcliffe, Leconfield and Spofforth. Topcliffe became the family's main residence, having a fairly substantial village, mill and church with two priests; Leconfield was a secondary residence, with a fishery providing 2,400 eels. All had several acres of meadow and woodland. Retaining Nafferton and Tadcaster netted him more mills and a fishery. Emma held land jointly with her husband worth £4 at Hambledon (given by her father) which, besides the usual villagers, Domesday records as having two slaves, a mill and woodland for four pigs. She also brought into the Percy landholdings Seamer manor, near Scarborough, for her dowry.

William rebuilt York Castle in 1070 and Whitby Abbey in 1077, appointing his brother Serlo as the abbey's prior. He then 'took the cross' and embarked on the First Crusade but in 1096, just in sight of Jerusalem, he died. He was buried in Antioch but his heart was brought back for burial at Whitby. Emma died four years later, aged about sixty-two, and was buried at Whitby.

The third Lord of Topcliffe was named after his grandfather by his father Alan, who lived quietly and died around 1135, aged sixty-eight, while on pilgrimage. William was the first Percy to fight on the borders, leading one of the four wards at the Battle of the Standard (so called for the four-wheeled cart upon which flapped the church banners of St Peter of York, St John of Beverley and St Wilfred of Ripon) when King David of Scotland invaded Northumberland in 1138, killing and pillaging indiscriminately. A shocked Richard of Hexham wrote that the Scots had 'massacred in the most barbarous manner children and kindred in sight of their relatives, masters in sight of their servants and servants in the sight of their masters, husbands before the eyes of their wives and carried off, like booty, noble matrons and chaste virgins and other women, naked, fettered, herded together and driven by whips and thongs, goaded with spears and other weapons by far to a greater extent than in other wars... when tired of abusing these poor wretches like unto animals, [they] made them slaves, or sold them for cattle to other barbarians'. On 22 August, the Scots rampage was blocked by English troops waiting for them in open fields 2 miles north of Northallerton. Fighting was ferocious; the Scots were decimated in three hours.

In 1149 William founded Sawley Abbey, although when he died in 1175 he was buried at Fountains Abbey. He was married to Adelize de FitzGilbert de Clare and they had two daughters, Matilda and Agnes. The latter married Josceline, the half-brother of Henry I's second wife, Adeliza, 'fair maiden of Brabant', who went on to marry William d'Albini, Earl of Arundel. She gifted her brother the Sussex estate of Petworth, which the Percys thereafter used as their southern home. Agnes bore Josceline seven children who took the surname of Percy. Their eldest son, Henry, was born around 1156. Peeris said of him, 'A noble man was he, gracious, good and fair.' Their youngest son, Richard, was born about 1170. After his father died, he was doted on by his childless and widowed aunt Matilda, Countess of Warwick.

In 1190 Henry married Isabel de Bruce of Skelton. They were married only nine years before he died and was buried in France. They had two sons: William, who was about five or six years old when his father died, and Henry, who was three years younger. Their uncle Richard seized their father's lands and title, and later rebelled against King John; named one of the baron overseers of Magna Carta, he was excommunicated by the Pope. When William was thirty-four years old he married twenty-one-year-old Ellen de Balliol on 1 July 1227. She was his second wife and gave birth to his son and heir, Henry, the following year. (In a generous spirit William, in 1231, granted his brother Henry the lease of the manor of Heyshott – part of the Petworth estate – for either a pair of gilt spurs or 12*d* every Easter.) In 1244, William regained his full inheritance on the death of his uncle but did not live long to enjoy it, for he died the following year and was buried at Sawley Abbey.

In September 1268, William and Ellen's son Henry married Eleanor de Warenne, daughter of John, Earl of Surrey and Alice de Lusignan, King Henry III's half-sister. (The earl was father-in-law of John Balliol, who was married to Ellen's sister Isabella.) Ellen died on 22 November 1281 having attained the great age of seventy-five years and was buried next to her husband at Sawley, having seen the birth of two grandsons and the death of her son, who died in 1272. Eleanor gave birth to her second son, Henry, on 25 March at Petworth, seven months after his father died. His older brother John died on an unknown date while in the custody of King Edward I, who had seized him to appropriate his scutage of knights' fees in order to fund his Welsh Wars.

Henry came into his Sussex and Yorkshire estates in 1293 and the following year married Alienora FitzAlan, daughter of Richard, Earl of Arundel. In 1296, John Balliol (King of Scotland since

1292) allied with King Philip IV of France to attack Edward I on two fronts. It proved to be a miscalculation for storms sank the French king's ships, leaving the English king free to deal with the Scots. Marching to Berwick, an important Scottish seaport, King Edward offered the defenders the chance to surrender. In reply they bared their buttocks at him. Astride his great warhorse, the king, 'angry like a boar pursued by wolves', ordered all, no matter the age or sex, to be put to the sword as his horse leapt effortlessly over ditches and palisades. Henry was knighted by the king that day. He can be glimpsed thereafter attending court and parliament, negotiating truces and fighting the Scots: 'a blue lion rampant on yellow was his banner ... very conspicuous'. During times of peace, Henry lived with his wife at Leconfield where a son, Henry, was born on 6 February 1301, followed two years later by William.

On 25 February 1308, their father was one of the shocked attendees at the joint coronation of Edward II and his wife, twelve-year-old Isabella, daughter of Philip IV. The king, in a spirit of devilment, entered Westminster Abbey attired in green robe and black hose (his royal robes being carried on a board) while his closest friend, Piers Gaveston, newly created Earl of Cornwall and carrying the crown, preceded him wearing royal purple silk trimmed with pearls. The Earls of Lancaster, Gloucester, Hereford, Surrey, Arundel, Warwick and Pembroke were distinctly unamused: upon confronting the king they directly told him their allegiance was to the crown, not to the person wearing it, and insisted he exile Cornwall. Edward II responded by appointing him Lord Lieutenant of Ireland, with the document witnessed by Henry Percy. Later in the year, Henry leased Wressle Castle and was given licence to crenelate his castles of Petworth, Spofforth and Leconfield. A year later, seeking a base near the Scottish borders, he purchased Alnwick Castle from Anthony Bek, Bishop of Durham for £4,666 (it had an annual income of around £475). To meet the asking price Henry borrowed £2,666 from Italian merchant bankers. Henceforth he was entitled Lord of Alnwick.

He rebuilt the keep, augmenting it with seven semi-circular towers, and added a great hall and kitchens on the east side of the court.

Cornwall proved an able administrator in Ireland and the earls allowed him to return in August 1309. He was restored to his lands and earldom. Over the next two summers, he and Henry Percy fought on campaign against Robert Bruce. Everything changed in September 1311, however, when the earls threatened to depose the king, peremptorily dismissed his servants and officers and forced Cornwall to sail to Brabant on pain of death, leaving behind his pregnant wife, Margaret. In January 1312 Edward invited him to return to visit his wife and newborn daughter. For a few months, the two friends lived quietly in York, joined by Queen Isabella, who fell pregnant while there. Rashly, on 3 April, Edward appointed Cornwall Justiciar of the North, replacing Henry Percy. An incensed Lancaster, threatening to kill Cornwall, marched towards York at the head of a large force. Cornwall and the king fled to Newcastle, leaving behind jewels and goods which took four days to catalogue.

On Ascension morning (4 May), Lancaster and Henry Percy approached Newcastle. Retreating to Tynemouth, Edward and Cornwall sailed for Scarborough Castle while Queen Isabella travelled overland to Darlington. Worried for the safety of his queen, the king rode to join her. Scarborough Castle was besieged by two forces, one led by Henry Percy and the other by Aymer, Earl of Pembroke. On 19 May, Cornwall surrendered to Pembroke, who took his prisoner southwards. Turning a blind eye, he allowed the Earl of Warwick to abduct him one night, and Warwick in turn handed the prisoner over to the Earls of Lancaster, Hereford, and Arundel. They took him to a place called Blakelow where they stabbed and beheaded him. Henry Percy, although arrested and imprisoned, was pardoned by the king in October 1313. The following summer Edward invaded Scotland and was defeated at Bannockburn but Henry Percy did not fight. He died at Alnwick Castle in early October, aged forty-one, and was buried at

Fountains Abbey. His wife survived him by thirteen years and was buried at Beverley Minster.

When he reached his majority Henry, second Lord of Alnwick, married Idonea, daughter of Robert Clifford. Their first child, another Henry, was born at Seamer Manor during 1321. Two years later, Edward II came to York, knighted Percy, and made him Warden of the Marches. In 1328, after his father had been deposed, Edward III granted Henry the castle and barony of Warkworth with 50 marks per annum for his support with 'men and arms all his life'. Two years later, Henry fought in the bloody and fierce Battle of Halidon Hill. Three Scottish brigades were decimated to one; a fourth was driven into the sea by King Edward, who bellowed, 'No quarter!', aping the Scots' own cry at the start of the battle.

The second lord's son Henry (nicknamed the Short) married Mary, daughter of Henry, Earl of Lancaster (and great-granddaughter of Henry III) at Tutbury Castle in September 1334 when they were both thirteen or fourteen years old. (Mary's brother Henry became Duke of Lancaster in 1351 and his daughter Blanche married John of Gaunt, son of Edward III, entwining the two families.) Henry and Mary had two sons: Henry, born on 11 November 1341, whom Peeris calls 'a lord of great might, born in Scarborough Castle, upon St Martin night', and Thomas, born in 1343.

In 1346 Henry the Short and his father were both fighting in wars: Henry junior fought at Crecy in France with the king; Henry senior confronted Scotland's King David II and his army of twelve thousand at a moorland place near Durham called Neville's Cross on 17 October. The English had with them longbowmen whose 6-foot yew bows could discharge yard-long arrows every five seconds in a descending black cloud of death. In the merciless hand-to-hand fighting which followed, many prominent Scotsmen were killed and the Scottish king was captured as he tried to flee. Two arrow wounds in his face were treated by a physician at Bamburgh Castle, but one arrow-tip could not be removed and he had painful headaches for the rest of his life.

Henry the elder died in February 1352 after a distinguished military career and was given an elaborate funeral at Alnwick Abbey. In his will he left his wife a psalter, two cups and a bowl; to his heir Henry the Short he bequeathed two enamelled basins (one having the Judgement of Solomon in its bottom and the other a Wheel of Fortune), two washbasins, two dozen salt pots, two silver goblets, a dozen spoons, six silver-gilt forks, a salt-cellar, all his suits of armour (excepting one for his son Roger, who also received £200, a sword of war, a ruby and a sapphire) and all 'the tapestries for the hall of the ancient arms of Percy', a sword of war and all his beds, tapestries and silver chapel ornaments in all his manors. To his son Thomas he bequeathed eighteen dishes and six saucers; to his daughter Margaret a bracelet and brooches, a ruby, two silver-gilt forks and an ivory table; to her sister Isabel he left dishes, a silver basin, a gold ring, a brooch, a pair of Paternoster beads and a book on the nature of animals in French. He left his brother William his horse, a crystal cup, a sword of war, a knife and three of the finest mares with foals at Leconfield, and to William's son (another Henry) he left 10 marks. He also left sums of money to his servants and officers and to various abbeys.

Henry the Short's son and heir was eighteen years old when he married twenty-year-old Margaret, daughter of Ralph, Lord Neville de Raby in 1358. In 1362 he took over his father's role as Warden of the Marches while his brother Thomas was gifted Wressle Castle for life in 1365 for the rent of one red rose a year by their father, who died on 18 May 1368 at the age of forty-six. His long Inquisition Post Mortem lists all Percy manors and parks in Yorkshire and Northumberland and shows they now owned a London inn with eight shops in Aldersgate.

Henry and Margaret Neville's first son, Henry, was born on 30 May 1364 (joined later in the nursery by three brothers and a sister). Margaret died in 1372, aged thirty-four. Three years later, Henry Percy and his friend John of Gaunt angered the Bishop of London in the affair of religious reformer John Wycliffe. Riled Londoners marched to Percy's Inn and broke into the house, tearing beds and hangings into pieces. Hearing the two were dining with the king's steward, they marched to John de Ipre's house. A breathless messenger rushed in shouting that the Londoners were nearly upon them: 'Up jumped the duke being then at his oysters and tumbling over a form, he scraped his shins and they both ran for their lives.' Reaching the river, they took a boat, not disembarking until it reached Kingston.

Ten-year-old Richard II, grandson of Edward III, was crowned on 16 July 1377. Attired in all white (even his buskins), he walked the short distance to Westminster Abbey under a canopy of purple silk carried on four silvered lances with silver bells. John of Gaunt, Duke of Lancaster bore the sword Curtana before him, held after Mass by his son (and the king's cousin) Henry Bolingbroke. After he made his coronation oath, the king's clothes were cut open so he could be anointed. He was crowned, invested with sword, ring, sceptre and orb and then lifted to his throne. Contrary to custom, Sir Simon Burley carried the king back to the palace, losing his shoe along the way. Before any banqueting began, King Richard created Henry Percy (entitled Lord of Petworth) Earl of Northumberland. Then, after tasting only a few dishes, the young lad retired.

The new earl's eldest son, Henry, eager to fight with his father, fought the Scots for the first time when he was twelve years old; they nicknamed him Hotspur, being always 'bloody with spurring, fiery red with speed'. Over the next four years father and son defended the borders (and later Hotspur took over his father's warden role). At the end of 1381 the earl married his second wife, Maud Lucy, daughter of Sir Thomas, Baron Cockermouth and widow of Sir Gilbert de Umfraville, who had died a year earlier. Peeris says of her, 'Second wife to this Henry, a noble famous man ... by this lady Lucy in their arms always, three luces silver beareth by Percys to this day.' The marriage eventually brought the castles of Prudhoe and Cockermouth into Percy possession.

In 1388 Archibald, Earl of Douglas invaded Northumberland via Redesdale, his foray 'visible enough from the smoke'.

Northumberland sent his sons Henry and Ralph to reconnoitre at Newcastle and remained at Alnwick to direct troops where they were needed to cut off any Scottish retreat. Henry and Ralph were spotted, and Douglas and Hotspur fought hand-to-hand. Unhorsing Hotspur, Douglas captured his pennon, shouting that he would fly it from Dalkeith Castle as he galloped away.

Spies then came to Hotspur to tell him the Scots had made camp at Otterburn. Hotspur marched his troops over 30 miles and, despite their tiredness, decided to attack immediately. The alarm call, 'Percy, Percy!' rang through the night from serving men lodged outside the main camp. As the English and Scots fought at close quarters, Douglas seized a battleaxe and, wielding it with both hands, 'gave such blows on all around him that no-one could withstand them ... and thus he advanced like another Hector' until he was struck down, speared in the shoulder, stomach and thigh, as was Sir Ralph Percy, who was severely wounded. He surrendered to Sir John Maxwell, telling him, 'I am so desperately wounded that my drawers and greaves are full of blood.' Sir John ordered his men to minister to Sir Ralph, whose wounds were staunched and bound, while Douglas died of his wounds on the field unnoticed. Henry was captured but released after his father paid a hefty ransom.

Hotspur married Elizabeth, daughter of Edmund Mortimer, Earl of March (and great-granddaughter of Edward III) and they had a son, Henry, born 3 February 1393; his sister Elizabeth was born two years later. Hotspur's uncle Thomas was created Earl of Worcester in 1397, having carved out a naval career, and his stepmother Maud died on 18 December 1398. When John of Gaunt died on 3 February 1399, many said it was from grief at Richard II exiling his son Henry Bolingbroke for ten years the previous year. In flagrant contravention of English law, Richard II then decreed an exile had no legal claim to his father's inheritance and seized his cousin Bolingbroke's lands.

At Whitsuntide, awaiting a fair wind to sail to Ireland, somebody whispered in the king's ear that Northumberland intended to be disloyal to him. When the pursuivant returned from delivering a royal summons for the immediate presence of the earl and his men, he gave the king a letter in which the earl stated the king had 'sufficient forces not to disfurnish the northern parts of their strength which would give the Scots opportunity to invade'. Richard took the letter as proof of incipient treason, and proclaimed the earl a traitor. In consternation, the earl and his family fled into Scotland.

While Richard II was in Ireland, Bolingbroke, now Duke of Lancaster, left France and landed at Ravenspur. Although he had declared he was merely travelling to his castle of Pontefract, by the time he reached Doncaster disaffected subjects had flocked to his banner, including Northumberland and Hotspur. Richard II was captured and taken to the Tower of London, where he was said to have abdicated in favour of his cousin. Henry IV's coronation took place on 13 October 1399. Northumberland carried one of the swords before the king and 'at the banquet, always standing around the king', at which were served three courses of delicacies including venison in frumenty, an 'enarmed' boar's head, pork jelly, eggs in jelly, cygnets, capons, pheasant, herons, sturgeons, stuffed piglets, curlews, pigeons, quails, snipes, coneys and various sauces and sweetmeats.

In the late summer of 1402 Henry IV set out to quell Owain Glyndwr's rebellion against the English but Welsh guerilla tactics, torrential rain and violent gales defeated his plans. In the north, Northumberland and Hotspur defeated an army of Scots at Homildon Hill, capturing many high-ranking prisoners for ransom, including Archibald, Earl of Douglas. While he was imprisoned at Warkworth Castle, he and Hotspur became friends. Against custom of ransom, a cash-strapped Henry IV insisted all Scottish prisoners should be brought to London. Hotspur brought all except Douglas. In the argument which ensued the king punched Hotspur who stormed out, saying, 'Not here, but in the field.'

The following summer, Hotspur accused the king of 'tyrannical government' and, with his sixty-year-old uncle Thomas, marched to reinforce Glyndwr who was fighting Prince Henry at Shrewsbury. The king, already on the march to aid his son, realised the new danger and sped to get there first. Hotspur, though heavily outnumbered, made a stand in a pea-field named Berwick. For three hours Henry IV, with two lookalikes, was in the thickest of the fierce battle while his son attacked the enemy flank, not stopping even when wounded in the face by an arrow. Suddenly a cry went up: 'Hotspur is dead!' His host of Scots and Welsh fled. Douglas, who had fought with Hotspur and lost an eye in the scrum, complained perplexedly, 'Have I not slain two King Henries with mine own hand?' The Earl of Worcester was immediately beheaded. After burial, Hotspur's body was exhumed in response to murmurs he was not dead. The king had it propped upright between two millstones before having it beheaded and quartered. His wife later gathered the pieces of the body and buried them in York Minster.

Having been too ill to mount a horse, Northumberland, despite not being at the battle, was imprisoned by the king. At the trial that followed, his peers declared him 'innocent of treason' and he returned to Warkworth. Embittered, he rebelled in May 1405 but fled into Scotland, taking with him Hotspur's wife and twelve-year-old son, after the king travelled north with the largest collection of siege engines ever seen. On 19 February 1408, still in a spirit of defiance, the sixty-seven-year-old earl was killed at Bramham Moor. The king had him decapitated to display his head on London Bridge. His body quarters were sent to Berwick, Newcastle, York and Lincoln, but were later interred at York Minster.

Petitioned by his aunt Joan Beaufort, Countess of Westmorland, upon his accession in 1413 King Henry V officially recognised Hotspur's son as second Earl of Northumberland. Returning to England, the earl married the countess's daughter Eleanor at Berwick. The couple gave a celebratory banquet for the king at Leconfield. There the future third earl was born on 25 July 1421 (followed by Thomas, Katherine, George, Ralph, Richard, William, Joan and Anne).

As Lord High Steward, Northumberland oversaw the coronation of Katherine Valois, the French king's daughter. He served with the king at Rouen and Melun but, like all Percys before him, his main role was to fight the Scots as Warden of the Marches. When Henry V suddenly died in 1422, Northumberland was appointed a member of the nine-month-old Henry VI's regency council and proved himself skilful in international and public affairs. Meanwhile, the dowager queen, only twenty-one at her husband's death, secretly married Owen Tudor, giving the king two prominent half-brothers in Edmund and Jasper. On the domestic front, the Percy family travelled to Beverley on Corpus Christi Day 1423 to see the plays, acted out on three-tiered wheeled stages. They had dinner and supper in the house of 'William Thyxhill, barber, at a cost of £4 4*d*' and enjoyed the event so much it became a yearly family tradition. Around this time, Northumberland was in conflict over land with the Archbishop of York which escalated regularly into violent skirmishes.

Aged fifteen, Lord Percy married fifteen-year-old Eleanor Poynings on 25 June 1435. In 1448, Henry VI gave him and his father licence to found a chantry within the chapel at Alnwick (a town recently enclosed and fortified by the earl), select a chaplain to instruct poor boys for free in grammar, and build a house for two chaplains to reside in and in which the scholars would be taught. The earl's only grandson, inevitably called Henry, was born in 1449, joining Anne, Margaret and later Eleanor and Elizabeth in the nursery.

In March 1454, news leaked out that Henry VI had been unable to move, feed or dress himself for nine months, his illness hidden by his wife Queen Margarete of Anjou with the aid of Edmund Beaufort, Duke of Somerset. Richard, Duke of York (descended in maternal and paternal lines from Edward III's second and fourth sons) insisted that, as heir apparent, he should be appointed Protector of the Realm. (Many, including Richard himself, believed he had a better claim to the throne, Henry VI being descended from Edward III's third son). Elevated into the role of Protector, York appointed as Chancellor his brother-in-law Richard Neville, Earl of Salisbury – Salisbury was also Northumberland's brother-in-law, and the two hated each other.

In January 1455 the king suddenly recovered his wits and found he was the father of a baby son, Edward. York, Salisbury and his son Richard, Earl of Warwick, in dispute with Somerset, feared their lives were now in peril, and they felt this was confirmed when the king summoned a great council at Leicester. They decided to intercept the king. On 22 May King Henry was travelling with the dukes of Buckingham and Somerset and also Northumberland when he was warned York was near with an army. He stopped at St Albans and 'pitched his banner at the place called Goslawe in St Peter's Street ... and commanded the ward and barriers to be kept in strong wise'. At first heralds moved back and forth in negotiations 'without any stroke smitten on either part', until the king said that those so bold as to raise people in his own land were traitors. Then York attacked between eleven and noon and 'broke into the town in three diverse places ... The Earl of Warwick ... ferociously broke in by the gardens' side between the sign of The Key and the sign of the Chequer in Holywell Street ... and suddenly blew trumpets.' Fierce hand-to-hand fighting left many men dead including Lords Clifford, Somerset and Northumberland. The family poem records, 'At St Albans, intending his master to save, He was slain, and there he lies deep in his grave.' Nominally this was the first conflict of what is now called War of the Roses, but it appears to have been taken as an opportunity to settle personal scores.

Desultory fighting between Lancaster and York continued, first at Blore Heath in autumn 1459. At Northampton in July 1460 Buckingham and Thomas Percy, Lord Egremont were killed guarding Henry VI, who was seized by Warwick. York was slain at Wakefield and his son and heir, slipping into London, was proclaimed King Edward IV on 4 March 1461. Twenty-five days later, at Towton, Lancastrian men facing into a blinding sleet driven by sharp winds were felled by Yorkist archers using the weather as an ally. The third Earl of Northumberland, seeing what was happening, ordered his men into close combat. The battle raged for ten hours and so many men were killed that blood flowed into streams and coloured the snow red for miles around. The earl was slain with his brother Richard. Peeris recorded of him, 'King Henry the sixth found him in great fidelity, And for his sake oftimes he stood in great perplexity. In conclusion, in his quarrel what should I more say? At Towton he was slain upon ill Palm Sunday.' The two brothers were buried at St Denys Church in York, opposite the family mansion called the Percy Inn on the north side of Walmgate. At Hedgeley Moor on 25 April 1464, the late earl's brother Sir Ralph, covering a retreat, fought until his arm could no longer wield a sword. He died covered in wounds.

A month later John Neville, Lord Montague, brother of Warwick and cousin of the third earl, defeated Lancastrians at Hexham. Having captured Somerset there, he had the Lancastrian leader beheaded. He wrote to King Edward, 'Henry of Windsor was the best horseman of his company for he fled so fast no one could overtake him.' Edward IV rewarded John Neville by granting him the earldom of Northumberland. Around the same time William Herbert was created Earl of Pembroke in place of Jasper Tudor, whose nephew, seven-year-old Henry, Earl of Richmond, was given into the custody of Pembroke's wife, Anne Devereaux, who later betrothed him to her daughter Maud.

In unknown circumstances, Edward IV had managed to capture Northumberland's fifteen-year-old son, imprisoning him in the Fleet (paying for Sir Henry Percy £1 *6s 8d* weekly for his table, with four persons attending him for two months and four days for £11 *3s 8d*), from where John Paston wrote to his wife, Margaret, in September 1465 that it was 'unseasonably cold' and that Lord Percy wished to be remembered to her. Soon after, Lord Percy was transferred to the Tower of London.

I

'SOME PRIVY TREASON'

Sir Henry Percy (our Henry Percy's grandfather-to-be) remained in The Tower, a fellow inmate of Henry VI who had been captured in July 1465 in Clitherwood. On 27 October 1469, Lord Percy was taken to Westminster and asked to swear fidelity to King Edward IV. Having done so, he was given his liberty and restored, becoming the fourth Percy Earl of Northumberland. The king, desiring a strong supporter in the north, soon appointed him Warden of the East Marches, partly in response to his nineteen-year-old brother, George, Duke of Clarence, having kidnapped him during his summer progress. Egged on by his father-in-law Richard, Earl of Warwick and Warwick's brother the Archbishop of York, George had imprisoned Edward at Middleham. The king had managed to escape to York in September. When Edward, Clarence and Warwick rode through London on 7 October, Sir John Paston noted, 'The king has good language of the Lords Clarence and Warwick, saying they be his best friends, but it is not what his household says.' Hoping to appease John Neville, the king created him Marquis of Montague. In private he complained he had only 'a magpie's nest to maintain it', despite George, his four-year-old son, being created Duke of Bedford, amid murmurs he was to marry the king's eldest daughter, three-year-old Elysabeth.

In March 1470, an uprising occurred in Lincolnshire. Artillery taken by Edward threw the commons into confusion and they ran away. Realising they were 'dupes and pawns' in a further scheme by Warwick and Clarence to depose him, Edward did not pursue them. Clarence and Warwick, seeing their plan foiled, escaped overseas to France. When York saw fresh unrest at the start of August, Edward travelled north only to find the rebellion over before he arrived. On the 5th Sir John Paston wrote to his brother that the king should hastily return to London for rumour was Lords Clarence and Warwick 'will assay to land in England every day, as folks fear'. The king's brother-in-law, the Duke of Burgundy, who was patrolling the Channel for Edward, also warned him he had been lured north and should return south. Edward ignored the advice.

When Burgundy's ships were dispersed by a sudden squall, Clarence and Warwick, with Jasper Tudor and John de Vere, took the opportunity to land on the south coast on 13 September. Edward rushed from York, sending out summonses for royalist troops to muster at Doncaster. In the early morning of 29 September he was roused from his bed by Alexander, his sergeant of the minstrels, saying enemies were near at hand to seize him.

Unmoving, the king replied, 'It is only Montague's men.'

'He is coming to take you,' insisted Alexander, 'he has changed sides.'

The king sent Alexander to wake his seventeen-year-old brother Richard, Duke of Gloucester, while he hastily dressed. They fled cross-country to King's Lynn to take ship. Having neither bag nor baggage, they paid for passage to Flanders with their rich gowns.

Henry VI was brought out of the Tower, lodged in the bishop's palace and dressed in clean robes. Queen Margarete and their son remained in France. Thirteen-year-old Henry Tudor, Earl of Richmond was removed from the care of William Herbert's widow and brought to London to meet his uncle the king. Edward's wife, Elizabeth Wydville, sought sanctuary with her mother and daughters in Westminster Abbey where she gave birth to her first son, Edward.

When Warwick heard rumours Edward was intending to return to England, he sent out commissions to raise troops. Mid-March 1471, Edward landed at Ravenspur. Proclaiming he had landed only to reclaim his inheritance, he was allowed entry into York and then Wakefield. Men began joining him. At Nottingham, leading a large host towards Warwick's force, he proclaimed himself King of England. At Banbury he met Clarence and the two brothers embraced. Reaching Barnet on the evening of Easter Sunday Eve, 13 April, a thick fog fell. Ordering silence, Edward used it as cover to set up camp near to Warwick's men. Fighting began at four in the morning. Warwick, seeing his brother Montague killed and the army in disarray, tried to flee the field but was killed. A luckier casualty that day was John Paston: he wrote to his mother on 30 April for money, complaining, 'By my truth, my leechcraft and physic, and rewards to them ... had cost me since Easter Day more than £6 and now I have neither meat, drink, clothes, leechcraft nor money...'

Queen Margarete and her seventeen-year-old son Edward landed at Weymouth on the day the battle was fought at Barnet. News of Warwick's death reached her at Cerne Abbey. Her son refused point-blank to leave and gave orders to the Duke of Somerset and Jasper Tudor to recruit men, the former from the West Country and the latter from Cheshire and Wales. Fully cognisant of their plans, King Edward ordered Gloucester to close its gates to the Lancastrian host moving north. Blocked from entering the city, the Lancastrians had to continue to Tewkesbury while King Edward force-marched his own troops to the town, intent on a confrontation.

The two forces engaged on 4 May. At the end of the ferocious battle Queen Margarete was a prisoner and her son was dead. Jasper and Henry Tudor fled to Tenby, where they took a boat bound for the Continent. Also dead on the field was the Yorkist

Sir Henry Stafford, Henry Tudor's stepfather. He and the widowed Margaret Beaufort, Countess of Richmond had married thirteen years earlier in a love-match. Only a few months previously, at Woking Palace, they had celebrated their wedding anniversary, feasting on curlew, plover and larks.

During the summer of 1472, Northumberland married Maud Herbert. Of this marriage Peeris wrote, 'A lady he married of ancient and high degree, Lord Herbert's daughter, Maud of benignity, Wise, politic, prudent and always gracious, To him true ... a lady most bounteous.' The earl's favourite residence was Warkworth Castle, which lay within a loop of the River Coquet. Preparations began for the couple to take up residence: walls were repaired (including those of the slaughterhouse) and gutters cleaned, the latter costing 8*d*; the mill and fishery were improved; John Frost and his fellows roofed the lord's grange and ox-house over six days at 4*d* a day among them. By Michaelmas, everything was ready for their arrival: the 'fish-house within the castle' had 170 salt salmon and 160 salt grilse. The earl's hounds were moved in, and straw was brought in as litter for oxen and horses and for mattresses in the castle for those without a bed.

Hosting a chapter of St George in his bedchamber at the Tower of London, in 1474 King Edward made Northumberland a Knight of the Garter and in July appointed him Constable of Newcastle and Warden of the East and Middle Marches for seven years (at a rate of 2,000 marks yearly in time of peace or truce, and 6,000 marks in time of war). Later in the year, Henry and Maud celebrated the birth of their first child, Eleanor. Northumberland was one of the knights taking part in the royal banquet at Windsor on St George's Day 1477 when the queen and her ladies attended the chapter wearing gowns of the order.

On 13 January 1478, at Leconfield, Maud gave birth to their son and heir, Henry. Later siblings joining him in the nursery were William, Alan, Joscelin and Anne. During this relatively peaceful time, the earl built a new gatehouse tower at Warkworth Castle, carving the Percy lion into its front. He enlarged the great hall by moving the outer walls, and made it brighter by installing larger windows on the courtyard side. At the dais end, a doorway gave entrance to a grand stairway which connected the hall to the great chamber on the first floor (and provided access to the private apartments). Between the hall and the kitchen he made a pantry and a buttery, with a stair leading to the beer cellar. The kitchen and pastry kitchen (which had its own oven) had deep fireplaces and stone channels to collect basting juices into a pot. Water was available from a lead tank.

Border hostilities resumed in May 1480 when Archibald Douglas, Earl of Angus attacked Bamburgh Castle and the villages around it. Richard, Duke of Gloucester was the earl's counterpart on the West March and Constable of Carlisle at this time, and while he and Northumberland mustered a large army, the latter moved with Maud to Alnwick Castle. He ordered 'a great cleaning of the hall and chambers of the lord and lady' and the purchase of white straw for beds and rushes to sweeten them, plus new window glass and iron for bands and hinges. Oats and peas were to be ground in the mill for his hounds.

At a council of war held at Durham, Gloucester's strategy was to divide the army: he would lead one detachment to Berwick; Northumberland would take the other to Jedburgh. Leaving orders for John Stother to buy oxen and sheep and deliver wine from Warkworth to Alnwick, the earl took with him fifteen wagons of provisions and materials of war. William Dower was paid 34*s* 8*d* for making over five score bows (using the earl's materials within Alnwick Castle). His tenants were paid various sums (between 5*s* and 40*s*) for 'carting arms and habiliments of war, and victuals' from Alnwick to Jedburgh, each wagon 5*s* in going and coming, totalling 75*s*. Buckan received 16*d* for carrying the earl's harness and a pair of garde-viands (bags for victuals). The surgeon received 13*s* 4*d* for tending a French gunner whose face and body were greatly burned. The earl replaced his clothing – cloak 5*s* 7*d*; tunic

3*s* 8*d*; shirt 14*d*; hat and a pair of shoes 7*d*; a pair of boots 2*s* 2½*d*; belt 1*d* and a purse 5½*d* with 6*d* in it; twelve pairs of laces 1*d* – and boarded him at a cost of 6*s* 8*d*. While the earl was absent John Buttre made a gun cart and new posts, and renovated the stable floors.

A harsh winter brought starvation and much killing on the borders. Artillery, including cannon and handguns, was hauled to Alnwick from Newcastle (having sailed from London) by 120 horses and in July 1482 an English army of 22,500 men mustered at Alnwick. Gloucester and Northumberland ordered divisional commanders to cross into Scotland using different fords. One division went to Newcastle and another to Berwick. The divisions in Scotland were to rendezvous and march together on Edinburgh. At the capital, Scottish lords quickly sued for a truce and gave up Berwick to England.

Nineteen days short of his forty-first birthday, to the shock of the realm, King Edward died on 9 April 1483. Twelve-year-old Prince Edward, residing at Ludlow, was proclaimed Edward V. On St George's Day he set off for London with an armed retinue of two thousand horse. When Richard, Duke of Gloucester arrived at Northampton with his retinue of six hundred horse, expecting to meet up with the new king as arranged, he was met instead by Anthony, Earl Rivers and Richard Grey (uncle and half-brother of the king). They explained they had sent King Edward 14 miles further south to lodge at Stony Stratford. Courteously, the duke invited them to dine and lodge with him. During the evening, Henry Stafford, Duke of Buckingham clattered into the town with three hundred horsemen and was invited to join them.

Next morning, Richard, as Constable of England, arrested Earl Rivers and Richard Grey. Later, after meeting up with King Edward, Gloucester had Thomas Grey, Marquis of Dorset, Sir Thomas Vaughan and Sir Richard Haute arrested and imprisoned. Buckingham and Gloucester, with the king, proceeded to London. The coronation was arranged for 22 June. Parliament was scheduled for 25 June and summons to attend were sent out on 13 May, as were letters of invitation to those chosen to be created Knights of the Bath.

On 13 June, Northumberland entered York to attend to business. The council gifted him mayn-bread, six gallons of Gascon wine and two pikes (pike was a luxury, and each cost between 3*s* and 4*s*). He was still in York two days later when Sir Richard Ratcliffe brought him an alarming letter from Gloucester dated 10 June. In it he requested York city council to send troops to London to aid and assist him and the Duke of Buckingham 'against the queen, her blood, adherents and affinity', who intended to murder them. The council immediately sent two hundred horsemen to London and began mustering troops to be sent to Northumberland, who was to go to Pontefract Castle. There, on 24 June, Northumberland was chief judge at the trial of Earl Rivers, Richard Grey and Sir Thomas Vaughan. They were sentenced to death; their execution was superintended by Sir Richard Ratcliffe the following day. Edward IV's children were declared illegitimate by the lords, and the reign of Richard III began on 26 June.

On the night of 4 July, in the Tower, Richard dubbed seventeen Knights of the Bath including Thomas Butler, Earl of Ormond and his son-in-law William Boleyn. The following morning, eager crowds lined the streets to watch the royal procession from the Tower to Westminster. King Richard rode by wearing an ermine-furred purple velvet riding gown over a blue doublet decorated with nets and pineapples. Queen Anne rode in a white damask litter, its gold silk ribbons fluttering in the breeze. Her white kirtle was decorated with silver wings and over it a white lace mantle with gold ribbons.

At the coronation, two days later, Northumberland walked before the king holding the unsheathed and pointless sword Curtana. John de la Pole, Duke of Suffolk (the king's brother-in-law) carried the sceptre and his son John, Earl of Lincoln carried the ball and cross. John Howard, Duke of Norfolk carried the king's jewelled crown between his hands; his son Thomas, Earl of Surrey held the sword of estate. The royal couple wore long-trained purple gowns; King Richard's train was held by Buckingham and Queen Anne's train by Margaret, Countess of Richmond. Walking barefoot on the red carpet, laid from the King's Bench to St Edward's Shrine, they were duly anointed and crowned. The banquet, set in Westminster Hall, began at four in the afternoon. The royal couple had changed into robes of crimson velvet embroidered with gold. The king was served his favourite dishes of peacock and swan.

A fortnight later, Northumberland entered York where he presented five bucks to the Lord Mayor to feast him, the aldermen and the soldiers who had travelled with him to London. He stayed in the city to help prepare it for the king's entry (for which he was gifted mayn-bread, two pikes, two tenches, three great eels and four gallons of Gascon wine). On 8 September, York citizens cheered until they were hoarse as, crowned and in royal robes, King Richard and Queen Anne, holding her son's hand, walked in procession through the streets to York Minster. Forty trumpets announced their arrival at the doors and the cheering swelled from inside to out. Prince Edward was knighted by his father, who gave him the gold wand, wreath and kiss that created him Prince of Wales.

The borders calm, Northumberland negotiated peace with Scotland in April 1484. On 26 June he arranged the marriage of Amicia Lewis to Sir Roger Hastings in his chapel at Leconfield. The following summer news arrived that Henry Tudor, styling himself rightful king, was attempting to invade England again. On 27 July 1485 Northumberland made his will before joining King Richard at Nottingham. On 7 August Henry Tudor landed at Milford Haven. On the 22nd, the two armies came in sight of each other near Bosworth in Leicestershire.

Richard set his troops in three battles: vanguard, main and rearguard. Norfolk commanded the vanguard, King Richard the centre and Northumberland the rearguard. Polydore Vergil writes that the battlefield was a marshy meadow: 'There was a marsh betwixt both hosts, which Henry of purpose left on the right hand, that it might serve his men instead of a fortress, by the doing thereof also he left the sun upon his back.' Combat began when the royal artillery opened fire. Oxford, commanding Henry's vanguard, made a flanking manoeuvre to attack Norfolk. For reasons never to be known, Northumberland did not commit his rearguard to the battle. Perhaps he was unable to engage because of troop positioning; perhaps he favoured Henry Tudor; perhaps before he could engage he saw Richard fall and be killed.

The York city council recorded that Northumberland was at Wressle Castle the day after the battle in which 'King Richard was piteously slain and murdered to the great heaviness of this city'. They sent a letter to ask him for his 'best advice'. The *Eboracum* recorded another council meeting on 24 August where it was stated, 'John Nicholson was sent to Wressle to the Earl of Northumberland with writing, appeared and showed' them that the 'earl was with the king at Leicester for the weal of himself and this city' and would meet them at the 'mill in the street without Walmgate-Bar' as previously arranged. Whatever the earl's position or thoughts, he was confirmed in all his titles and offices by the new king, Henry VII.

In April 1486, Northumberland, after meeting the king at Pontefract, escorted him to York. For his entry, King Henry rode a courser and wore an ermine-furred, black-satin-lined cloth of gold robe. Some 3 miles from the city the royal party were met by city officials and citizens, all on horseback. A mile from the city all the churchmen and a great number of men, women and children on foot and lining the way shouted out the king's name in welcome. At the city gate, as two roses – white and red – sprang up with a gold crown descending to hang over them, a man dressed as Ebrauk (the city's founder) handed the keys of the city to the king. At the bridge over the River Ouse, an enthroned King Solomon gave his sceptre to the king. Citizens leaned out of windows on both sides of the street, casting out wafers and comfits as the king rode past. At the Common Hall on Coney Street, King David presented King Henry with a 'sword of victory'. On Stonegate the Virgin Mary descended from heaven to praise him, saying she would ask her son to send him grace.

On St George's Eve, having been crowned in the morning and having taken his dinner and void while served by Garter Knights, the king went to the minster to hear Evensong. Next day he heard the Requiem Mass for the dead. Northumberland personally foiled an attempt made upon the king's life at this time, quickly seizing and hanging the principal movers. Henceforth he was often at court: at Greenwich in November 1486; with the king at Newcastle in August 1487 (supplying the king's table with thirty salmon from Warkworth); in attendance on Queen Elysabeth's coronation on 25 November 1487; and in February 1488 at Greenwich, where he was appointed Sheriff of Northumberland (required to annually render only £100 per annum into the Exchequer).

Through the end of the year and part of the next, he was embroiled in litigation regarding the estate of Sir Guy de Brian. Although he was heir general in fee simple and by entail, parts of his estate were being claimed by others – among them Eleanor Beaufort, widow of James Butler, fifth Earl of Ormond and Wiltshire (who had since married Sir Robert Spencer), and Thomas, seventh Earl of Ormond, who was James's brother. After mediation, certain castles were distributed to the contestants: Countess Eleanor retained certain manors for life, remaindered to the Earl of Ormond after her death. Northumberland, descended from Lord Guy's elder daughter, was judged to have the better title and in an enrolment, signed on 16 December 1488, he was acknowledged as heir general to various manors and castles in Somerset, Devon and Dorset.

A new burden of heavy taxation was exacted by Henry VII in February 1489 (to raise funds to aid Anne of Brittany against

Charles VIII of France), causing much unrest in York. King Henry ordered Northumberland to deal with it. On 24 April the earl wrote an urgent letter from his manor of Seamer to Sir Robert Plumpton, requesting him to come with armed followers 'as many as ye may bring with your ease, such as ye trust, having bows and arrows' to be with him upon Monday night next at Thirsk. Before they could arrive, the rebels, whose ringleader was John Chamber, confronted the earl and murdered him at Blackmore Edge near Topcliffe on Wednesday 28 April. On 30 April, the Earl of Oxford wrote to Sir John Paston that the rebels had said 'they would pay no money; my Lord of Northumberland hearing thereof and that they were but naked men, addressed himself towards them without any harness in peaceable manner, trusting to have appeased them'. Rumour abounded that only a few of his retinue, among them Sir Hugh Hastings, attempted to rescue him from the mob; that some bore him a grudge for his inaction at Bosworth Field. Peeris wrote:

> In our days not seen so detestable a thing!
> Their own natural lord the commons so murdering!
> He good commanding them in the king's name
> To do their duty and keep themselves from blame.
>
> Both knights and gentlemen that day with him he led
> To whom he gave fees and was especial lord;
> But in his great need all suddenly from him fled.
> Some privy treason was the truth to record...

Thomas, Earl of Surrey, who had recently been released from the Tower, was sent by the king to deal with rebels and traitors continuing in riotous assembly. He quickly captured John Chamber and hanged him on a higher-than-usual gibbet, hanging his chief men on a lower storey around him. Shortly afterwards, Surrey was appointed Lieutenant-General of the North and Warden of the

East and Middle Marches. He and his family took up residence at the castle of Sheriff Hutton.

Poet Laureate John Skelton wrote an elegy, 'Upon the Dolorous Death and Much Lamentable Chance of the Most Honourable Earl of Northumberland', which he gave to the slain earl's twelve-year-old son, Henry, now the fifth earl:

> I wail, I weep, I sob, I sigh full sore
> The deadly fate, the doleful destiny
> Of him that is gone, alas, without restore,
> Of the blood royal descending nobly,
> Whose lordship doubtless was slain lamentably
> Through treason, against him compassed and wrought,
> True to his prince in word, in deed and thought
>
> I say, ye commoners, why were ye so stark mad?
> What frantic frenzy fell in your brain?
> Where was your wit and reason ye should have had?
> What wilful folly made you to rise again
> Your natural lord? Alas, I can not fain:
> You armed you with will and left your wit behind;
> Well may you be called commons most unkind.

In his will, the earl bequeathed 3,000 marks to his daughter Eleanor and 2,000 marks to his daughter Anne (to be paid on their marriages) and 40 marks yearly to William Rilston 'during his life to abide with my wife and heir'. His executors – Sir Thomas Burgh, Sir Guy Fairfax, Sir John Pickering, William Poteman and William Rilston, Thomas FitzWilliam and Edmund Thwaites – were to have governance of his heir and all his children while they remained unmarried until they were eighteen years of age, when each one could 'have and occupy the lands and tenements' pertinent to them. William was bequeathed 1,000 marks yearly from lands in the southern counties for the term of his life so long as he served his brother Henry, the heir apparent, with loving and lowly disposition. In a similar vein, he left 200 marks to Alan and the lordship of Holderness and to Joscelin 300 marks and the manor and lordship of Poynings. Annual gifts of money were bequeathed to extended family members and various servants. A codicil, dated at Newcastle on 24 February (but no year), was added after Maud had died which shows she was buried at Beverley Minster and he intended to lie with her. Maud had been embalmed, placed in a fair stone coffin and buried in cloth of gold, wearing embroidered silk slippers on her feet. Their joint blue marble tomb had a canopy and spandrils full of heraldry. Five priests were to sing masses daily for his and Lady Maud's souls.

The cost of 'embalming, leading and chesting' the earl cost £13 *6s 8d*. The wax of the hearse, timber and painting of it and 400 torches (*2s 8d* each) came to £84 *19s 8d*; the standard, banner, coat armour, 12 banners and 100 pensels in sarcenet and 60 buckram escutcheons to cover chair, hearse and church came to £26 *6s 8d*. Some 40 poor men – the age of the earl when he died – bore torches on horseback from Wressle to Leconfield at *2s* each, as did 100 men on foot at *6d* each; ditto from Leconfield to Beverley on the day of burial. A £20 reward was given to two officers of arms coming from London. Mourning gowns were provided for 12 lords, 20 gentlewomen, 24 gowns with hoods for lords and knights, 60 gowns with tippets for squires and gentlemen, 200 gowns for yeomen and 160 coarse black gowns for poor folk and torchbearers and 100 gowns for grooms and gentlemen's servants. In all, 400 yards of coarse black cloth was used for hangings in the church and around the hearse, rails and ground, with the black cloth costing £428. Provision was made for five hundred priests and one thousand clerks to attend. Dole at the burial was *2d* to every poor body that attended – there were 13,340, costing £123 *6s 8d*. The costs and expenses of meat and drink, and horse meat came to £266 *13s 4d*. The subtotal arrived at was £1,037 *6s 8d* and excluded items coming out of store, expenses for mortuaries, arms, his henchmen and the Master of the Horse (besides the cost of the monument).

The fifth earl and his sisters were sent by the king to live with his mother, Margaret Beaufort, at Coldharbour, her house in London. It was a comfortable, well-furnished house with glazed windows and a new chimney (which cost £28 18*s* 2*d*); she created a herb garden in the well-tended grounds, which stretched down to the Thames. The earl's three younger brothers were made wards of Buckingham and Surrey on 25 May for the sum of 80 marks, paid into the Exchequer annually.

2

'GOODLY FRUIT'

On 14 December 1490, Margaret Beaufort arranged for Eleanor, the earl's elder sister, now sixteen years of age, to marry Edward Stafford, Duke of Buckingham, who was two months short of his thirteenth birthday and also a ward at Coldharbour House. The fourth earl's executors agreed King Henry would receive the sum of £4,000.

In the same month, with regard to the Percy–Brian estate, Thomas, Earl of Ormond requested that certain manors in Dorset and Somerset be transferred into the possession of Sir Robert Spencer and his wife, Eleanor Beaufort, Countess of Ormond and Wiltshire. Eleanor was the daughter of Edmund Beaufort, second Duke of Somerset, uncle of Margaret Beaufort.

The earl soon blended into court rituals. One such occurred on Saturday, 1 November 1494 when the royal family gathered in the Parliament Chamber with other nobles and attendants. The Garter King of Arms entered first, followed by Edmund, Earl of Suffolk holding a rich sword pommel upward, the Earl of Northumberland with a gold rod and the Earl of Derby (Margaret Beaufort's husband) bearing the ermine-furred cape and rich coronal. Behind them George, Earl of Shrewsbury carried three-year-old Prince Henry, second son of the king. The Marquis of

Dorset and Thomas, Earl of Arundel led Shrewsbury and the little boy to the king, who created his son Duke of York, with an income of £1,000 per year. (The king paid for Northumberland's robe at a cost of £2 6*s* 8*d*).

To honour his son, and for the pleasure of his 'fairest young princess', five-year-old Margaret, the king arranged jousts to begin a week later. Seated in a stand covered in blue arras with gold *fleurs-de-lis*, with gold cushions for comfort, the king and queen gathered around them an audience of dukes, earls and gentlemen including Thomas, Earl of Ormond and his son-in-law Sir William Boleyn. Spectators – royals, nobles and citizens – wore a medley of rich and bright colours, giving the tiltyard a festival air that was augmented by cheers and exclamations of delight. Lord Abergavenny gave a display of dressage on a small black horse; the challengers of the joust issued out of Westminster Hall into the tiltyard wearing the king's colours of green and white, their harnesses sparkling in the sun from spangles and jingling bells.

On the second day, Ladies Elizabeth Stafford, Anne Percy and Anne Neville (daughter of Ralph, Earl of Westmorland) and Anne St Leger (daughter of the deceased Anne Plantagenet, Duchess of Exeter), all riding white palfreys and wearing white damask gowns, led into the tilt three knights and a squire. The challengers jousting that day entered under crested pavilions, their horse harnesses chequered black velvet, each lozenge with a rose, either red or white: the Earl of Suffolk, under a red sarcenet pavilion crested with a gold lion with white and green spangled feathers, had as his motto 'For to Accomplish'; the Earl of Essex, his pavilion dark tawny and bearing the crest of a flying silver falcon with a bruised wing, had 'Our promise made'; Sir Robert Curzon followed under a black pavilion with a red dragon head crest bearing the motto 'Thereto we be ready'; and last was John Peche, his pavilion light tawny crested with a plumed and crowned gold lion, and his motto 'In every thing'.

On the third and final day, to gusts of laughter, two knights rode in with horses trapped in paper: one in torn pieces and the other with a drawing of two men playing dice. The herald declared, 'One lance and then to swords.' They charged at each other; each missed. Taking up their swords, upon raising his blade to give his opponent a great stroke one knight found his weapon flying backwards out of his hand. As his opponent courteously returned it to him, he struck him with it on the helm and mimed the sting he had received, while the other reeled about unsteadily.

Each day of the joust ended with a supper and dance at which the 'fair and noble ladies' decided who had won a prize, bringing the winner to Princess Margaret to present it. On the first night Anne Percy and Anne Neville chose John Peche, who received a prize of a gold ring with a ruby; on the second Elizabeth Stafford and Anne Neville selected the Earl of Suffolk, who was given a gold ring with a diamond. In like form the Countess of Northumberland and Lady Elizabeth Herbert presented to the squire Thomas Brandon a gold ring with a ruby. The last night, 13 November, before a banquet for all the nobles and knights, Anne Percy and Anne Neville gave the princess a gold ring with an emerald to present to the Earl of Essex.

The record of the Countess of Northumberland at this event reveals that Margaret Beaufort had married the fifth earl to her kinswoman Katheryne Spencer, youngest daughter of Eleanor Beaufort and Sir Robert Spencer (who was one or two years younger than her bridegroom). Katheryne's older sister by six years had been married in 1490 to Sir Thomas Carey of Chilton Foliat. In the king's chamber accounts of May 1493 is a note of offerings of *6s 8d* at four unnamed marriages. It is possible Henry and Katheryne married in this year; however, if so, Margaret's views on premature cohabiting may have meant they had not yet begun their married life together.

Around Maytime 1495, John Skelton, residing in or visiting the Howard family at Sheriff Hutton, wrote a long poem called

The Garland of Laurel which he dedicated to some ladies who were making him a caplet of laurel: one was a teenage Elizabeth Howard, the eldest daughter of the Earl of Surrey:

> To my Lady Elizabeth Howard:
> To be your remembrancer, madam, I am bound,
> Like to Aryna, maidenly of port*
> Of virtue and conning† the well and perfect ground;
> Whom dame Nature, as well I may report,
> Hath freshly embeautied with many a goodly sort
> Of womanly features, whose flourishing tender age
> Is delightful to look on, pleasant, demure, and sage.

During that year, Elizabeth's eldest brother, twenty-two-year-old Lord Thomas, married Anne of York, the queen's sister, which made him uncle to the king's children.

Since 1492 King Henry had been vexed by a pretender to his throne called Perkin Warbeck. Various European heads of state had supported Warbeck's claim to be Richard, second son of Edward IV, including King James IV of Scotland. In 1497 he and Warbeck undertook to jointly invade England, but the pretender did not get the support he expected and they were forced to retreat. King Henry thought to 'continue the war his enemy had started' and asked Parliament to agree a tax to raise funds. Contemporary Polydore Vergil wrote, 'Money-men were sent out everywhere to collect the money ... while other men paid, the Cornishmen ... refused to pay the appointed tax, exclaimed that they could not bear its weight.' Cornish rebels, ignoring wiser heads, marched towards London.

At news of the uprising, 'noblemen and brave knights came to London from all sides, each one leading the company of soldiers

---

* Meaning 'bearing'.
† Meaning 'knowledgeable'.

he had recruited'. Among them were Thomas Howard, son of the Earl of Surrey, 'a distinguished and vigorous young man', and Sir William Boleyn with his twenty-year-old son Thomas beside him. Northumberland was placed in command of the 'Northern Horse' he had raised. The Cornish throng encamped on Blackheath outside the capital. They thought the king had to be panic-stricken as he appeared to have done nothing, but he had 'deliberately refused to oppose the mob, so that he might suddenly surround it more safely'. The king's army met the rebels on 17 June, and in the fighting that ensued over two thousand men who resisted were killed and countless were captured, 'including the leaders of the mob, who were executed shortly thereafter'.

Believing King Henry distracted by southern events, King James determined to invade England again. He underestimated northern strength and vigilance. The Bishop of Durham, Richard Fox, with his own strengthened garrison, joined forces with the Earl of Surrey, who had also anticipated trouble and recruited a 'goodly number of soldiers', augmented by experienced northern nobles and their men, all notable for their martial skills – Neville, Dacre, Lumley, Scrope, Ogle, Clifford, Conyers and Darcy – and 'likewise the brave and prudent knights' of border families such as Bulmer, Gascoigne, Pennington, Ellerker, Constable, Stapleton, Heron and Fenwick. Among their number was seventeen-year-old William Percy.

At sight of the English, the Scots fled towards Scotland, harried by Surrey who, by force-marching his men, endeavoured to overtake them. Lack of provisions compelled him to give up the chase. A month later, peace was concluded between the English and Scottish kings, to be sealed by a marriage between James and Princess Margaret when she was of age. Warbeck was given a polite request to leave Scotland. Thinking he would get backing from the disaffected Cornish, he landed in the south, mustered men and besieged Exeter Castle but lost courage and removed to Taunton. When a host of armed and armoured knights arrived there under Buckingham, 'a young man endowed with great spirit and virtue of character', Perkin rushed to take asylum at Beaulieu. Surrendering to the king's mercy, he was at first treated well but confined at court. After attempting to escape, he was lodged in the Tower of London.

In March and May 1498 respectively, King Henry granted Edward Stafford and Henry Percy special livery of their lands although neither had quite attained their majority of twenty-one years. As they attended the chapter of the Order of St George in 1498, it seems that both had been elected Knights of the Garter during the preceding year. Skelton had written a poem about the Garter Knights, the flavour of which can be understood from one verse:

> O knightly order, clothed in robes with garter!
> The queen's grace and thy mother clothed in the same;
> The nobles of thy realm rich in array, after,
> Lords, knights, and ladies, unto thy great fame:
> Now shall all ambassadors know thy noble name,
> By thy feast royal; now joyous mayst thou be;
> To see thy king so flourishing in dignity.

Her wards now grown, Margaret Beaufort took a vow of chastity and moved to Collyweston Manor in Northamptonshire, which she renovated to suit her own comfort. It had 'a chapel, library, counting house, great parlour, guest chambers and a jewel house'. She curtained and covered her bed in white damask and had cushions made for her two chairs: red velvet for one and russet cloth of gold with a blue fringe (her colours) for the other and a table covered with a tablecloth decorated with Tudor roses and her portcullis badge.

In control of his own destiny thanks to an income said to be over £3,000 a year, it may well be that Northumberland moved with Katheryne away from court to spend time at his homes in

Yorkshire. The earl particularly liked Wressle Castle near York and Leconfield Castle, slightly harder to reach, near Beverley. In York itself, at Walmgate, the earl owned the substantial mansion called the Percy Inn. (They would also reside at times at Topcliffe near Thirsk and the manor house at Petworth in Sussex. The castles of Alnwick and Warkworth seemed to have been demoted to bases for warfare against the Scots.)

The emerging tops of towers would have been the countess's first view of Wressle Castle. Access to the castle was via the main village road, with houses on either side. A wooden bridge arched over the moat into the garden between moat and castle, leading to a walled orchard in which the earl created arbours and mounds 'wreathen about with steps like turnings of cockle shells to come to the top without pain' to view newly created topiary beds and grass-covered alleys for bowling and walking. A deer park lay beyond to the north in which peacocks wandered. Before long, the earl added herb gardens (and would then stipulate no herbs were to be purchased, the cooks having them fresh from the garden) and two large pleasure fishponds. One gardener was employed to keep all in good order; he received a yearly wage of £3 *8d* and his duties included attending 'hourly in the garden for setting of herbs and clipping of knots and sweeping the garden clean'. (In 1517, a formal moated knot garden was added and a 'keeper of the new garden' employed at a yearly wage of 26*s* 8*d*.)

On the east side, a five-storey gatehouse (with guest lodgings) fronted a courtyard surrounded by ranges on four sides, a tower at each corner. The south-west tower, the Lord's Tower, contained her husband's private rooms and personal buttery. The countess's rooms were in the south-east tower on the second floor, which partly extended over the High and Nether Chapels on the floor below. Between the two towers was the Great Chamber (used as the family room and dining chamber). This had richly carved ceilings and a carved wooden border of foliage with carvings: a stag emerging from woodland; a bareheaded hunter with quiver and horn kneeling with his cap on the ground; a man holding a horse and on his left two greyhounds; a chained boar; a crowned lion and a chained unicorn with a coronet; and around them all decorations of crescents, crests, helms, badges and devices. As were the panels on either side of the doors, which depicted St George and the dragon, St Catherine with wheel, a man bearing a standard in one hand and a chain in his other. In several rooms the Percy motto was carved: '*Esperance en Dieu ma Comforte.*' (Sculptural wooden panels were also installed at Leconfield, described as a large, moated, eighty-three-room house with a spacious court and gardens.) The fifth earl beautified two newel staircases at Wressle which had octagonal screens covered with wooden sculptural panels, connecting the rooms and rising to the roof leads, which had a crenelated walkway linking the two towers.

Above the countess's rooms was the earl's library, which he called Paradise. In it, whether built by himself later or already in place, was a closet, described by Leland as being 'of eight squares, latticed about and at the top of every square was a desk, ledged to set books on coffers within them ... and by pulling, one or all would come down breast high in slots and serve for desks to lay books on'. Among the earl's books were Chaucer's *Canterbury Tales*, which had been his father's, John Hardyng's *Chronicle*, Lydgate's *Proverbes*, *Siege of Thebes*, *Troy*, *Assembly of Gods* and *Verses on the Kings of England*, as well as Peeris' family chronicle. The ground floor would later see the nursery, the schoolroom and the private chambers of the children.

The west range contained the great hall, at the north end of which, in the north-west tower, were the kitchens, buttery, pantry, pastry and larder; nearby was a separate bakehouse. The north range housed fair garderobes, storerooms and other household offices such as the spicery and ewery. The north-east tower, called the Constable's Tower, was where the constable and the steward had their chambers. (In later building projects, the earl added a base court with stables and lodgings, a laundry and a two-storey building inside the south-west corner of the moat which had a banqueting room on the first floor and a bathing room below, using water from the moat. It may have been used for swimming – the moat was regularly cleaned (which took twelve days annually, a boat being specifically kept for the purpose). In the middle of the orchard he constructed a two-storey study retreat or office (doing the same in his garden at Leconfield).

Henry and Katheryne's first child, Margaret, was born in late 1499 or early 1500. Around this time the earl had pulled together ceremonial ordinances and compiled a book for his household: the first eight concerned childbirth and christening, so we have an idea of the details. The countess's chamber was hung with verdure tapestries (or plain material) to make it warm and secure. Windows were covered to block out light, which was considered harmful. Between her bed and chamber door, a traverse was hung 'overthwart the chamber for keeping it secret and close for seeing in at the door when it is opened'. Before retiring for her lie-in, she was conducted from her chamber 'through the hall to the chapel' to attend Mass. After partaking of a void she retired, attended only by her women (and female friends) and a midwife, who would help deliver the child and cut the umbilical cord with soft woollen thread.

Forty days after giving birth, the countess was churched. Sprinkled first with holy water, she attended Mass in the chapel and offered a candle. Margaret would have been christened within a week of her birth. An ordinance provides advice on ordering and preparing the church and church porch. It cannot be known whether Margaret was baptised at the church or the castle chapel. Whichever venue, household chaplains and servants (particularly the earl's gentlemen ushers) would have been involved with any influential visitors. Walls would be hung with arras and carpets laid on the floor. A traverse was made around the font and inside it were a basin of water and a bowl of coals to ensure warmth. Someone would have been appointed to bear 'the salt' before the child and others appointed to carry torches, which would be lit when the baby was named. Those attending would partake of the void and the godparents' gifts were taken to Katheryne's chamber while the baby was returned to the care of her nurse and rockers.

There was controversy in 1500 when John Gorynge of Burton in Sussex accused Northumberland of keeping him 'more like a prisoner than a ward' for he 'pretends to have the ward and marriage of him' and further accused him of 'taking into his own hands John's lands and rents of his farms and part of his goods'. Summoned to appear before the Star Chamber (so called because of the painted star ceiling), the earl claimed John was his lawful ward for his grandfather held parcels of ground in the Honour of Petworth by knight's service and had died in his homage, while the complainant would not reach full age until Michaelmas; therefore the earl had entered the lands, being entitled to a 'mownter and a heriot' on each parcel of land, and had taken six oxen and a horse. He asked for the complainant to be punished for his slander. John counter-claimed he had no knowledge of his grandfather holding any lands by knight's service nor had any proof been given. No outcome was recorded but John stayed in the area and married in the same year after he came of age.

Northumberland was in attendance in June 1500 when King Henry and Queen Elysabeth met with Archduke Philip of Burgundy in Calais in the Church of Our Lady of St Peter's. The Calais chronicler recorded that both Northumberland and Buckingham wore cloth-of-gold gowns, that the duke's courser had a 'trapper enramplished with little pretty bells of silver and gilt', and that the Earl of Suffolk had a silk hat garnished with a chain of gold and the 'goodliest plumes of white Ostrich feathers that ever I saw'. The chronicler also recorded that seven horse-loads of cherries had been ordered and 'there lacked no cream, strawberries, nor sugar, bake venison, spice cakes, nor wafers; there were couched great plenty of wine and beer' along with other wines and hippocras, pippins and green ginger and other confections, and that at the banquet was 'the greatest number of young kids that ever I saw' as well as an English fat ox and venison baked into cold pastries.

The king's chamber accounts of 1501 contain a memorandum that the queen had received from the king a chain of gold valued at 5 marks which she had given to 'my Lady of Northumberland', but when this occurred is not recorded. During this year, the earl and countess had a second daughter (who appears to have died young) who was christened Maud; happiness mixed with sorrow, for on 16 August 1501, Katheryne's mother died in her sixty-ninth year.

Sixteen-year-old Katherine of Aragon arrived at Plymouth on 2 October 1501. She had travelled from Spain to marry Prince Arthur, the king's eldest son. With plague rife in London, the original plan had been for Katherine to travel to Gravesend and be conveyed to the Tower in a barge converted as a lodging, escorted by Buckingham and Northumberland in their own barges, entertaining her with music as she travelled. Instead she travelled overland, which much excited the people, who flocked to see her pass by. Outside London, she was lodged at Lambeth Palace. On 12 November, she left the palace after dinner and rode into St George's Field where she was met by the Archbishop of York, bishops and prelates, Prince Henry, the Duke of Buckingham and the Earl of Northumberland. (The presence of the Countess of Northumberland is not mentioned, but few of the ladies attending were named so she may still have been there.) Margaret, Duchess of Buckingham was definitely absent, for on 18 September at Penshurst she had given birth to her third child and only son, Henry. (His two sisters in the nursery were Elizabeth, born in 1497, and Catherine, born in 1499. Another sister, Mary, later joined them in the nursery but her date of birth is unknown.)

They rode to London Bridge where the procession began. The Mayor of London, in crimson satin and gold collar and with the city's sword borne before him, was followed by the black-velveted recorder, the sheriffs and twenty-four aldermen in scarlet. Riding through the packed streets, they cleared a passage, followed by the king at arms and heralds 'in coat armours of velvet and gold ... and divided the common people right orderly'. People hung out of windows and crammed the roofs to watch the procession pass, cheering the six gallants of the Earl of Essex, who wore ostrich-feathered hats and clothes of yellow sarcenet, as they curvetted their coursers to ring the silver bells on their trappers. Following them were Northumberland's men, and then those of his ducal brother-in-law, with trumpets, shawms and sackbuts announcing their coming.

The cheers grew even louder as the princess appeared, riding upon a mule alongside Prince Henry at her right hand. She wore a carnation-coloured broad-brimmed hat, tilted so her face could be seen, held in place on her light auburn hair by a gold lace. As the princess reached the broadest part of Gracechurch Street, a canvas-painted timber-and-stone castle stretched into the shop windows on either side, its battlements depicting Tudor roses and on the top a red dragon holding an iron staff and wearing a gold crown. Riding beneath the wings of the pageant, the party came to the Conduit in Cornhill where, seated on an ornamental bench, the Archangel Raphael blessed her. In Cheapside, between the Great Conduit and the Standard, was a throne with a picture of Prince Arthur. Beneath him were four stars running swiftly between heaven and earth showing zodiac creatures, the wheel turned by three armed knights. At the Standard lions, dragons and greyhounds surrounded a bejewelled God sitting on a throne, itself surrounded by burning wax tapers set in gold candlesticks, with angels singing sweetly about him. At this last stop, the king secretly rented a merchant's chamber to watch the procession wind by the window. With him were Prince Arthur and the Earls of Oxford, Derby and Shrewsbury. At the window of another chamber, Queen Elysabeth, with the Countess of Richmond, princesses Margaret and Mary and many of their ladies, enjoyed the spectacle.

The sixth and last pageant was at the Little Conduit, near the entrance to St Paul's churchyard, where Katherine was met by the seven Virtues. Honour sat in the centre of three seats, and on purple velvet cushions on the chairs either side of her was a sceptre and a coronet. The Mayor of London stopped there so he could present the princess with silver basins filled with coins. After being met at the cathedral door by the Archbishop of Canterbury and other prelates, Katherine made an offering at the Shrine of St Erkenwald before retiring to the bishop's palace.

On 14 November, excited crowds gathered hours earlier than they had two days before so as not to miss fifteen-year-old Prince Arthur passing by on his way to St Paul's. At the cathedral he changed his attire for his white satin wedding finery to await Katherine. She arrived wearing a white satin gown with sleeves and bodice with so many pleats it resembled men's clothing. In Spanish fashion she wore a farthingale under her skirt. Her coif of white silk was bordered with gold, pearl and precious stones. Inside the cathedral, the walls were hung with arras of biblical scenes. A raised walkway ensured the young couple could be seen by those watching as they went to the high altar for the Mass of the Trinity. Leaving the cathedral hours later, a pageant had been set up, a *riche-mont* covered in trees, herbs, flowers and fruit with wine for a river for all to dip their cups in and enjoy. To joyful music the bridal party entered the bishop's palace for the three-course meal (twelve, fifteen and eighteen dishes) set up for them with 'delicate dainties and curious meats' served by lords and knights.

Northumberland attended upon King Henry on St Paul's Day, 15 January 1502, at the king's newly restored Richmond Palace, to witness the proxy marriage in the queen's great chamber between Princess Margaret and King James of Scotland in the person of Patrick, Earl of Bothwell. The new Queen of Scots dined with her mother at her table, 'both at one mess covered', after which a joust was held. During this year, in the king's chamber accounts a memorandum records 'that the Earl of Northumberland took away the daughter and heir of Sir John Hastings of York, the king's ward, who died through his default, whereby the king's grace lost 4,000 marks, wherefore an action is to be taken against him of ravishment of ward'. On 1 April 1502 Northumberland was appointed to a court of oyer and terminer for London and its suburbs which took place at the Guildhall.

York city council held a meeting in which they decided that when the earl and his wife came into the city on Saturday 16 July, they – and many of the commons – would welcome them at Trinity Kirkgarth and present them with a gift of 'two maynbread, three gallons red wine, two gallons claret, two gallons white and one-gallon Hippocras, two cygnets and two great pikes', taken afterwards to the Walmgate mansion. Then, as had become customary for the earl, the household moved to Leconfield in November (it took seventeen carts to move everything). The Beverley town roll shows that around Christmastide the earl honoured the twelve governors of the town of Beverley with an invitation to Leconfield Castle to breakfast with him. In return for their courteous reception, and in token of the honour they had received, the governors sent the earl ten capons, four swans, six young herons, two bitterns and four shovellers. (They also paid Robert Green's expenses in riding about to purchase them and the 'oats and sheepshearts' with which to feed the birds and transport them to Leconfield, plus a present to the earl's cellarer of 3*s* 4*d* and 20*d* to the porter.)

It is more than probable that during the second half of this year – and feasibly at the end of the year – the earl's third child, his son and heir Henry, Lord Percy, was born. At this point, the family versifier concluded his work:

He has married a lady most gracious and good,
Katheryne Spencer, mirror of humility,
Which descended from the royal Somerset blood,
To King Henry the seventh she a-next by consanguinity,
God sendeth them goodly fruit of his benignity,
Margaret, Maud and young Lord Henry Percy.
God augment in them grace by his tender mercy.

3

'GAMBADES PLEASANT TO SEE'

On Saturday, 14 July 1503, at Dringhouses just south of York, the Earl and Countess of Northumberland awaited the arrival of thirteen-year-old Margaret Tudor, Queen of Scotland. They were to escort her to Kirk Lamberton to meet her thirty-year-old husband, James IV. John Yonge, Somerset Herald, recorded the event: Northumberland rode a fair courser with gilt stirrups and gold-edged crimson velvet footcloth reaching to the ground, while three henchmen rode before him and two footmen ran beside him. He wore a crimson velvet gown with slashed sleeves edged with gems, as was his open collar, and 'made gambades pleasant for to see', silver bells tinkling on his harness, to entertain Margaret as they travelled. All his knights, who included Sir John Hastings, Sir Robert Aske and Sir Lancelot Thirkeld, were dressed in velvet liveries and great chains.

The earl's retinue of three hundred mounted knights joined the queen's cavalcade of five hundred while Northumberland's own herald rode ahead to prepare towns and villages for the queen's arrival. For a public entry, Queen Margaret dismounted from riding pillion behind Sir David Owen to change into richer dress and travel in a cloth-of-gold-covered litter carried by two palfreys, one at the front and one at the back, while her coterie of minstrels played music.

The queen was welcomed at York's Micklegate Bar by Sir John Gylliot, Lord Mayor of York. While his robes and horse harness were crimson, his footmen were in green and the aldermen in scarlet. Courteously, Margaret invited the mayor to ride by her side. The people thronging the streets, attired in their best clothes, made for a multi-coloured backdrop. Nobles and gentry looked out from house windows. After hearing Mass at the Minster, Margaret made her offering and was lodged in the archbishop's palace.

On Sunday morning at nine o'clock, Margaret, dressed in a cloth-of-gold gown, a gold girdle falling down her skirt to the ground and a jewelled necklace around her neck, awaited the city officials. They presented her with a standing silver piece, inside of which they had placed a hundred gold angels. She prettily thanked them for their gift. The procession was put into order: the Cross was followed by the church officers and lords. The Earls of Kent and Northumberland in cloth of gold (the latter dressing his three gentlemen of honour in long, gold-embroidered jackets) followed. The Bishops of Moray and Norwich preceded the Lord Mayor, followed by the Earl and Countess of Surrey (acting as Margaret's guardians until her coronation). The queen joined the procession after the officers of arms. Mass was sung in Northumberland's chapel in the Minster where the queen made offerings. Returning to the palace after the ceremony, she welcomed her kinswoman Countess Katheryne with a kiss and they sat down together to chat.

The following day, at eleven o'clock, the journey resumed. Northumberland had put on an ermine-furred tinsel gown. At Newcastle, like York, the arras-hung streets and the windows were full of people keen to watch Margaret pass by. All the ships and tops sported gaily coloured banners. That evening, Northumberland gave a banquet which, because of games, dances, sports and songs, lasted until midnight. When the party arrived at the earl's deer park at Alnwick on 27 July, Northumberland invited Margaret to enjoy a day's hunting. She killed a buck with her own bow, and the gentlemen present, led by the earl, hailed her as 'Diana of England'. That night and the next she lodged at Alnwick Castle before completing her journey. Presenting Margaret to King James, the earl elected to wear a jacket of beaten gold and embroidery under a purple cloak edged with cloth of gold. And thus the fifth earl earnt his sobriquet 'the Magnificent'.

Relations remained strained between the Percy earls and the archbishops of York, in this instance Thomas Savage. During the summer, one of Northumberland's servants had been murdered by William Dixson, who was acquitted by 'some craft and subtlety contrary to justice' by the archbishop, at which the earl had made complaint to Sir Reginald Bray. The following year, on 23 May 1504, Northumberland travelled through Fulford just outside York with an escort of thirteen armed riders. A little earlier, the archbishop had passed through the town with eighty armed riders, a few of whom dawdled behind. Intercepting the earl's party, two rode deliberately between the earl and his men, causing his horse to stumble and fall to its knees. The earl, striking one of the interlopers in the face, exclaimed, 'What, is there no way sirs but over me?' The man's companion aimed a crossbow at the earl, but before he could fire it another of the archbishop's men sliced the bow. The archbishop complained to King Henry that the altercation was caused by Northumberland; the earl disputed this accusation. King Henry summoned them both to the Star Chamber. Each was ordered to enter into a bond of £2,000 to ensure their future good conduct.

In Yorkshire, Henry, Lord Percy was joined in the nursery by two brothers: Thomas, born in 1504 (or early 1505), and Ingram, born in 1506. During this latter year Northumberland appeared before the Court of Common Pleas to answer charges regarding the earlier 'ravishment of Elizabeth Hastings'. He was fined the extraordinary amount of £10,000. No clear picture has emerged as to what happened: six-year-old Elizabeth, after her father's death, died in 1502 while in the earl's household. Her mother, Catherine Aske, in her Will of February 1507, left a chain of gold to her brother Sir Robert, asking him to 'cause a stone to be laid over my husband at Norton Priory and another over me in the parish church of Aston-cum-Aughton, and if he think it to be done, to lay one for my daughter Elizabeth in Hemingbrough Church' (near Selby). In her list of bequests, she left to Our Lady of Hemingbrough a piece of cremel (lawn cloth) and a Venice of Gold lace set with pearl along with a kirtle of black damask and a corprax case (for linen cloth for the altar).

In the twenty-fourth year of his reign, Henry VII died on 21 April 1509 at Richmond Palace, leaving his seventeen-year-old son Henry to peacefully inherit the throne. On Wednesday 9 May, to the sound of trumpets and minstrels, the king's corpse entered London under a gold canopy on a chariot drawn by seven great coursers, surrounded by innumerable torches, to travel to St Paul's. As a Knight of the Garter, Northumberland followed the chariot with the king's crowned and robed effigy on its top. At the cathedral, the coffin was met at the west door, carried by twelve of the guard, to the hearse where vigil was kept day and night. After the usual ceremonies the following day, the procession began anew at one o'clock. The coffin was transported from St Paul's, along Fleet Street, past Charing Cross to Westminster Abbey. Carried to the high altar, the coffin was placed under 'a curious light of thirteen principal standards richly decked with banners'. After the dirge, knights were appointed to keep vigil.

Three solemn Masses were held before six o'clock the following morning, and offerings were made after the Requiem Mass. The Duke of Buckingham offered a testament of gold; the Earls of Arundel and Northumberland the king's coat armour; the Earls of Shrewsbury and Surrey the king's shield; the Earls of Essex and Kent his sword; and the Earls of Derby and Arran (the Scottish lord) the king's crowned helm. Sir Edward Howard, in full armour minus the helm, rode his courser up to the rails of the hearse, where he dismounted. The horse was received by the heralds while Sir Edward was presented between the Earls of Essex and Kent before disarming in the vestry. He returned dressed in a black gown. Buckingham and Northumberland laid palls upon the coffin. At the last, Sir Edmund Carew, on the second step of the high altar, offered the king's great banner and Sir Edward Darrell the king's standard. After removal of all the ornaments, the plain wooden coffin was placed into the vault beside that of Queen Elysabeth, who had died six years earlier. Among those receiving black mourning livery were Northumberland's sister Anne and his brother Joscelin, who was one of the king's cupbearers (and soon to retain the office under Henry VIII), and Thomas Boleyn, Esquire of the King's Body. The total length of cloth purchased came to more than 18,000 yards.

The new king held a chapter of the Order of St George at Greenwich on 18 May. The knights elected Thomas, Lord Darcy, and three days later Henry VIII appointed him Warden of the East Marches. Other appointees within the royal household were Sir Edward Poynings, comptroller; George, Earl of Shrewsbury, steward; Sir Charles Somerset, chamberlain, Sir Thomas Lovell, treasurer of the Household; and the Earl of Surrey, treasurer of the Exchequer. The Earl of Oxford retained his hereditary role of great chamberlain.

Henry VIII married the widow of his brother Arthur, twenty-three-year-old Katherine of Aragon, on 11 June in a simple private ceremony at Greenwich; Shrewsbury was one of the two witnesses. Eleven days later, on Friday 22 June, the pair travelled by royal barge along the river to the Tower of London. The king was resplendent in an ermine-furred purple gown over a gold damask satin doublet. At dinner, he ordered the twenty-six men due to be made Knights of the Bath the following day to serve his dishes 'in token that they shall never bear none after that day'. Among them were Richard Ratcliffe, Lord Fitzwater; Lord Scrope (of Bolton); Henry Clifford; Thomas Boleyn; Henry Wyatt; and Henry Sacheverell.

On Saturday, in brilliant sunshine, Henry and Katherine left the Tower to travel to Westminster. Vivid tapestries were hung from shops and houses, a vibrant backdrop to the huge crowds, railed in on one side, who loudly cheered the passing procession. First came the new Knights of the Bath wearing their hooded blue gowns with blue and white silk tassels on one shoulder. Edward, Duke of Buckingham, in a costly gown of needlework and with a jewelled collar about his neck, rode ahead of the king who was astride a horse trapped with gold damask. His ermine-furred robe was of crimson velvet over a gold jacket covered in diamonds, rubies, emeralds and pearls competing with his huge collar of ballas rubies. A golden canopy was carried over him by the Barons of the Cinque Ports and Sir Thomas Brandon rode after him, wearing cloth of tissue embroidered with gold roses and a gold baldric. All the lords, knights and esquires followed.

Queen Katherine, wearing white satin, sat in a litter carried by two white palfreys. A jewelled coronet kept her long hair from her face. Her attendants, in coloured silks, followed in chariots. Among them were the Countesses of Oxford, Surrey, Shrewsbury, Essex and Derby and the Ladies Elizabeth and Anne Stafford, Elizabeth Boleyn, Anne Percy (given the degree of a baroness and allowed a crimson velvet gown edged with tawny cloth of gold) and Mabel Clifford (who had only tawny velvet to edge her gown).

After the banquet and evening prayers in St Stephen's Chapel, the royal pair retired to sleep in the Painted Chamber. At eight the next morning, they left Westminster Hall to walk to the abbey on a striped ray cloth carpet. As soon as they entered, the carpet was immediately cut up by souvenir hunters. After the joint anointing and crowning, the great estates paid homage to the king. Afterwards they all returned to the palace for the banquet, the first course signalled by fanfare. Buckingham, riding a huge charger with richly embroidered trappings, entered alongside Shrewsbury riding a horse decked in cloth of gold, to oversee the service of many dainty dishes and subtleties with their strange devices and mottoes.

For the following day an entertainment had been arranged in the tiltyard, decorated to look like a woodland with trees, bushes and ferns. A band of men entered, all wearing gold plumes and a costume of white velvet with gold roses on one side and green velvet with gold pomegranates on the other. Another group of men, their green attire embroidered with gold brambles, then rode in. Around them were foresters blowing horns. White and green palings, like a fence, with gates were erected and fallow deer brought in to roam. The park gates were opened and greyhounds were let loose. The deer, chased and killed, were presented to the queen and her ladies. After the joy came sorrow, for the next day the king's grandmother, Margaret Beaufort, died; her page, Henry Parker, believed she took ill after eating a cygnet.

A few weeks later, quick to share tittle-tattle, especially if he thought it tinged with treason, Lord Darcy wrote to the Lord Privy Seal, Richard Fox (now Bishop of Winchester), that Northumberland's servants, returning from London after the coronation, had been heard to grumble that 'their master should rule all from Trent north, and have Berwick and the marches'; that Darcy received the grants before King Henry was crowned and believed they were thereby 'of none effect' and had complained that 'if their lord had not rooms in the North as his father had it should not long be well'. Lord Darcy suggested that if Fox thought it pertinent he should show his letter to the king.

Parliament opened on 21 January 1510. Northumberland, with the other lords, was arranged in procession in the queen's great chamber at Westminster.. The line-up began with esquires, knights, young lords, bishops and abbots flanked by officers of arms, dean and almoner and the Garter Knights. Lord Henry Stafford (to be created Earl of Wiltshire) bore the sword of state and his brother Buckingham bore the cap before the king. During the session many things were debated: the annual expenses for the King's Household (£19,394 16*s* 3½*d*), assignment of money for his Great Wardrobe (£2,015 19*s* 11*d*), repeal of a statute for fishing in

Iceland, coroners to take no fee when investigating bodies slain by misadventure, and cancellation of Northumberland's £10,000 fine and recognisance of £5,000.

During that January, Sir Thomas Boleyn, although in his early thirties, was part of the coterie around Henry VIII enjoying his 'innocent pastimes' and was one of the twelve green-clad Merry Men who burst into the queen's chamber armed with bow and arrows, dancing with the ladies before departing. (He was also a skilled jouster for, on 23 May, he jousted alongside the king against Sir Edward Howard and Christopher Willoughby.)

The investiture of Stafford took place on Sunday 3 February at Westminster. The king, and the lords standing around him, watched as Northumberland and Shrewsbury, wearing their robes of estate, led in Lord Stafford, who was preceded by his sword carried by the Earl of Derby. In April, Northumberland attended the chapter of the Garter held at Greenwich. At the ceremony, the king's almoner, Thomas Wolsey, was chosen to be the order's new registrar. The following day, after Mass for the Dead, Lord Thomas Howard, Surrey's eldest son, was elected; when he was called, the Garter was put around his thigh by Buckingham.

England was delighted when, on New Year's Day 1511, between two and three in the morning at Richmond Palace, Queen Katherine gave birth to a son. To honour her and celebrate the birth, her husband immediately arranged a joust for after her churching. Erected in the tiltyard was a forested mountain. In the midst of the Savage Forest was built a golden castle, and at its gate a gentleman weaved a garland of roses for the prize. On 12 February, to the sound of trumpets, four knights emerged from the mountain: Sir Loyal Heart (King Henry) rode a grey courser under a gold and purple pavilion embroidered with gold 'H's and 'K's; his three aides – Valiant Desire, Joyous Hope and Good Wish – had pavilions of crimson damask, each topped by a great gold 'K'. In the jousting that followed Sir Loyal Heart broke more lances than the others, while a thousand onlookers cheered and marvelled at the king's prowess. King Henry entered a pavilion near the tilt and came out riding upon a grey courser with white roses made of fine gold on its harness. Wearing a tight, straight coat with straight sleeves, cut in places and fastened with ribbon, he made his horse leap and turn, and turned his hooves against the tilt to beat the boards like a drum, resounding as if it was the shooting of guns. Stopping, he turned to the queen and made her a lowly obeisance.

On the second day of jousting Sir Charles Brandon, wearing a long russet satin robe like a religious recluse, with his horse also in russet, entered silently to neither drum nor music. He petitioned the queen to allow him to run, if it would please her. As she assented, he threw off his robe to reveal his armour beneath. Henry Guildford, in russet within a russet castle, followed him. Then entered two pilgrims of St James dressed in black with horses trapped in black but edged with gold scallop shells; they turned out to be the Marquis of Dorset and Sir Thomas Boleyn. Henry, Earl of Wiltshire, clothed in cloth of silver, entered shortly after with a crimson damask pavilion, embroidered with gold roses and arrows, a silver greyhound on its top bearing a tree of gold pomegranates, the branches so large that it 'overspread the pageant in all parts'.

Once again, after the joy and merriment, sorrow followed. The young prince died at Richmond on 22 February and was buried at Westminster Abbey five days later. A week earlier, on 15 February, Anne Percy married William FitzAlan, Lord Maltravers (heir to the Earl of Arundel) in the presence of the king, who made an offering of *6s 8d*.

At Michaelmas (the start of his financial year), Northumberland continued his extensive household ordinances in a new book. The immediate household then comprised the earl and his wife; Henry, Lord Percy and his brother Thomas; their brother Ingram in the nursery, which was shared with his sister Margaret (and sister Maud before she died); and the earl's brothers, William, Alan and

Joscelin (although the latter two were usually at court). Divided into fifty sections, the book detailed duties, hours of attendance, periods of rotation, diets, wages and allowances, graded by status and all strictly administered by a council composed of the earl's highest gentlemen officers: chamberlain, comptroller, treasurer, secretary, clerks of the kitchen and signet (and who sat at their own 17-foot 'knights' table' in the great chamber, as did the countess's two or three ladies and any kinswomen). The domestic household accounted for 166 people, with further provision made for 57 strangers every day. In 1511–12 the household wage bill came to £154 *6s 8d*; the total sum for one year (including the wages) was recorded as £933 *6s 8d*. (Northumberland's average income between 1515 to 1527 was just under £3,400 a year.)

What is called the Northumberland Household Book begins with Comptroller Richard Gouge and Clerk of the Kitchen Thomas Percy (in 1514 Robert Percy and Gilbert Weddell). After recording goods remaining in store, they are tasked with compiling a list of provisions required for the forthcoming year (noting seasons and prices to be paid). In the first year: 123 beefs (100 fat at Hallowtide and 23 lean after Midsummer to be fattened), 667 muttons (similarly divided), 25 pigs (porks), 28 veals, 60 lambs (10 at 12*d* each from Christmas to Shrovetide and 50 at 10*d* each to serve from Easter to Midsummer), 140 stockfish and 942 saltfish, 9 barrels of white herring, 10 cades (a cade was a barrel of 500) of red (smoked) herring, 5 cades of sprats plus figs, spices and hops for brewing, 1½ barrels of honey and the same of oil, 4,087 lbs of wax for sises, prickets (a spiked candle), quarions (square-shaped wax with a wick) and torches, 39 lbs of rosin for torches and 2 lbs of wick. For Lent: 180 salt salmon at *6d* each, 3 firkins of salt sturgeon and 5 kegs of salt eels. The spices, ordered yearly, comprised pepper, currants, prunes, ginger, mace, cloves, sugar, cinnamon, almonds, dates, figs, nutmeg, rice, saffron, grains (of Paradise), galingale (like ginger), salt and anise.

Other requisite items included oats for the horses, wood, coals and charcoal (an amount for Christmastide as smoke from sea-coal could harm the arras) plus thirty sacks of charcoal for distilling flavoured waters (such as water for the stone, rose, parsley, oak leaf, primrose and other wild flowers and herbs), red, rose and white wines (including a Vin de Greave) from Bordeaux or Gascony and sweet wines. For the horses they listed the mowing and making of hay and shoeing them. (The list did not include the daily tallies from the bakehouse, woodyard or outlying farms for things such as butter, eggs and vegetables, nor venison from his parks and fish from his rivers.) On top of all this, the earl reserved certain foods for himself (and his guests and sometimes his chamberlain and steward) which did not figure on the list, which enumerates forty-seven varieties of wildfowl including swans, peacocks, cranes, bustards, herons, redshanks and bitterns all of which were reserved for 'principal feasts'. He preferred to purchase leather pots instead of earthenware for serving meals and reserved the use of his pewter for Christmas, Easter, the St George feast, Whitsun and All Saints, it being too costly to be used commonly.

In later years, the earl endeavoured to economise. He ordered all trencher bread to be made from the mill's meal, horse-bread to be baked in the bakehouse, all beer to be brewed in the brewhouse, vinegar (40 gallons) to be made in-house from broken wines and mustard (160 gallons) to be made by the groom of the scullery (and not purchased from the sauce maker). Stockfish was only to be purchased when saltfish was dear and 'no lambs to be bought when they are at their dearest'.

Mass was performed every morning at six o'clock. Officers met between seven o'clock and half-past eight to scrutinise supplies and prices, to undertake any planning required, make out duty rosters, discuss shortcomings in provisions (or servants) and note who would be dining in, this latter to calculate the number of messes required. (A mess was a dish which served four persons.) Festival days were accounted separately as visitors 'exceedeth the ordinary' and at those times the earl decreed accounting was to be made twice daily after dinner and supper at principal feasts 'to prevent officers forgetting for long bearing of it in their minds'.

The family had breakfast after Matins, around seven o'clock. The earl and countess would each have on meat days (with trenchers) 'two manchets (fine bread), a quart of beer, a quart of wine, half a chine of mutton or a chine of boiled beef' and on fish days, replacing the meat, two pieces of saltfish, six 'baconed herrings' or a dish of sprats or three white (salted) herrings. Henry and Thomas, who appeared to have shared a room before Henry received his own chamber and servants, received on 'flesh days' half a loaf of household bread, a manchet, a pottle of beer, and a chicken or three mutton bones boiled; on fish days a dish of butter, a piece of saltfish a dish of sprats or three white herrings. In the nursery. Lady Margaret and Master Ingram received 'a manchet, quart of beer, three broiled mutton bones' and on fish days 'a dish of butter, a piece of salt fish, a dish of sprats or three white herrings'.

Between ten and eleven (eleven to noon on fish days), dinner was served in strict ceremony, just as it was for supper. The yeoman of the ewery would see every board cleaned and covered with fine linen tablecloths (87 yards of yard-wide linen was purchased annually for all the napery, carefully measured and cut) smoothed out by rods. Basins, towels and jugs of water were made ready (so diners could wash their hands and faces and ensure their nails were clean). Tables were set with salt, napkins and trenchers (precisely cut four-inch-squares of dry bread). The duties of gentlemen waiters, carvers and servers saw covered dishes brought from the kitchen to the dresser. From there they would be ceremonially placed on tables, perhaps first going to the carver (for items to be carved into bite-sized pieces). The yeoman of the cellar poured drinks on command, given to the cupbearers. The earl had his own personal waiter, carver, server, cupbearer, pantler, butler and ewerer with two yeomen of the chamber; his wife had her own cupbearer, carver, server and waiter.

Once the table was cleared the void would be brought in, usually wafers, spices, battered cheese and fruit. The children as they grew older would be taught, among other things, to eat daintily, to place bones in a bowl set for the purpose, not to put elbows on the table (wisely as tables were usually boards set on top of trestles) and to use the tip of a clean knife to place salt on food or trencher. Supper was served around four or five in the afternoon (a little later in wintertime while rooms were lit), followed by music, dancing or an entertainment. The castle gates were shut around nine o'clock in the summer. When the earl retired, his attendants, while he prayed privately, conducted the 'all night', making his bed, lighting candles, and delivering the evening livery: both he and the countess received bread, beer and wine, six white wax candles and three syses; Henry, Lord Percy and Thomas and Lady Margaret (in the nursery with Ingram) were allowed three white lights with bread and a pottle of beer. All the offices were locked securely for the night.

Festival days marked the year. A formal procession to the chapel, the earl with his sword borne before him, began Christmas Day. The chapel's singing men (three bass, four tenors and four countertenors) performed the nativity while the six chapel children (who sang treble) performed 'Gloria in excelsis Deo'. Dinner, with special dishes, was served in the great hall hung about with arras. Smaller banquets were served on the feasts of St Stephen, St John, Holy Innocents and St Thomas. On Holy Innocents, a Barn Bishop would arrive either from Beverley or York and receive 20*s* in reward. These ordinances reveal glimpses of the children as they grew: on New Year's Day, three minstrels (playing tabor, lute and rebec) played first at the earl's chamber door and then his wife's, and received in reward 13*s* 4*d* from the earl and 6*s* 8*d* from the countess. Mimicking this, when the children were older they played at Henry's chamber door and received 2*s*, then at the chamber doors of his younger brothers, who each gave them 8*d*.

Twelfth Day and Night were the culmination of the season. For dinner in the great hall, a great carpet was laid on the floor betwixt hearth and screen. Tables were covered with carpets overlaid with linen tablecloths, as were dressers and a five-height stage displaying plate. On the high table the great gold standing salt was placed, with a smaller gold salt for the assay, and gold spoons and carving knives. The earl and countess sat alone (this time no 'Reward' seats – places at table given as an honour). Henry, Lord Percy, when he was 'at age', was seated with his father. At the board end, a gentleman usher knelt giving attendance and two chaplains said grace and acted as almoners (they collected leftover food and drink to give to the poor).

Perpendicular to the dais were set three long tables. The chamberlain's table, below the earl, included the countess's ladies and gentlemen strangers, was laid with two silver salts (without covers) and silver spoons. The dean of the chapel oversaw the next table, set with three salts, with the chapel staff (a surveyor, sub-dean, epistler, gospeller, organ player, two secretaries including William Peeris, who wrote the plays), a riding chaplain and also a chaplain for Henry, Lord Percy (who waited upon him daily) and a master of grammar (who was probably employed when Henry attained the age of six or seven years) and the gentlemen and children singers. The steward's table, below the countess, seated the council and head officers. If necessary a table was set up in the gallery for strangers and their dishes were brought to them via the little door at the back of the kitchen.

On Twelfth Night all tables and cupboards were covered with linen as before and cushions were brought in for the earl and countess. The yeoman of the cellar and groom of the mouth brought in the couple's cups and brought the plate from the cellar to be placed on the cupboard. After Evensong, standard bearers came into the hall to ensure it had been well lit. The great procession formed: the marshal waited at the hall door to lead in the children, gentlemen and dean of the chapel, shown where to stand by two yeomen ushers. The gentlemen, in ascending order of rank, entered, followed by officers and council and the comptroller, treasurer, steward and herald walking in pairs. The earl walked in the centre of the procession and behind him came his brother William (and, as they came of age, his sons Henry, Thomas and Ingram), the chamberlain, the countess and Lady Margaret (before she married), ladies and gentlewomen, with the rear of the procession brought up by the yeomen. All in place, the revels began. Gifts were given by the earl to his family, household and guests.

Disguisers entered the hall (and if any were women they came in first) with torches borne before them by yeomen waiters, who returned to light the entrance of the male disguisers and then stood to one side. Minstrels and musicians played, as they did for the Morris dancing that followed, entering the hall from the earl's tower. Sometimes a comedy play was performed (the earl had a troupe of twenty actors). The music would start up for the dancing. The master of the revels would introduce a gentleman to a lady for them to dance together. Afterwards she would be returned to her seat with an obeisance from her partner, who departed.

The main event of the evening was the bringing in of the Wassail cake (one each for the earl and his wife). The yeoman of the pantry brought in salts, carving knives, bread and trenchers. Two yeomen ushers and two gentlemen ushers preceded the marshal bearing his white rod. He led in the herald, treasurer, comptroller and steward. Whoever was last cried, 'Wassail!' thrice as he entered. One groom, a towel upon his shoulder, carried the earl's Wassail cake to him, and another did likewise for the countess. The chapel sang the carol, with minstrels playing, until everyone had tasted the cake. A two-course banquet of several dishes came next, followed by the void (comfits, spiced sweetmeats and hippocras). Afterwards, minstrels played music for dancing. Anyone disposed to games was provided a table with cards and dice. And when the earl and his wife retired, all the chapel went before them singing carols, out of the hall, through the knights' chamber until they reached their own rooms.

All the excitement over, the earl broke up the household and retired to his 'secret house' (to the smaller lodges to live 'privately'). Servants were placed on board wages and lodged in the town or stayed with friends or family until the earl reassembled the household on 11 January.

As the children grew, living privately had different permutations: at first the earl and his wife sat at the high board with his brother; later all his children sat with them; then just the three boys after Margaret married and then, when he had his own chamber and his own waiting gentlemen, Henry sat at the table with his father and mother while his brothers waited upon them, Thomas as carver and Ingram as server.

Candles were offered at Mass on 2 February. On Shrove Tuesday night, the chapel performed a play in the great hall which was followed by a disguising and Morris dance. If the earl was at home for the feast of St George, he was led through the knights' chamber and into the great chamber. During dinner and supper minstrels played. The following day a Requiem Mass was held for the souls of all Garter Knights who had departed, at which the earl gave an offering of 4*d* and a further 4*d* for his father; Henry, Thomas and Ingram offered 1*d* each for their grandfather.

On Maundy Thursday, the earl (if at home) gave 'as many russet cloth gowns with a hood, linen shirts, bread, meat and ashen cups of wine and penny pieces in leather purses as he counted years' and one for his age to come. After the ceremony he removed his own lambskin-lined violet gown (made purposely for the occasion) and gave it to the poorest man present. One of his chaplains delivered on behalf of his wife as many groats of her age and one to come to that number of poor men, and the same for Lord Percy and his brothers. On Good Friday, the earl and his sons crept to the Cross and the earl offered 4*d*, and 2*d* for Henry and 1*d* each for Thomas and Ingram. On Easter Eve the family partook of communion and on Easter Sunday morning enjoyed the play of the Resurrection, enacted in the chapel. Ascension Day was celebrated with a High

Mass at which the earl offered 12*d*, his wife 8*d* and Henry and his brothers 1*d* each.

Besides a herald, a pursuivant (not allowed a servant), an armourer and two falconers, the earl had a master of horse who supervised a team of grooms, which also included one for the hounds (hunt), one who helped the family mount, a sumpterman (for packhorses) and one for the chariot. The earl's own horses numbered thirty-three. When riding locally he would be attended by his master of horse, two grooms and two henchmen (gentlemen's sons). When roaming further afield, his riding household comprised thirty-six henchmen in four groups: five went ahead as harbingers, the next group travelled with clothes and necessaries, and one of the other two went before the earl while the other followed him.

As he grew older, Henry, Lord Percy was given his own stable by his father. He was obviously old enough at this time to go hawking and hunting, for he had a little nag (the name given to reliable, sure-footed and even-tempered horses) to ride when he did so. He was also provided with an ambling horse for his daily journeys, a great double-trotting horse for travelling in winter, 'a curtal (a great double-trotting horse) for riding out of town and a gambalding horse to ride in towns'. He also had a great ambling or trotting gelding to carry his 'mail with his stuff for his change when he rides'. His younger brothers had a nag each.

4

'THEIR SPURS FLASHING...'

On the international stage, Henry VIII provoked the French in autumn 1511 by joining the Holy League, created by the Venetians and Katherine of Aragon's father Ferdinand to defend the Papal States from French hostility. In response, King Louis XII of France manoeuvred James IV of Scotland into making war on England the following summer. When the Scots attacked Berwick, a thirty-thousand-strong army was sent north with the Earl of Surrey at its head and Northumberland as one of its captains. In January 1513, Henry Percy's fifteen-year-old cousin Elizabeth Stafford was forced into marrying Surrey's eldest son, the forty-year-old widower Lord Thomas Howard. Buckingham, knowing his daughter was in love with his ward Ralph Neville, Earl of Westmorland, tried to persuade Howard to marry another daughter but the man was adamant he would only have Elizabeth.

The following month, Northumberland received a letter of royal command instructing him to provide three hundred archers and a hundred each of demi-lancers and billmen on foot, all well equipped, and prepare himself to travel overseas. A follow-up letter revealed he would be given shipping and passage for six horses, five captains, ten horses, five petty captains, five horses, a hundred demi-lancers, a hundred horses, four carriages for himself and twenty-four horses – all to be ready by 28 May at Dover or Sandwich. He was to pay his and his retinue's passage and for any horses or carriages above his allotted allowance. He was to receive monthly wages of £439 9*s* 8*d*.

Sir Thomas Boleyn, returning from his embassy to Margaret of Savoy, Governor of the Low Countries (and Holy Roman Emperor Maximilian I's daughter), was stranded at Calais on 11 May. His mission had been to persuade the emperor to join the Holy League. Before leaving for home, he had arranged for his six-year-old daughter Anne to join Margaret's household. In the early days of June, Margaret wrote to him, 'I have received your letter by the Esquire Bouton who has presented your daughter to me, who is very welcome ... I find her so bright and pleasant for her young age that I am more beholden to you for sending her to me than you are to me.' (Claude Bouton was Margaret's Flemish envoy who was returning from a diplomatic mission to Henry VIII; he and Anne's father were well acquainted.) Six months later Anne was joined in the household by two compatriots: six-year-old Anne Brandon (daughter of Charles, styled Viscount Lisle after his betrothal to his ward, the eight-year-old heiress Elizabeth Grey) and Charles's adopted daughter Magdalen Rochester (born sometime in 1505 and adopted after Charles had saved her from drowning). During the summer, Lord Percy's uncle Joscelin left the north, being appointed the king's cupbearer at court, receiving a monthly wage of 18*s* 9*d*.

Lord Percy and his brothers may have been excited to observe the preparations their father was making for war, watching weapons and campaigning equipment being packed into coffers and carts. Just for himself, their father was taking six sumpter horses to carry plate (including two silver salts, twelve silver spoons, a washing basin, standing cup and four candlesticks), a trussing bed, quilt, feather mattress and cushions, his armour, money and iron-hooped barrels of wine. Another sumpter horse and a wagon carried the earl's apparel, the exhaustive detail of which gives an insight into the degree of finery an earl brought with him: four arming doublets (worn under armour), one each of crimson and green satin and two quilted white satin; a gross of white silk and a dozen white silk and Venice gold arming points, plus sixteen dozen for the earl's hose in equal amounts of crimson, black, green and tawny; black silk ribbons for doublets and sleeves; three pairs of white arming hose with laps and several pairs of hose in scarlet, crimson, black, tawny and white; Milanese coats of mail and one of plate, helms and leg harness; an arming coat in green edged with silver and lined with black sarcenet, and one cloth of silver edged with green and a cloak of crimson satin edged with green; two white satin arming platelets lined with linen to wear under his harness and bolster to wear about his middle for bearing the cuirass; linen shirts to wear under his armour; a furred russet nightgown; six black bonnets and six scarlet night bonnets; coifs, girdles and hatbands; two pair of black leather boots, two pair of night buskins (one pair red, the other black cordwain furred with black lamb), twelve pairs of arming shoes – black, white, red and yellow – and a pair of arming shoes in white leather covered with black velvet. He also took kerchiefs, garters and gloves. His horse harness was to be equally fine, with a 'change for every day and another when meeting princes which be the king's friends'.

For bodily ills he took with him six tiny bottles: one holding *aqua vitae*, one water for the stone, two for water of oak leaves (used to treat haemorrhage, diarrhoea and dysentery), and two spare. For his own tent, the earl had a foldable stool of ease covered with tawny leather, a cupboard (which served as an altar), four folding tables (two for himself, one for his clerk to write upon and one for the pantry/cooks to use for dressing his meat), with accompanying folding forms and thirteen three-legged stools with seats of black leather. A seven-horsed wagon was packed with items for kitchen, pantry, buttery and cellar: kettles, a large-handled iron frying pan, a saucepan, pots and ladles, gridirons, tongs, four iron spits, knives (including two leeching knives), a spade to make a kitchen trench, a great leather bottle (carrying thirty gallons of water), a gallon-bottle of verjuice, four gallons fine mustard, three gallons of vinegar and a sack of white salt. Spices, only delivered to the cook when the earl's meat was dressed, included 4 lbs pepper, 4 sugar loaves, ½ lbs of mace, ¼ lbs of saffron, 3 lbs prunes, 4 lbs small raisins, 3 lbs rice flour, ½ lbs of saunders (red sandalwood); 4 lbs ginger and 3 lbs cinnamon. There were also candlesticks, lanterns, wax torches and 7 lbs of prickets and 12 lbs of mortars for lighting. Practical items were also packed: iron mattocks for setting tent poles and stakes; spades (to dig trenches of ease), three scythes for cutting grass for the horses and axes to cut wood for fires.

The weapons packed included 420 bows with corresponding sheafs of arrows and red and black leather arrow cases, halberds for the billmen and lances for the demi-lancers. A close cart pulled by six horses carried 'all manner of secret stuff' and three carts pulled by five horses each carried the hovels, tents and pavilions to house his army and included the ironwork, armoury and saddlery – and slings to convey horses aboard ship – which included horses for gifts for the Dukes of Burgundy and Brittany. The earl also saw to the making and packing of liveries for his captains, petty captains and gentlemen and heraldic bannerolls, guidons, banners and escutcheons (including white crescents upon red and black paper for his lackeys' lodgings). An entry in the Household Book reveals that, with his officers and servants receiving king's wages by the day, the earl ordered Thomas Percy to ensure that those attending him overseas should have no household wages – these would restart when they returned. He also appointed one William Worme, a gentleman usher of the earl's chamber, to be his cofferer (treasurer) and his general receiver of his lands in 'the north parts'.

Did Henry, Thomas and Ingram watch with pride as their father, 'the Grand Captain of his own retinue', rode off to war in the hot June weather? Did they see the troops of 523 men set off with their captains – Sir John Normanville, Roger Lascelles, John Lamplugh, Cuthbert Musgrave and William Middleton? Embarking from Dover for Calais on 16 June, Hall described Northumberland's company: 'The lords and gentlemen so well-armed and so richly apparelled in cloth of gold, of silver, velvets of sundry colours pounced and embroidered, all petty captains in satin and damask of white and green, yeomen in cloth of the same colours.'

According to the diary of John Taylor, Clerk of the Parliaments, Northumberland was ordered to join Shrewsbury (Lieutenant of the Vanguard) at the siege of Thèrouanne, setting off on 29 June. A day later, Taylor watched from the sea walls as King Henry arrived with his fleet, 'saluted with such firing of guns from the ships and from the towers, you would have thought the world was coming to an end'. While the gunners, pioneers, demi-lancers and Almains (totalling some 9,466 men) disembarked, the king enjoyed meeting ambassadors and participating in entertainments. Thomas Wolsey, with Charles, Viscount Lisle, oversaw the unloading of the king's bed of estate, several sets of armour, fourteen fine horses (with their silver-belled trappings of gold and crimson), the blue, yellow and white fabric tents and pavilions (and animal toppers), the gigantic Twelve Apostles cannon (each cast with an image of an apostle), the king's travelling wooden house (which by itself took up fourteen wagons) and all the other provisions and supplies for the army, the culmination of thousands of receipted orders. Wolsey also saw to the welfare of the soldiers by employing between eighty and ninety surgeons and physicians and drawing up Statutes of War which forbade acts of sacrilege, robbery or violence towards civilians, firing houses and entering houses where women were lying in childbed.

King Henry set off from Calais on 21 July. John Taylor, travelling with him, recorded that on '1 August, pitched the camp at the first milestone from Thèrouanne; heavy rain in the night which lasted day and night following, with violent wind; the soldiers up to their knees in mud'. En route the king had hanged three Germans for disrespecting churches, had provisions from Calais intercepted and lost two of his Apostles, one captured and the other stuck in a pond. Workmen sent to retrieve the latter were slain by the French. Taylor wrote on 4 August they had joined the besieging army and Emperor

Maximilian had visited the trenches. He described him as 'of middle height, with open and manly countenance; pallid complexion; has a snub nose and a grey beard. Is affable, frugal, an enemy to pomp.'

At daybreak on 16 August, while cavalry attacked the besiegers to distract them, a separate company of cavalry led by Louis d'Orleans, Duc de Longueville attempted to sneak supplies to the starving garrison. They were spotted by Northumberland's archers, who dismounted and unleashed arrows upon them. Surprised, they turned tail, 'their spurs flashing' in the bright sunshine as they retreated so fast they left behind lances, standards and bits of horse armour. The earl's light horse pursued them for 3 miles, capturing many noble persons, including the Duc de Longueville (who was sent to reside in the Tower of London). John Carr, a Yorkshireman in Northumberland's troop, was singled out and knighted by the king for his bravery at what became known as the Battle of the Spurs. Thèrouanne surrendered on 22 August.

While King Henry visited Margaret of Savoy at Lille on 12 September, Shrewsbury moved the army to besiege Tournai. There, on 16 September, Northumberland received astonishing news that would have already seen his sons bursting with pride. On 9 September, English and Scottish armies met and fought on Flodden Field. In the melee Sir Guiscard Harbottle, Constable of Prudhoe Castle by Northumberland's appointment, fought in hand-to-hand combat with King James, who 'laid upon him so heavy a blow using both hands that it descended from his shoulder down his side and left him lifeless on the ground'. Surrey then engaged the Scottish king, killing him a mere spear's length away. The earl's brother William was second-in-command of the left wing with the Alnwick archers, fighting lustily alongside his father-in-law, seventy-year-old Sir Marmaduke Constable. Surrey dubbed William a knight banneret for his outstanding bravery. (For his own bravery, the following year the Earl of Surrey regained his dukedom as second Duke of Norfolk; his eldest son, Thomas, became Earl of Surrey.)

In 1514, domestic matters in the north saw Northumberland, now returned home, enter Preston Manor on 22 March to secure George Harbottle, son of Sir Guiscard, whom he believed to be rightfully his ward. (Sir Guiscard was the son of Margaret Percy (granddaughter of the second Earl of Northumberland) and Sir Ralph Harbottle of Horton.) Sir Guiscard had betrothed George to Margery, the daughter of Lord Ogle (who had died the previous year). George's mother, Jane Willoughby of Wollaton, complained to Wolsey (now Bishop of Lincoln and the king's leading councillor in all state matters) disputing the wardship and complaining that the earl had sold her son's wardship and marriage to Lord Ogle's widow, Margaret Gascoigne, who had leased out Horton Manor to Thomas Lisle.

A few weeks later, Venetian ambassador Sebastian Giustinian, newly arrived in London, was invited by King Henry to celebrate the festival of St George at Greenwich. The few attendees included the Duke of Norfolk and Charles Brandon, now Duke of Suffolk (rumour was rife this title was granted to allow him to court Margaret of Savoy after they had flirted together). In his report to the Doge, Giustinian described King Henry as 'the handsomest potentate I ever set eyes on, above the usual height with an extremely fine calf to his leg, his complexion very fair and bright, with auburn hair combed straight and short, in the French fashion, and a round face so very beautiful, that it would become a pretty woman, his throat being rather long and thick ... Plays well on the lute and harpsichord, sings from book at sight, draws the bow with greater strength than any man in England, and jousts marvellously.' In another report he wrote the king was 'very fond indeed of hunting, and never takes this diversion without tiring eight or ten horses, which he causes to be stationed beforehand along the line of country he may mean to take, and when one is tired, he mounts another, and before he gets home they are all exhausted. He is extremely fond of tennis, at which game it is the prettiest thing in the world to see him play, his fair skin glowing through a shirt of the finest texture.'

Upon discovering duplicitous activities by Ferdinand and Maximilian, King Henry ordered Wolsey to negotiate a peace treaty with France. The treaty was sealed with a betrothal between Henry's sister Mary and King Louis (his last wife, Anne of Brittany, had died in January). Peace was proclaimed at Greenwich on 7 August when Louis d'Orleans, Duc de Longueville (who had been lodged in comfortable apartments in the Tower and often visited court) took seventeen-year-old Princess Mary's right hand and espoused her on behalf of the French king, thirty-five years her senior, giving her a gold ring which she placed on the fourth finger of her right hand. After Mary, wearing her night attire and lying in the bridal bed, was touched just above her ankle by the Marquis of Rothelin's 'naked leg' (bare from mid-thigh to his feet), the marriage was considered consummated. On 14 August, Sir Thomas Boleyn wrote from Greenwich to Margaret of Savoy 'with humble heart to his very dear and beloved lady', saying the new Queen Mary wishes 'to have with her *ma fille, la petite Boulain* ... I do not know how to refuse to do so, and I beg you very humbly that you will give and grant to my daughter to return by way of my people whom I send to you for this cause', thanking her for the great honour she had shown his daughter Anne.

News came in the autumn of the death of Cardinal Bainbridge, Archbishop of York, who was believed to have been poisoned by his servants. Thomas Wolsey was given the archbishopric by the king. Described by Hall as 'eloquent and full of wit', Wolsey immediately began remodelling York Place (near Westminster Palace). Bricks arrived by barge from Battersea for the building of a new hall, great chamber, kitchens and wine cellars. The gardens and orchards were also renewed. From Scotland, information came that Queen Margaret, on 1 September, had secretly married Archibald Douglas, the young Earl of Angus.

The weather being fair, Queen Mary's wardrobe, stable and riches had already been shipped when, on 2 October, the king waited in the early morning hours to say goodbye to her at the waterside. Among those accompanying her were the Duke and Duchess of

Norfolk, the Earl of Surrey, Lord Edmund Howard and Sir Thomas Boleyn. Mary begged her brother to remember she was marrying Louis, who was 'aged and very sickly', for his pleasure and that he had promised, should Louis die, she could marry a man of her choosing afterwards. The wedding of Mary and Louis took place on 9 October, and almost as soon as the ceremony was over King Louis discharged all her servants except six of her youngest ladies, one of whom was Mary Boleyn. She complained bitterly that she was left only with those who had little experience of the world.

At Christmas, the chronicler Hall recorded that King Henry – and with him Charles, Duke of Suffolk and two others – entered court wearing cloth-of-silver mantles lined with blue velvet, with great capes (emulating those Portuguese grandees wore), in gold-embroidered doublets, coats and hose. Four ladies in gold bonnets and blue velvet gowns, hooped in the Savoy fashion, danced with them. Three of the ladies were Mistress Carew (the young wife of Nicholas Carew) and Ladies Guilford and Fellinger. The fourth, who danced with the king, was Elizabeth Blount, the king's fourteen-year-old mistress who had captured his eye after his return from France. Hall more romantically said she had captured the king's heart with chains of love in his 'fresh youth' and described her as a fair damsel who 'in singing, dancing and all goodly pastimes exceeded all other'. The record of this mummery also mentions one Master Boleyn, marking perhaps the first appearance of Anne's brother George, presumed to be about ten years old at the time.

Between autumn 1514 and spring 1515, Henry's sister Margaret, now fifteen years old, became the second wife of twenty-two-year-old widower Henry Clifford, son of the tenth Baron Clifford of Skipton. His first wife was Margaret Talbot, daughter of George, fourth Earl of Shrewsbury; they had grown up together at court. For the wedding, the manor chapel (including the two altars at the chapel door) was covered with the best arras and carpets were placed on the floor. The altars bore images of the saints, silver and gilt candlesticks, basins, ewers, cruets and chalice and a cross upon a stage. Cushions were set before the altar for the couple to kneel on. Margaret, who slept in her mother's chamber, was helped to dress. The ushers placed the procession according to rank while the chamberlain ordered two unmarried lords to lead the bride to the chapel door, the gentlewomen following behind her in pairs.

After the ceremony, Margaret returned to her mother's chamber to await the signal for her wedding dinner, led to the table by two gentlemen ushers who removed the board to allow her to easily seat herself, with Countess Katheryne sitting at the end of her table. There were two (possibly three) courses: the first course at a wedding was always brawn with mustard, served alone with sweet wine. This was probably followed by a frumenty or pottage, and, being a joyous celebration, perhaps dishes of venison, young herons, capon, pheasant, a fish dish, a meat or pork and cheese pie, fritters, sweetmeats or marchpane, a tart and fruit. If there had been a third course they might have been served cream of almonds, partridge, a meat pie, bread puffs and cheese with fruit (and it being winter the fruit would most likely have been roasted apples).

Margaret rested in her chamber while the hall was voided. When all was ready and the minstrels in place, a gentleman usher signalled for her mother to take her daughter by the hand, with all the ladies following, and bring her to the hall where she was presented to her uncle William for the first dance. Supper was served after that, and once the eating was done the bride and groom sat together to watch a disguising. At bedtime, all the men were told to depart, leaving only women around her to lead her to the bedchamber, where Henry was sitting in the bed in his shirt, a gown cast about him. All the following day Margaret stayed in the chamber attended only by women. On the third day she went to the chapel to offer a taper. In the Household Book new rules appeared: 'My Lord uses and accustometh to give yearly to the servant of his son-in-law that hath married his lordship's daughter if he be upon New Year's Day with his lordship and sends his Lordship a New Year gift 13*s* 4*d* and ... similarly in reward to his daughter's servant 6*s* 8*d*.'

Meanwhile, shock news arrived from France: On New Year's Day 1515, King Louis was discovered dead in his bed at six o'clock in the morning. His son-in-law, twenty-year-old Francis Valois, was now king, for his fourteen-year-old wife Claude was not allowed by French law to ascend to the throne. The widowed Mary, now designated *La Reine Blanche*, retired to a darkened room in Cluny Palace where she was supposed to remain secluded for six weeks. Instead, pestered by the new king, she took a drastic measure: Suffolk, sent to France by King Henry, wrote to Wolsey on 5 March that Queen Mary 'would never let me be in rest till I had granted her to be married; and so to be plain with you, I have married her heartily and have lain with her, insomuch as I fear me that she be with child'. As regards the king, he had 'rather died than he should be miscontent'.

The king was, in fact, very 'miscontent' and exacted a heavy price: Suffolk was to pay yearly to the king during his wife's life £4,000 of her dower (which left her £6,000) and to hand over all plate and jewels given to her by King Louis. Mary, reminding Henry of his promises, wrote he had known her 'good mind' to the Duke of Suffolk. The two had an open marriage ceremony on 30 March in France. Mary and her new husband returned to England on 2 May and were married again on 13 May at Greenwich in 'presence of the king and queen and such other nobles and estates as then were attending in court'. Mary Boleyn, along with Mary's other maids, returned to England with their mistress. Her sister Anne, at an unknown date, became part of Queen Claude's household, becoming close friends with Claude's sister, four-year-old Renée. On 30 May Suffolk wrote from Greenwich to Archduchess Margaret that he had been grateful for the reception of his daughter Anne, 'whom he had intended to leave permanently with her' but the queen, his wife, was 'desirous of her presence'; Magdalene remained with the archduchess.

The previous summer, Wolsey had been granted a ninety-nine-year lease for an annual rent of £50 on a manor lying 20 miles south-west of London. Hampton Court, a day's ride from Windsor, was easily reached in a few hours by barge via the newly built water-stairs at York Place. He now began commissioning the best carpenters, joiners, painters and gilders (some from as far away as Italy). A moat was dug. A herb garden was planted with parsley, thyme, caraway and coriander. Two great kitchens and a smaller one for his personal use were built. Stone came from Reigate and Barnet, timber from Weybridge and Reading, and thousands of red baked bricks arrived daily. By May 1516 a glazier had put in 65 feet of window glass on both sides of the gallery for views of gardens or the river. Some 280 guest chambers (mostly double lodgings) were completed. All principal apartments had baths and toilet facilities.

Wolsey was not alone in building. Since his return from France, Northumberland had completed his own projects, finishing by painting his Wressle garden house (his summer study or reading room) with a poem on the counsel of Aristotle to Alexander (at Leconfield he had an alternative translation of Aristotle's advice painted). Castle rooms were adorned with proverbs, poems which stressed the fickleness of fortune and the perils of flattery and greed, along with several verses of instruction, such as:

If thou surfeit in drink, forget not that,
Avyse the oft thou come not in that snare,
Withdraw thy hand, feed not thyself to fat,
Drink that suffice thee and other while thou spare,
Too much drink makes men of wit bare,
And the wine thereof is not to blame,
But the drinker bringeth himself to great dissame.

Believe not the saying of every wight,
For some reporteth all otherwise,
Than ever it was for malice and disport,
And some hath of custom and of guise,
To feed folk with faining and flattering lies,

Give little trust therefore to such speaking,
For many one be found contrary to their saying.

When fortune hath given thee high felicity,
Yet wisely look about for suddenly thou may fall,
After great wealth follows sharp adversity,
False fortune turneth as doth a ball,
In trust of her is no surety at all,
Her wanton play is so full of peril and blame,
That the end is woe which began with game.

To have to do if it fortune thee
With him which is not equal to thy might,
To thy uttermost power show never thy cruelty,
For by chance thou may come to the same plight,
For it is seen in tournament and in fight,
That fortune changeth all suddenly,
And he is overrun which had the victory.

As the time requireth so make thyne expense,
Measure thy hand after thy degree,
According to the time and also the presence
So that thou spend no more than needeth thee,
To thy assured friends be liberal and free,
And when thy mind is to make such cost,
Provide always wisely that it be not lost.

No thing to fortune thou apply,
For her gifts vanish as doth fantasy.
The more thou receiveth of her gifts most unsure,
The more to thee approacheth displeasure.
Then in blind fortune put not thy trust,
For her brightness soon receiveth rust,
Fortune is fickle, fortune is blind,
Her rewards be fickle and unkind.

The world is round like a ball,
And to dalliance it doth thee call,
But I hear another sound,
Which bideth and other way rebound,
For fear of a worse that may confound.

The bathing houses were covered with poetic commentary:

The Part Sensative
The surmounting pleasure who can express,
Which is in harmony of song and the sweetness,
All pensiveness it putteth away,
And with mirth and solace driveth forth the day.

The Part Intellective
On such momentary pleasure if thou set they mind,
The joy that is everlasting thou may never find;
Joy here and in heaven thou canst not obtain,
Vanitas vanitatum all that is but vain.

The Part Sensative
Rich apparel, costly and precious,
Maketh a man lusty, comely and glorious,
Vestueries of estate wrought preciously,
Causeth men to be honoured and much set by.

The Part Intellective
In such apparel if thou set thine affection,
In thy soul it will cause sinful infection;
It will not excuse thee, I tell thee plain,
Vanitas vanitatum all this is but vain.

Besides the verses, there were also drawings of allegorical figures coupled with verses covering gardens, wisdom, friends, good counsel, good manners and music – especially of song and musical instruments such as harp, clavichord and lute:

> He that fingereth well the keys of the clavichord maketh a good song,
> For in the mean is the melody with a rest long,
> If the tunes be not pleasant to him that hath no skill,
> Yet no lack to the clavichord for it doeth his good will.
>
> A slack string in a virginal soundeth not right,
> It doth abide no wresting it is so loose and light,
> The sound board crased since the instrument,
> Through misgovernance makes notes which was not his intent.
>
> A shawm maketh a sweet sound for he tuneth base,
> It mounteth not too high but keepeth rule and space,
> Yet if it be blown with too a vehement wind,
> It maketh it to misgovern out of his kind.

Nor did Henry, Lord Percy escape his father's 'good intent'. His chambers were painted with improving commentaries, such as:

> A
> He that made this house for contemplation
> Minded specially exercise of learning and virtuous occupation,
> And Adolescencia which thinketh himself wise
> Shall know himself better by virtuous exercise.
>
> B
> For what intent is this made I cannot say
> But Youth of nature is inclined to play.
>
> A
> It is hard to know as writes Solomon
> The passage of a ship which suddenly is gone

More hard it is in youth to perceive
Whereto he will draw or what he will receive
What availeth knowledge, what availeth speculation
But Youth bear them away for his own good information.

B
He that in his memory good learning will bear away
Needeth not to be a disciple and study all day.

A
By diligence of study great grace thou may obtain
The pain is soon past, the profit doth ever remain,
And if thou have thine appetite by sensual pleasure,
The pleasure soon vanishes; the dishonesty abideth ever.

B
Virtuous exercise is good, what then
Yet at times to be at ease coveteth every man.

In light of the earl's literary interests, grooms of the chamber were required to tend to the fires in the 'houses in the garden and other places where my lord shall sit about his books'. The earl was as economical with fuel as he was with any other supplies, and detailed ordinances exist ruling on the allowances involved.

Northumberland seems neither to have attended Parliament nor the ceremony at Westminster Abbey on 18 November when Thomas Wolsey, now forty-two years old, received his cardinal's hat from the Pope. He would henceforth be seen only in robes of scarlet or fine crimson taffeta or satin, with red gloves, a red hat and shoes of silver gilt set with pearls. On 24 December, in the presence of the king at Eltham Palace chapel, Cardinal Wolsey took the oath of office of Lord Chancellor, making him the most powerful man in England apart from the king.

5

'WHEN HE IS BETTER LEARNED'

On Friday 18 January 1516, Lord Henry Percy became an uncle. An entry for expenses writes of 'my Lord's gift, and my Lord Percy's, at the christening of Master Harry Clifford £20'. The earl turned his thoughts to his son and heir's marriage. It appears that marriage negotiations began during the early weeks of the year after George Talbot, Earl of Shrewsbury suggested Henry Percy marry his daughter Mary. In February, all England celebrated when Queen Katherine had been delivered of a daughter at four in the morning at Greenwich. Three days later, the girl was christened Mary.

In April, Northumberland was ordered to meet Queen Margaret at Berwick Bounds. Deposed as regent after marrying Angus, she had been replaced by the Duke of Albany. Claiming her life was in danger, she had fled Scotland before giving birth to a daughter, also Margaret, the previous October at Harbottle. She had then fallen ill, but was sufficiently recovered to visit her brother. Northumberland, whose wife stayed at home, escorted Margaret from Berwick to York. Reports had it he 'acquitted himself of his trust faithfully, but without any effort at display'. The city made up for any lack. The day after her entry on Monday 14 April, she was taken by Sir John Carr on a gaily decorated barge from the water gate of St Mary's Abbey to 'the pike garth', where he had put on a great banquet for her.

On Wednesday she continued her journey to London, where she was welcomed by her brother. Sir Thomas Boleyn was given the honour of being carver to her for forty days. Northumberland had left York as he was making a separate journey to London, summoned to appear before Wolsey on 16 April in the Star Chamber in respect of George Harbottle. With great humility he confessed himself guilty in the matters objected against him, asking Cardinal Wolsey to intercede for him with the king. Custody of George and his lands was given to his maternal grandfather, Sir Henry Willoughby of Wollaton (although the case came up years later in another context.)

On 30 April 1516, George Talbot, Earl of Shrewsbury, wrote from his Lodge of Worksop to Dr Cuthbert Tunstall saying his house was stricken with the plague and he was 'sorry to hear my Lord of Northumberland is committed to the Fleet but hopes the king will shortly be good lord to him, and that the earl will take no displeasure, as it might hurt himself'. Shrewsbury's servant Thomas Allen wrote to inform him on 6 May that Northumberland was still in prison and, four days later, while sending Shrewsbury 'ten pasties of congers, the greatest and fattest he ever saw', mentioned in his letter that 'this day the Earl of Northumberland shall be delivered out of the Fleet'. On 16 May, Sir Richard Sacheverell wrote to Shrewsbury about an interesting dialogue he and Buckingham had while walking after supper in the duke's garden. Buckingham had taken him by his arm and said, 'Sacheverell, the cause that I sent for you is to let you know part of my mind. The last day at the court it fortuned my Lord Cardinal and me to sit together without any company.'

Wolsey had suggested his son should 'come to the King and the Queen, and to be acquainted. And I said to him that I had but one son, wherefore I would be loth he should come.' (At that time, contagion was rife in London.) The cardinal had then asked, 'Why do ye not marry him?' to which the duke had replied, 'I wist not where.' To this the cardinal suggested Lady Salisbury's daughter or one of Shrewsbury's daughters. And now he had moved Sir Richard to write to Shrewsbury regarding cross-marriages between the two families, and had said he was 'content to tarry till Monday come sennight' for the answer, adding that the only news he had was that 'my Lord of Northumberland came forth of the Fleet on Saturday and was with the king on Wednesday in his Privy Chamber'.

Shrewsbury wrote to Mr Ursewick (once Margaret Beaufort's confessor) saying he wished him to continue his good offices in the matter between Northumberland and himself, writing that Buckingham had 'proposed cross marriages' and desired him to beseech Northumberland to 'remain in his good mind'. He was apparently worried that 'if Buckingham knew, he might try to change his purpose'. He then wrote in reply to Sir Richard that he was much bound to the duke for still wishing to offer the earl his son as he had promised 'that I should have him better cheap by 1,000 marks than any other man. Howbeit, when he came to the point that I desired to know what sum he would ask, it was so great that I never desired to speak of the matter since, for I trust with a little help to marry all my daughters with that sum that he asked with one of them.'

On 24 May, Thomas Allen, besides sending Shrewsbury black, russet and yellow satin (the best in London), shoes, paper, currants and red wax, wrote:

> Mr Ursewick spake with my Lord of Northumberland who remains in the same mind ... The question hath been asked of my said Lord for the marriage of his son, of Sir William Compton and divers others: he hath made answer, 'I have concluded with my lord of Shrewsbury.' When asked when he would bring his son to court, he answered, 'When he is better learned, and well acquainted with his wife; shortly after he shall come to the court.'

No information has come to light as to when Mary Talbot was born. She was probably two, or possibly three, years younger than Henry Percy. Nor is it known if they ever met, although a rumour has arisen they had and disliked each other intensely. Whatever the truth, the betrothal did not take place. An indenture dated 1 December 1517 was agreed between George, Earl of Shrewsbury, Lord Steward of the Royal Household and Thomas, Lord Dacre of Gilsland (Warden of the West Marches and a border lord) for a marriage between Mary Talbot and Lord Dacre's son and heir, William, Lord Greystoke (by right of his mother after her death in 1516). William was born on 29 April 1500. (Decades later, William would marry Mary's sister Elizabeth, who was born in 1507.)

Worme's accounts record Northumberland as being in London from 31 May to 3 August and his expenses amounting to £100. A further entry reveals he went to Petworth: 'Monday, 25 August 1516, for my lord's cost at Petworth and homewards £30.' On 11 September he purchased a horse for Master Poynings (and other causes) which cost £10 and paid £100 to Sir Henry Clifford for his marriage money as well as paying £120 to 'my lord's creditors' at London. (The accounts, which are mutilated, appear to be partial records for, according to the earl's household book, Worme would have recorded sums in and out – and from whom and why – in his own account book so that every Saturday he could present the earl with a balanced and precise record of the weeks incomings and outgoings, with the amount of money actually on hand as at that date.)

On 7 May 1517, Henry VIII wrote from Richmond to the earl to thank him for his attendance on his sister, Queen Margaret, at 'her late repair hither' and now, with his 'dearest sister' returning to Scotland, 'we wot and desire you to put yourself, and the lady your wife, in a readiness to accompany and conduct her' on her return to York (expected to be 29 May) and attend upon her up to Newcastle. The earl appeared reluctant, for he wrote to the king suggesting Clifford or Dacre have the honour. Receiving no reply, he wrote from Leconfield on 24 May to Shrewsbury, sending by his servant a copy of the king's letter showing the royal desire for his wife to attend, and requesting he ask the king to excuse her as 'she is not in case to ride', although she would gladly do so if she could. He himself intended 'to meet the queen without York and wait on her to Newcastle, eschewing of further charge'. On 3 June the Earl and Countess of Shrewsbury attended on Queen Margaret until she reached Doncaster, and she was honourably received by Lord Darcy on entering Yorkshire and at York by the Earl of Northumberland and the Mayor, while the countess remained at Wressle.

Hall records that the king made plans for his summer pastime but the 'Sweating Sickness turned all his purpose. This malady was so cruel that it killed some within three hours, some within two hours, some merry at dinner and dead at supper. Many died in the King's Court.' Michaelmas term was adjourned but the sickness continued all the rest of the year. Wolsey had stayed at his post although he was ill in June and in August, with quinsy and the Sweat, with many of his household dying. Giustinian wrote to the Doge on 11 November that the king was moving from place to place because of the plague and that some pages had attended him in the morning and died by the evening. Court was dismissed and courtiers and officials fled to their own estates. The king and cardinal intended to absent themselves until after the Christmas holidays or longer if the plague continued. The king, his company decreasing, kept no solemn Christmas that year for fear of infection, 'so fervent and infectious' was the Sweat. On 24 January 1518, Giustinian wrote that Wolsey had arrived back in London and that the king, after a brief appearance, 'departed immediately to Windsor, where he will remain till Easter'.

As Cardinal Wolsey preferred his noble attendants to come to court when they attained fifteen years, he may have expected Lord Percy to arrive at the end of 1517 or the beginning of 1518. It is more than doubtful Northumberland would have risked his son going to Wolsey's household while plague and sickness raged, however, and deaths were only just abating by autumn 1518.

The peace between England and France was read and sworn at St Paul's on 3 October 1518, with agreement for a personal interview between Henry and Francis to take place. The Cardinal of York sang High Mass. Later that day, at his own dwelling, the cardinal gave a sumptuous supper for the court. 'The whole banqueting hall being so decorated with huge vases of gold and silver that I fancied myself,' wrote Giustinian, 'in the tower of Chosroes, where that monarch caused divine honours to be paid him.' After supper twenty-four masquers appeared, half of them male and half female, all dressed alike in fine green satin covered with cloth of gold, and performed dances. When they removed their visors, the two leaders were the king and his sister Mary. Among the other dancers were Nicholas Carew, Francis Bryan, Anne Browne, Anne Wotton and Elizabeth Blount.

Two days later, as part of the peace treaty, the betrothal between Mary, King Henry's daughter and the dauphin, eldest son of King Francis, was celebrated. King Henry stood in front of his throne with his wife and his sister on either side. Princess Mary stood in front of her mother 'dressed in cloth of gold, with a cap of black velvet on her head, adorned with many jewels'. Once all parties had assented to the marriage contract, the Cardinal of York placed a diamond ring on Mary's finger and blessed her. Giustinian in his letter dated 25 October wrote that the ambassadors were preparing to depart and that 'the queen is near her delivery, which is anxiously looked for', with everyone praying for a son. On 10 November, Queen Katherine gave birth to a stillborn daughter (the fourth girl out of seven, or possibly eight, pregnancies) when she was in her eighth month. Henry was then twenty-seven years old and his wife thirty-two.

Sir Thomas Boleyn was sent to France by King Henry to arrange the interview between the two kings. Margaret of Savoy wrote to Henry VIII on 23 January 1519 that her father, Emperor

Maximilian, had died at the city of Veltz on 3 January. All Europe waited to see who would become the next Holy Roman Emperor: Charles of Castile, Francis I or Henry VIII. The 'meeting and embrace' between the kings was put on hold.

On 16 February 1519, Henry Percy's cousin Henry Stafford, not quite eighteen years old, was married to fifteen-year-old Ursula Pole, daughter of Margaret Plantagenet, Countess of Salisbury. She brought with her a dowry of 3,000 marks. They continued to live within the Duke of Buckingham's household with guardians to watch over them.

Northumberland's terse accounts from this time reveal he was in London between Friday 20 May and Wednesday 8 June 1519. With King Henry dubbing Henry, Lord Percy a knight before Trinity term was over, it seems this was the time the young man arrived to take up his public duties in the cardinal's household. He was probably given the usual parental homily that he should in 'all things reverence, honour and obey' the cardinal as he would his own father, 'esteeming whatsoever he was told or commanded'. Northumberland had returned to Wressle by 27 June but had returned to London around 6 July, presumably for the solemn Mass sung at Paul's on 8 July after nineteen-year-old Charles of Castile was elected Emperor Charles V. (William Worme was sometimes an inefficient and inaccurate record keeper, recording incorrect dates, days, years and amounts with no explanations by them; however, it does seem whenever the earl travelled he borrowed money to help with cashflow; on this occasion the earl borrowed money from Lord Dacre, Sir Edward Ratcliff, John Lamplugh, the Earl of Worcester and Sir Thomas Lovell.)

Wolsey's household would have been a familiar environment to Lord Percy, for it was, like his father's, a replica of the royal court. What would have been different was that Wolsey had 'about five hundred persons in his household according to his checker roll'. His privy chamber comprised a chamberlain and vice-chamberlain, twelve gentlemen ushers, six gentlemen waiters, nine or ten lords (allowed two or three servants of their own, although in 1521 the Earl of Derby was allowed five). Lord Percy appears to have had two servants: one who waited upon him and one who brushed and dressed his stuff. The lords and gentlemen, although an addition to ceremonial occasions, were not purely to augment Wolsey's grandeur, despite being expected to jump dutifully to his every instruction, for the sons of peers and gentlemen might make fruitful connections, gain knowledge of national and international affairs and learn the art of governing.

In further contrast, Henry Percy would find himself surrounded by luxurious furnishings and hangings (and possibly warmer chambers). Beautiful works of art appeared everywhere as the cardinal appreciated fine things. On display were gold, silver and gilt plate – goblets, cups, flagons, bowls, basins, ewers, plates and dishes, many decorated with his cardinal's hat and crosses, salt cellars (including one decorated with scallop shells having a boy with a serpent on its cover) and candleholders, including six candlesticks with leopard heads.

The head officers – the steward, treasurer and comptroller (heading their own tables to accommodate staff and sittings) – oversaw Wolsey's great chamber. George Cavendish, one of Wolsey's most trusted gentlemen ushers (who wrote the *Life of Cardinal Wolsey*), stated 'a mess for the young lords and another for gentlemen' was always kept in the chamber. When in residence, the cardinal kept three tables for guests, courtiers and petitioners, each supervised by an officer of his household, while he ate separately of special dishes. In his private kitchen Wolsey had a master cook (who wore velvet or satin with a gold chain around his neck) overseeing two grooms, six assistants, two yeomen of the larder as well as any combination of yeomen, grooms and pages working in catering or the scalding house, scullery, buttery, pantry, ewery, wafery, cellar, laundry and woodyard. The other kitchen, servicing the great hall, had two master cooks, clerks of the kitchen, a surveyor of the dresser, a clerk of the spicery, a yeoman of the scullery and two others in his silver scullery.

Outside, two yeomen and two grooms acted as gate porters. Besides his master of the horse, a yeoman of his barge, a farrier, a yeoman of the stirrup and grooms for the hundred horses and six mules, the cardinal had four footmen with rich running coats and a serjeant-at-arms. All his servants were dressed in a livery of crimson velvet, the front and back of their tunics bearing the gold letters 'TC' for Thomas Cardinalis, with the device of the red hat. Chamber attendants were the usual cupbearers, carvers, sewers and waiters, to the number of forty, with a further six yeomen ushers, eight grooms and forty-six yeomen who attended upon the cardinal daily. His master of the wardrobe had a staff of twenty to assist him to keep the great jewelled robes, gowns, copes, capes and hats as well as the linen.

Working alongside his secretaries, the cardinal kept his own lawyers, auditors and surveyors. Other officers were his personal physicians, apothecary, herald, armourer, tent keeper, confessor, two almoners, four minstrels and a fool. His chapel comprised a dean, subdean, gospeller, epistler and choirmaster of twelve boys and sixteen men, and twelve singing priests and a servant to look after them. In the vestry he kept a yeoman and two grooms.

Departing from his houses, Wolsey was preceded always by two tall cross bearers and two pillar bearers (always 'in-waiting' in his anteroom or great chamber). In term-time the cardinal proceeded from his private rooms to his public offices: to the Star Chamber on Mondays, Tuesdays and Thursdays, where 'he neither spared high nor low, but did judge everyone according to right' in suits and causes; and to the Court of Chancery on Wednesdays, Fridays and Saturdays, where he had more staff in the form of various officials such as the clerk of the crown who attested all letters and writs issued under the Great Seal, and the clerk of the hanaper as well as two principal secretaries, two of whom were Brian Tuke and William Knight.

Wolsey began his day saying the daily office with his chaplain. He then attended to his own routine business. After two Masses in his privy closet, he prepared to leave York Place for Westminster Hall at eight o'clock in the morning. Wearing robes of fine scarlet or crimson satin, taffeta or damask, with a black velvet tippet of sables about his neck, he entered his presence chamber holding 'a fair orange filled with vinegar and confection against pestilent airs'. Waiting there to attend him to Westminster were the 'noblemen and gentlemen of his household'. Borne before him was 'first, the Great Seal of England, and then his cardinal's hat by a nobleman or some worthy gentleman, right solemnly, bareheaded', then the two great crosses of silver, the two great pillars of silver and his pursuivant, holding a great silver mace. The gentlemen ushers cried, 'On, my lords and masters; make way for my Lord's Grace!' In this way he passed through the hall. Outside, his crimson-velvet-trapped mule with gilt stirrups awaited him. About him he had four footmen holding gilt poleaxes and before him his cross bearers and pillar bearers mounted on great horses trapped in red scarlet, and so the procession wended its way through the streets of London.

'He used every Sunday to repair to the court, being then for the most part at Greenwich, in the term, with all his former order, taking his barge at his privy stairs, furnished with tall yeomen standing upon the bayles, and all gentlemen being within with him, and landed at the Crane in the Vintry,' it was said. He then rode his mule – crosses, pillars, hat and Great Seal before him – to Billingsgate where he reboarded his barge to be rowed to Greenwich, there received by the chief officers of the king's house (the treasurer and comptroller) and escorted to the king's chamber. His crosses would be placed on one side of the king's cloth of estate. When he departed he would leave in like procession. 'And when it pleased the king, for his recreation, to repair unto the cardinal's house, as he did divers times in the year, at which time there wanted no preparations or goodly furniture, with viands of the finest sort.' The cardinal devised banquets, musical interludes, masques and mummeries, gorgeous and costly, to entertain the king: 'There wanted no dames, or damsels, meet or apt to dance with the maskers, or to garnish the place for a time, with other goodly disports.'

Meanwhile, in France, Sir Thomas Boleyn, godfather in proxy for King Henry VIII, wrote on 7 June from Poissy to Wolsey that 'on Sunday last, about ten at night, Henri, the king's young son, was christened and had presented, on behalf of King Henry, the salt, cup and layer of gold', which greatly pleased King Francis. The £100 Wolsey sent he had 'bestowed on the nurse, four rockers, the gentlewomen of the queen's chamber, and an offering of twenty nobles'. In England, on 15 June, eighteen-year-old Bessie Blount gave birth to King Henry's illegitimate son, who was christened Henry FitzRoy (and although Elizabeth had been Henry's preferred dancing partner for her beauty, high spirits and energy, the king did not renew their relationship). On 6 September, Sir Thomas Boleyn wrote from Blois to Wolsey resigning his comptrollership to take up his new appointment of Treasurer of the King's Household.

Giustinian, having left England in July, arrived back in Venice to pouring rain on 6 October. Giving his report to the Signory on England and its principal characters four days later, he described Wolsey as 'very handsome, learned, extremely eloquent, of vast ability and indefatigable ... He is pensive and has the reputation of being extremely just: he favours the people exceedingly, and specially the poor; hearing their suits, and seeking to despatch them instantly; he also makes the lawyers plead gratis for all paupers ... He has a very fine place, where one traverses eight rooms before reaching his audience chamber and they are all hung with tapestry...' He also said that when he first arrived in England, 'the Cardinal used to say to him, "His Majesty will do so and so"; subsequently, by degrees, he went forgetting himself, and commenced saying, "We shall do so and so"; at this present he has reached such a pitch that he says, "I shall do so and so."' Despite

Giustinian's views, a perusal of letters between king and cardinal show that if Henry agreed with Wolsey's advice or decisions he let things be; if he did not he would quickly overrule his minister, showing a detailed grasp of affairs, plans or situations. Of the Duke of Buckingham, Giustinian observed he was extremely popular and 'that, were the King to die without heirs male, he might easily obtain the crown' – a sentiment no doubt caught by receptive ears.

Jousts were held at Greenwich on 21, 27 and 28 October to honour the marriage of Henry Courtenay, Earl of Devon to Gertrude Blount, daughter of Baron Mountjoy (the queen's chamberlain), on the 25th. Devon's party had bases and trappers of russet velvet and cloth of silver engrailed, lozenged and cross-lozenged with cloth of gold, each with gold trueloves. The king, Sir William Kingston and Henry Percy's twenty-four-year-old cousin William Carey were in harness, trapper and base of russet velvet and cloth of silver on one side, double and cut with the other side purple tinsel.

On 1 February 1520, in the king's presence, four masked gentlemen in blue satin entered the queen's chamber at Greenwich, bringing with them a lady on a wagon; on its pillars were devices for challengers to come and run certain courses on 12 February. The joust was to celebrate the recent marriage of Mary Boleyn and William Carey (who was also third cousin to the king). Mary's father, still in office in France, was forced to miss it, not getting leave to depart until March. The king, 'intending to answer the challenge' of the joust, ordered made a saddle, trapper, base of russet velvet, lozenged with cloth of silver damask, edged with cloth of gold damask and in each a branch of eglantine embroidered in damask gold. Four gentlemen waiters were dressed in russet and white damask. Being an excellent jouster and tennis player, William would have been popular with the king and, like Henry Norris, was a gentleman of the Privy Chamber; both were paid wages of £8 *6s 8d* per quarter.

Beyond England's borders, however, all was not well. At the beginning of April it became clear to the king that Ireland was in a state of disorder, and he duly appointed the Earl of Surrey, on Wolsey's advice, to pass into that country, taking with him 'divers gentlemen that had been in the garrison of Tournai, and one hundred yeomen of the King's Guard, and other to the number of a thousand men. Where he by his manhood and wisdom brought the Earl of Desmond and divers other rebels to good conformity and order…'

6

'CONFERENCE OF TRIVIALITIES'

Since the previous March, there had been feverish instructions and preparations regarding the planned 'Embrace' between King Henry and King Francis. A field for jousting was selected while commissioners arranged arming lodges, galleries for the ladies, stands and security arrangements. On 19 March 1520 they began arranging for the building of a palace, sending details to Wolsey on 26 March 1520: '... the King shall have three large chambers ... the greatest chamber' would be 124 feet long, 42 feet wide and 30 feet high, 'which is longer and wider than the White Hall'; the second chamber, 'to dine in' would be 80 feet by 34 feet and 27 feet high, 'which is larger than the greatest chamber in Bridewell'; and the third chamber for his highness to withdraw in would be 60 feet long and 34 feet wide. For the queen there were to be 'three chambers as large, a gallery to the king's lodgings, a chapel and two closets'. The cardinal was to have three chambers next to the king. All three were to have lodgings in the chateau accessed by a secret covered gallery.

Timber was coming from Holland and they required '250 carpenters, 100 joiners, 30 couple-sawyers, 40 plasterers and 1,000 of wainscot' and for Vertue, the king's master mason, to be sent with 150 bricklayers. Painters, tailors, glaziers and others were recruited. Lower walls were built from local stone and formed an undercroft in which to house kitchens, pantry, buttery, cellar, spicery, ewery (private and general), a room for plate, scullery, saucer and wafery. Canvas placed on wooden board was painted to emulate the stone below and used to create the upper walls. Glaziers installed windows using 5,000 feet of 'the best glass that could be gotten'.

Lists of lists were made: of Arras tapestry (to be taken across and hung forty days before the interview between the kings); of chapel ornaments; of the king's tallest guards who would be selected, armed with bows and arrows and supplied with two sets of coats (one with goldsmith's work showing the king's device on a scarlet base, the other red with a rose and crown imperial on the breast); of ships (which to be used for the crossing, which to scour the sea during the passage); of duties for various household officers; of the hobbies, palfreys and harness; of hounds, greyhounds, horns, leashes, collars; of gifts selected for foreign estates; and of provisions of food, drink and lights. A mummery was also to be written for the banquet, comprising fifty noblemen and noblewomen in five companies (their apparel to be devised at the king's pleasure).

Similar lavish preparations were being made on the French side. At Tours, an army of workmen and women, having procured 35,000 ells of canvas (some dyed black, white, tawny and purple for the king's colours) were producing sumptuous tents and pavilions. Fustian, taffeta and thousands of pounds in weight of ribbons, hundreds of pounds of silk fringe in black, white, tawny and violet, buckram, cotton thread, silk, cord, wool, leather, rope, straps, and a great number of pegs and nails were purchased. Fine linen was brought from Holland to use as windows. And 'yards upon yards of cloth of gold and cloth of silver, of gold and silver toile, velvet and satin purchased from Florence, Milan and Lyons', used to make an endless number of heraldic devices, *fleurs-de-lis* and crosses. (After the meeting, many of the silks were resold to a silk merchant.) The final wage bill just for the tent makers came to £4,600.

On Monday 21 May, King Henry and Queen Katherine with all the court began the move from Greenwich towards the sea. There was more business to attend to first, however, for the king had agreed to a meeting with Emperor Charles V before his departure. On Friday, the emperor's ships were spotted off the coast. Cardinal Wolsey and his noble retinue (which probably included Lord Percy) rode to Dover where, on the Saturday, lack of wind prevented the emperor's ship coming into port. Near evening, while his ships fired their cannon, he boarded a little boat to be brought to land, a gold cloth of estate with a black eagle held over him. Wolsey met him with reverence and conducted him by torchlight to the castle. Sir Edward Poynings, Warden of the Cinque Ports, brought the castle keys to him but the emperor refused them, saying he knew he was as safe in England as if he were in his own realm. During the evening, his retinue arrived on English soil. About two in the morning, King Henry arrived at Dover by torchlight. The emperor rose to greet him.

In the 'full morning' they rode together to Canterbury to celebrate Whitsunday. Entering the cathedral, they were met by Wolsey in procession. A purple carpet led to a 'kneeling desk' for the two, with gold brocade cushions. The king knelt on the left to honour the emperor. The Archbishop of Canterbury offered them the cross to kiss and sprinkled them with holy water. Rising, they were conducted to the high altar, to another canopied kneeling desk with gold cushions. Kneeling again, the archbishop presented them with the wood of the holy cross to kiss, and then commenced the hymn, *Veni Creator Spiritus*. When the music ceased, the two royal men left.

At the first porch of the palace, twenty-five of the handsomest and best-apparelled ladies of the court awaited them. Lining the corridor were twenty of the queen's pages in chequered gold brocade and crimson satin. At the top of a staircase of fifteen marble steps, a tearful Queen Katherine waited. She was dressed in an ermine-lined cloth-of-gold gown with a beautiful string of pearls about her neck. Embracing her nephew, she took him to partake of breakfast in a private chamber. Emperor and king returned to the cathedral for High Mass. They walked side-by-side to the high altar and seated themselves in a pew level with the fourth step. It was covered in gold brocade embroidered with roses and its floor carpeted in crimson velvet. Both men wore simars:* the emperor's, particoloured, was half gold and half silver stripes on gold; the king's all gold, lined with lynx fur. The cardinal, in ermine-lined crimson camlet, sat in a gilt chair on the fifth step, while on a lower step Queen Katherine sat with her sister-in-law Mary, as dowager Queen of France. Queen Katherine wore a violet velvet gown with gold-embroidered roses over a silver lamé petticoat; Mary was also in silver lamé, her gown joined by gold cords with pearls for tags. All went to dinner after the ceremony, followed by dancing.

Whit Monday followed the same form. The emperor wore a sable-lined gold brocade gown. The king's simar was one half gold, the other half grey velvet, with slashed sleeves joined by jewels for buttons; his black velvet bonnet was edged with white feathers. Queen Katherine wore a petticoat of cloth of gold over black, slashed and laced with gold and black cords with tags of pearls and jewels. Over it she wore a particoloured gown in gold and violet, with gold-embroidered and pearl flowers in relief. Her headdress was in Flemish style with a long veil. Around her neck were five strings of pearls and a pendant of St George on horseback slaying the dragon, all drawn in diamonds. Once again Mass was celebrated and everyone departed for dinner, after which there was dancing, although the emperor did not take part. A sumptuous banquet, began at nine in the evening. Buckingham entered riding a white hobby. Halfway to the table he dismounted and made obeisance. Riding to the table, the hobby was led away while he knelt to serve the bowl of water to the king and

* Simars were newly fashionable fur-lined, knee-length, open-fronted robes.

emperor as Suffolk held the towel. The cardinal sat with Katherine and Mary. They were served by the emperor's servants. At another table sat ladies who had 'enamoured youths' standing behind them. The Count of Capra took his role so seriously he fainted (or feigned swooning for his mistress's delight) and was carried out to recover himself. No one went to bed until three in the morning.

On Tuesday, emperor and king rested in the morning before sitting in council until just before sunset. An hour later, in the light of tall wax torches, emperor and king departed Canterbury, where 5 miles on they took leave of each other: the emperor to Sandwich for Flanders and King Henry and his court, with twenty-seven ships, to Calais.

The English host headed to France numbered nearly 6,000 persons and just over 3,000 horses. The king's retinue held 4,544 people, the queen's 1,260, and Wolsey, with many more attendants allowed than the estates, took 300. Given the numbers, although neither Henry Percy nor Anne Boleyn appear in the lists of those in attendance at the Field of Cloth of Gold, their positions and connections mean it is highly likely that both were in service at the event. It is impossible to mention more than a few of those present. The Duchess of Buckingham attended the queen, but among all the wives of lords and knights attending Queen Katherine – including all the Boleyn family and those related to them – there is no mention of Katheryne, Countess of Northumberland. The Dukes of Suffolk and Buckingham, Marquis of Dorset and the Earls of Shrewsbury, Northumberland (appointed to be a judge of the lists), Westmorland and Devonshire attended the king. Among the knights mentioned were Sir Thomas Boleyn, Sir Henry Wyatt, Sir William Paston, Sir Edward Boleyn and many others. William Carey was mentioned as one of the Esquires of the King's Body.

The Duke of Buckingham, although vehemently decrying the great expenditure 'for the future spectacle of foolish speeches' at a 'conference of trivialities', did not restrict his purchases. By the end of the year he had debts of around £4,546. Northumberland's account summaries reveal he too took out loans for ready cash: from Thomas Semar, mercer and alderman of London, 'in wares the value of £1,000, which was made in ready money £677', and 'of William Buttrey, mercer, as a loan in ready money and goods £338 10*s* 9*d*', and of Nich. Vannachien, a Florentine merchant, £80 10*s* 'as in the price of 11½ yards of cloth gold of tissue, raised after £7 a yard'. Before leaving home he also borrowed amounts from various people totalling £120.

Henry Percy's first sight of Guisnes on 4 June would have been the open gates of an embattled towered gatehouse. Images of great men of war such as Hercules and Alexander stared down at those arriving, with a view of a great castle through the gatehouse arch. Those passing through the gates came to four gold lions surrounding a pillar with a Cupid above them with his bow ready to send arrows of love into people's hearts. In front of the palace was a spacious courtyard and lawn with a blue-and-gold fountain. Bacchus, the god of wine, oversaw flowing streams of Malmsey and claret wine into silver cups bearing the motto '*Faite bonne chere qui voudra*'.

Each corner of the palace had a round tower, the walls between them set with many windows. Venturing inside, there were halls and chambers leading one into another. Wood-planked floors were strewn with rushes; the ceilings were covered with light, fine silk with roses and the walls were hung with tapestries of foliage and flowers, nature scenes or just plain white and green silk. Each public room had hanging centrally from its ceiling a large ornamental lantern shaped like a crown but the windows made rooms so bright with light everyone felt like they were in the open air. 'In every chamber in place convenient were cloths of estate, great and large of cloth of gold, of tissue and rich embroidery, with chairs covered with like cloth ... and great cushions of rich work of the Turkey making.'

Anne Boleyn, serving Queen Claude, would have found herself in a bright and colourful city of two thousand tents erected just outside of the town of Ardres. Queen Claude's tent and her two smaller pavilions were embellished with gold and silver toile, violet satin with *fleurs-de-lis* and 16,224 ermines (created with black velvet on silver cloth). Louise, the king's mother, had a tent of crimson satin and purple velvet decorated with *fleurs-de-lis* and 14,284 silver crosses mounted on crimson satin. The king's tent, covered in gold brocade, was decorated with gold lilies on three azure velvet bands. It was sixteen paces in diameter and had a corridor eight paces wide. Woven hemp ropes were tricoloured, plaited in white, tawny and black. On the summit of his tent was a gigantic St Michael standing on a gold ball, holding a lance and shield with the arms of France, the saint's pedestal having twelve zig-zag rays of light arrowing to the ground. The interior walls were covered in azure velvet and gold toile, decorated with gold lilies.

Three smaller gold-brocaded tents adjoined to serve as wardrobe, private chapel and council chamber, and around them were fifteen tents covered in crimson satin. One was a banqueting hall with a foot-high brick foundation, decorated inside with tapestries and a ceiling made to look like a night sky with stars, moon and planets. All the tents and pavilions were decorated with golden apples and banners with the royal arms. Besides those craftsmen created 211 smaller gold apples used as window cords, ends of masts and candle holders, and 75,544 gold *fleurs-de-lis* mounted on blue velvet. An eyewitness said the cloth of gold, gold devices, lilies and apples were very beautiful in the sunlight.

At a pre-determined time on 7 June, signalled by artillery, King Henry rode a beautiful charger to the Vale D'Or. Cardinal Wolsey rode beside him, followed by the Papal Nuncio with the Archbishop of Canterbury, the Spanish ambassador with the Duke of Buckingham and the Venetian Ambassador with the Duke of Suffolk, followed by the earls, lords and gentlemen. The retinue comprised about five hundred altogether, all splendidly attired in cloth of gold and silk. They stopped at the top of the valley.

In a simar of silver brocade, closed by silver cords with jewels for tags, sleeves set with diamonds, rubies, emeralds and pearls, with a similarly bejewelled white-plumed bonnet, the king glinted and sparkled as he moved, dazzling all who looked at him.

On the other side of the valley the French party had similarly entered and reined in their horses. Slowly, the two kings descended to the valley floor, their respective constables bearing naked swords. They stopped, about two casts of a bowl from each other. Into the expectant silence a trumpet sounded. The two kings spurred their horses, like combatants about to engage, raising their hands to remove their bonnets so they could embrace bareheaded. Dismounting and embracing again, they entered arm-in-arm into a richly jewelled cloth-of-gold pavilion, made comfortable with Turkey carpets on the floor and chairs with cushions. Wolsey and the Admiral of France entered after them. The constables remained at the entrance, their swords bared still. English officers served great pots of wine to the Frenchmen, who cheered them. The English nobles remained unmoving, not leaving their array even when the Frenchmen came to speak fair words to them. The two kings then emerged, revealing the French king was wearing a simar of cloth of silver, and over it a jewelled purple satin cloak and on his head a coif of damask gold set with diamonds. Hall described him as 'a goodly prince, stately of countenance, merry of cheer, brown coloured, great eyes, high nosed, big lipped, fair breasted and shoulders, small (thin) legs and long feet'.

On Sunday 10 June, the two kings swapped courts to dine with each other's wives. Queen Claude greeted Henry wearing a cloth-of-gold robe with gold frieze over a gold kirtle, the diamond called *la pointe de Bretaigne* at her breast. Her sleeves ended with bands of diamonds at her wrists and her headdress was smothered in diamonds, rubies and emeralds. The king, removing his bonnet, made reverence to her, one knee on the ground. Rising, he kissed her and then all the princesses and ladies with her. Claude took his hand and bade him sit beside her. As twenty-four trumpets sounded, delicate dishes were brought in by lords and gentlemen in gold vessels. Music played while people ate. It was above four hours before the king and queen removed into another room to talk at leisure. When the dancing was to begin, all changed into masquing gear. At the serving of the void – spices, fruits and jellies – artillery was fired to signal the two kings were soon to depart. Henry, after kissing the queen, the duchesses and all her ladies of court (which no doubt included Anne Boleyn), mounted his bay charger, giving it the spur to make it bound and curvet. According to a French eyewitness, 'The king of England is a very handsome prince, honest, tall and straight, in manner gentle and gracious, rather fat, and with a red beard, large enough and very becoming.'

The royal women met for the first time on Monday, bringing retinues of richly dressed and bejewelled ladies. Queen Katherine arrived in a beautiful litter covered with gold-embroidered crimson satin. Mary arrived in a litter of cloth of gold, wrought with lilies, with 'L&M' joined together with porcupines. Queen Claude, dressed in cloth of silver over cloth of gold, arrived in a silver-encased litter covered with gold knots; 'Madame' Louise was carried in a litter of black velvet. Queens Katherine and Claude exchanged greetings and sat together on the glazed balcony with their favourite ladies around them. The ambassador of the Marquis of Mantua wrote to his master that the English ladies were 'neither handsome, graceful nor richly clad', and very disapprovingly wrote that one of the English ladies in front of the platform 'took a large flask of wine, and putting it to her lips, drank freely, and then passed it to her companions, who did the like and emptied it. Not content with this, they drank out of large cups, which, during the joust, circulated more than twenty times amongst the French lords and those English ladies.' For the next three hours, the two kings jousted fully armed, breaking many lances and showing they were equal in skill and strength.

Wednesday was meant to be a jousting day, but the wind was too strong for lances to be couched. Because the kings and many ladies were at the camp, there was dancing. Jousting took place on Thursday and again the queens came to watch as the two kings entered the field, challenging all comers. Then entered the Earl of Devon, and in his bend the Lords Montague, Herbert, Leonard Grey and Masters Arthur Pole, Francis Bryan and Henry Norris with four others, apparelled so that on one side embroidered against blue velvet there was a man's heart burning and a lady's hand holding a garden pot pouring water on it; the other side bore white satin embroidered with gold letters. On Friday and Saturday combats were performed on foot at the barriers, thrusting and casting lances and swords both short and two-handed, and then the lists were closed.

During the night, a chapel was erected and a platform built with two oratories. Seats with gold canopies were placed to one side for Cardinals Wolsey and Bourbon and beneath them benches for bishops, ambassadors and others. Spectators assembled on Sunday morning at around ten o'clock, when the kings mounted the platform steps and knelt at one oratory; Katherine and Claude similarly knelt at the other. Cardinal Bourbon brought the Gospel for the kings to kiss; he presented it first to Francis, who said Henry should do so first, and Henry in turn refused the honour. Suddenly, a great gold and silver dragon, 'four fathoms long, and full of fire', appeared in the air. Frightening people – some thought it a comet, others a monster – it passed over 'as fast as a footman can go, and as high as a bolt shot from a crossbow'. It was described later in a poem as having 'eyes ablaze, and with quivering tongue it licks its mouth which opens wide; the dragon hisses ... it enfolds itself in circles of varying size, with mighty coils, and, compacted, twists itself into a swift spiral'. At the Agnus Dei, the Pax was kissed by the kings, each once again giving the first honour to the other. Cardinal Bourbon then presented it to the queens, who likewise politely declined, and instead kissed each other. Once Mass was finished, all went to dine. The event was over.

The following day, English retinues removed to Calais. While many sailed back to England, the king and queen, with the cardinal and a diminished retinue, waited at Calais for a second meeting with Emperor Charles on 10 July. The king's retinue for this meeting comprised the Archbishop of Canterbury; the Bishops of Durham, Armagh, Ely and Exeter; the Dukes of Buckingham and Suffolk; the Marquis of Dorset; and the Earls of Shrewsbury, Northumberland, Essex, Derby, Devonshire, Westmorland, Stafford, Worcester, Kent, Wiltshire and Kildare. Also attending were Sir Thomas Boleyn, Sir William Kingson, Sir Arthur Plantagenet, Sir John Seymour and Sir William Paston.

In Calais, a banqueting house had been built 'with sixteen principals made of great masts, betwixt every mast 24 foot'. In the middle, eight great masts bound together with iron held up the azure canvas ceiling which was painted with stars, sun and moon. Around the walls tiered balconies had been built for onlookers, as had a stage for musicians and singers. On the painted walls were landscapes of mountains, woods and meadows with animals, villages and windmills. And on another part blue waves of a sea against a clouded sky with birds and upon the water ships blown by winds, and beneath them fishes and marine monsters. 'From the ceiling there hung large chandeliers ... and between every two chandeliers there was a human figure in the air of wicker-work, and covered and clad with silk or cloth, and bearing torches in their hands'; these were alternate men and women in different foreign costumes. 'Below these lights were cornucopias, with foliage, which likewise served for candlesticks, being fixed on the masts. Round the centre-mast tables were placed, forming a square, and other tables all round for the company.' On the day the banquet was to be held, 'the wind began to rise ... rain blew out above a thousand torches and tapers ... and all the King's seats that was made with great riches that could be ordained, besides all other things, was all dashed and lost'.

When the Imperial party arrived, they were lodged at the Staple; with the loss of the banqueting house, they were served in the king's house. At their ensuing conference, ways and means – forceful or peaceable – were discussed as to how Charles V might pass through Italy so he could be crowned Holy Roman Emperor by the Pope. On 14 July, the emperor, accompanied by King Henry, both riding dapple-grey horses, rode together for 4 miles, their retinues and ambassadors following. The two sovereigns embraced each other, caps in hand, and parted: the emperor returned to St Omer, and the king to Calais, arriving at Dover on 18 July.

The months following the Field of Cloth of Gold saw Northumberland peacefully attending to domestic affairs. A truce of one year had been made with Scotland, so the borders were relatively quiet. At Beverley, one of the earl's servants was ordered to present a deer to the twelve governors and was given *8d* in reward. The earl's bearward, John Grene, was given *6s 8d* for the exhibition of his dancing bears in the marketplace and *2s* was given to the 'trumpets of the Duke of Buckingham for playing' before the twelve. In similar vein, the Duke of Buckingham remained at Thornbury working on his gardens, erecting bowers and a summer house and in the autumn stocking his parks and fishponds. In February 1521, Northumberland sent a servant to Buckingham to tell him he was making a visit to Hailes and the two travelled there around 14 March.

On Monday 8 April, a royal messenger arrived at Thornbury. The king had summoned the duke to court. He rode to Westminster and entered his barge at Tothill on the Thames. Suddenly, his barge was boarded by the Captain of the King's Guard, Sir Henry Marney, and a hundred yeomen. After ordering them to land at Hay Wharf, Marney commanded the duke's servants to go to the duke's manor of the Red Rose in St Laurence Pountney while Buckingham, stunned to find he was accused of high treason, was escorted to the Tower of London via Thames

Street. The shock to Northumberland and Lord Percy must have been immense, not to say disquieting.

At eight in the morning on 13 May, the duke was brought to the Bar, the Tower Axe before him. After the indictment was read out, he declared, 'The charges are false and untrue and conspired and forged to bring me to my death.' Witness depositions were read out and the witnesses brought forward to affirm their evidence. The duke spoke for more than an hour, eloquently refuting all the charges. The peers deliberated, and when the duke was returned to the Bar he was told his peers had found him guilty. The duke expressed that he had never been a traitor but that he would forgive them his death and desired them to pray for him. On Friday 17 May, at about eleven o'clock, the forty-three-year-old duke was led to Tower Hill, escorted by a five-hundred-strong guard. He made a short speech to the spectators, many of whom wept, and asked them to pray for him, saying that he died a true man of the king, whom he had offended only through his own negligence and lack of grace. Asking the executioner to despatch him quickly, and offering him forgiveness, the duke removed his gown. His eyes blindfolded, he laid his neck on the block. Four misaimed strokes later, neither flinching nor making a sound, his head finally toppled to the ground. His corpse was placed in a coffin and carried by six men to the church of the Austin Friars.

Henry Percy's aunt Eleanor was now a widow. With all the ducal property now belonging to the crown, his cousins were disinherited. Three weeks later, at St George's Chapel, the deceased duke was expelled from the Order of the Garter and his crest, banner and sword were thrown into the choir, where they were retrieved by officers of arms and discarded in a ditch. Inventories valued the duke's plate at £2,494 and all his lands at 7,358 marks yearly (just above £4,905). Wolsey, after recovering from a bout of fever which left him unable to eat, left Greenwich on 18 May for Hampton Court. He wrote to a correspondent's enquiry that the Earls of Wiltshire and Northumberland were 'quite free from suspicion'.

On 27 June, Wolsey was informed that the growing hostility between Francis I and Charles V was escalating into war: the latter had driven the French out of Navarre and the former had declared he would crush the young and inexperienced emperor before invading Castile at the beginning of July. King Henry offered himself as a mediator between the two. Other news came from Lord Dacre that the Duke of Albany was intending to invade England on 2 September. With difficulty, Wolsey induced George, Earl of Shrewsbury, decrying the indisposition of his body, to take upon himself the charge of Lieutenant in the North, as he informed Sir Thomas Boleyn on the quiet to tell the king. On 8 July, Richard Pace, with the king at Windsor during an unseasonably rainy July, informed Wolsey 'the king still complains of pains in his head' and Wolsey was to order the matter as he pleased but did not 'mislike' the French news of agreeing to a mediation. On 21 July he wrote the king was 'glad to understand that the emperor and French king have agreed to send their ambassadors to meet Wolsey at Calais'.

On 2 August, Wolsey landed at Calais. He took with him the Bishops of Ely and Durham. Lord Percy is not mentioned as attending, although the retinue did include his close friend Thomas Arundel (who was the same age as Henry), Edward Stanley and James Butler. The cardinal carried with him various commissions in different combinations, all dated 29 July, signed by the king. He had the power to settle the differences between the two rulers, to foster closer amity with one or the other, or to make war on Francis alongside Charles. The French king, mistrusting everyone, sent an army of French and Swiss into Italy while the emperor sought to wrest the duchy of Burgundy from France. The distrust grew more profound when the rumour Wolsey meant to visit the emperor in Flanders proved true. Sir Thomas Boleyn was sent to the emperor at Brussels in September to present Wolsey's written advice suggesting the emperor should raise two thousand foot in Flanders and the same in Hainault, one thousand in the Low Countries and two hundred men-at-arms at the passages to resist French attacks.

Meanwhile, in Ireland, the Earl of Surrey wrote to the king from Dublin on 16 September asking to be recalled, saying he had 'held office for eighteen months and now suffers so much from the flux he believes he will lose his life'. The king replied to him that he was sorry to hear of his illness and was agreeable for his return as long as he found a suitable deputy and he was 'to propose to Sir Piers Butler pretending to be Earl of Ormond as of himself, to take the office' (he was married to Margaret FitzGerald, daughter of the Earl of Kildare). Regarding the 'pretending', Sir Piers, who was a distant cousin of the seventh earl, had begun calling himself the eighth earl after Thomas Butler's death on 3 August 1515 (at Rochford), but the claim was hotly contested by his two daughters, Margaret Boleyn and her widowed older sister Anne St Leger (who had two sons, George and James). In his will, Ormond left his daughters seventy-two manors in England as well as certain lands in Ireland. He left his grandson Sir Thomas Boleyn an ancestral white ivory horn garnished with gold, for it 'to continue still in his blood'.

To the king's request for Wolsey to return to England to administer justice and government, the cardinal replied on 30 October that he had written to the Papal orator to stop the divorce suit made by Queen Margaret at Rome. Furthermore, he concluded with important news:

> Finally, Sir, I have considered the request and desire made unto Your Grace by Sir Piers Butler, contained in his letters, which I think very reasonable; and surely, Sir, the towardness of his son [James Butler] considered, who is right active, discrete and wise, I suppose he, being with his father in that land, should do unto Your Grace right acceptable service. ...

> And I shall at my return to your presence, devise with Your Grace, how the marriage betwixt him and Sir Thomas Boleyn's daughter may be brought to pass, which shall be a reasonable cause to [delay] the time for sending his said son over unto him, for the perfecting of which marriage I shall endeavour myself, at my said return, with all effect.

Wolsey had brokered many marriages in the past so must have presumed that this would be easily accomplished. And Anne Boleyn, in her fifteenth year, was of marriageable age.

7

'GREW SUCH A SECRET LOVE'

In January 1522 the French ambassadors complained to Wolsey of 'suspiciously unfriendly English acts', saying all English students had left Paris and Boleyn's daughter, in Queen Claude's service, had suddenly been called home. These were indications that the English intended to make war, they said, and not a sign of 'continued friendship'. Cardinal Wolsey told them the students had seen the confusion in France and decided to 'consult their own safety'; as for Anne Boleyn, he had recalled her 'because he intended, by her marriage, to pacify certain quarrels and litigation between Sir Thomas Boleyn and other nobles'.

George Cavendish wrote of Anne that 'being very young, she was sent into France, and made one of the French queen's women ... and then was she sent for home again; and being again with her father, he made such means that she was admitted to be one of Queen Katherine's maids, among whom, for her excellent gesture and behaviour, did excel all other'. As Treasurer of the King's Household and a member of the Privy Council, Sir Thomas was well placed to gain a position for his daughter. The poet Thomas Wyatt found her beautiful, witty and graceful in speech. His grandson George wrote in his memoir that there was 'presented to the eye of the court the rare and admirable beauty of the fresh and young lady Anne Boleyn, to be attending upon the queen. In this noble imp, the graces of nature graced by gracious education, seemed even at the first to have promised bliss under her aftertimes.'

On Shrove Tuesday, 4 March, a supper at York Place was arranged by Cardinal Wolsey to entertain the king and Imperial ambassadors. When it was finished, Wolsey brought the whole company into a great, well-lit chamber hung with arras. At its nether end stood an embattled castle, the Chateau Vert, with three towers. In each tower a banner was displayed: one of three torn hearts, one a lady's hand gripping a man's heart, and the third a lady's hand turning a man's heart. Eight masked ladies in the upper chamber, wearing white satin gowns in Milan fashion and bejewelled Venetian gold bonnets, were custodians of the castle. Each lady's name was embroidered in gold on her dress; they were Beauty, Honour, Kindness, Constance, Bounty, Mercy, Perseverance and Pity. In a chamber beneath them were ladies of India (children of the chapel dressed up); their names were Scorn, Disdain, Danger, Jealousy, Unkindness, Malebouche and Strangeness.

A man called Ardent Desire entered, his costume of crimson satin decorated with gold flames. He led a band of eight lords wearing gold caps and blue satin mantle-cloaks; their names were Amorous (King Henry), Nobleness, Youth, Attendance, Loyalty, Pleasure, Gentleness and Liberty. Ardent Desire called upon the ladies to surrender their castle. Scorn and Disdain refused. In response Ardent Desire said, 'The ladies must be won.' At a great boom of guns, the lords ran at the castle, throwing dates and oranges while the ladies of India defended it with rosewater and comfits. At the last Lady Scorn and her company fled, leaving the lords to capture the ladies and lead them into a dance. After the dancing finished, they 'disvisered'. The ladies, according to the list made by Gibson in his accounts, were Mary, the French queen; Gertrude Blount, Countess of Devon; and mistresses Anne Boleyn, Mary Carey, Jane Parker, Anne Browne, Elizabeth

Dannet and one unnamed.* Henry Percy, being present, would have seen the new and graceful addition to the court circle.

At the end of April, Sir Thomas Boleyn and his son George were granted, among other offices, fees and manors, Buckingham's Kentish manors of Brasted and Penshurst and its park. A few months before, William Carey had been appointed keeper of the manor of Newhall, renamed Beaulieu by the king, who had purchased it from Sir Thomas Boleyn. In the north, Henry Percy's brothers Sir Thomas and Sir Ingram were knighted by their uncle William after bravely fighting the Scots in the Merse and Teviotdale. In May, Sir William Percy, Philip Dacre and Lord Ogle slew Lance Carr, one of the worst borderers in Scotland, and forty persons with him, receiving royal thanks for their efforts.

Emperor Charles arrived at Dover at four in the afternoon on Monday 26 May. It was a quick visit arranged so that he, along with the Duc d'Alva, the Prince of Orange, the Count of Nassau and the Marquis of Brandenburg, could view the English fleet. They were received by the Marquis of Dorset and Earls of Northumberland, Shrewsbury, Essex, Devon and Worcester. Northumberland borrowed money to cover his 'costs to Canterbury £66 13*s* 4*d*' (this time from Lords Dacre and St John, Sir Henry Clifford and Sir Thomas Lovell and others). Included among the knights ordered to attend were Sir Thomas Boleyn, Sir William FitzWilliam, Sir Richard Sacheverell and Sir Arthur Plantagenet. Cardinal Wolsey arrived accompanied by the Earls of Surrey and Wiltshire with thirty-six knights, a hundred gentlemen, eight bishops, ten abbots, thirty chaplains all in velvet and satin and seven hundred yeomen. Henry Percy was probably of that number attending the cardinal.

* Although Anne's name appeared third in Gibson's account and the name Perseverance comes third in Hall's narration, Anne could as easily have been Constance – or any other, except perhaps Beauty. It is notable that Anne used an armillary sphere for a device, which symbolised constancy.

When they met, the cardinal embraced the emperor on the sands and took him by the arm. Taking horse, they rode together to Dover Castle to await the arrival of King Henry. On Friday, 'the King brought the emperor aboard his new ship' called the *Henry Grace a Dieu*, and afterwards had them rowed around all his great ships, including the *Mary Rose*, at safe anchorage in Dover Road. To the king's great pleasure, the Imperial guests highly praised all his ships and artillery, saying 'they never saw ships so armed'. Vice Admiral FitzWilliam wrote from the Downs to inform the king that the *Henry Grace a Dieu* 'sailed as well and rather better than any ship in the fleet. She weathered them all, save the *Mary Rose*; and on a wind, there would be a hard choose between them.'

On 2 June the Imperial party came to Gravesend. Travelling in thirty barges, they landed just before six in the evening at Greenwich. They were welcomed into the palace by the king and all his nobility and at the hall door by the queen and all the ladies. Charles dropped to his knees in Spanish fashion to ask his aunt's blessing. Two days later the king honoured the emperor with a joust, himself leading a band of nine. Hall provides little description. Fortunately, Gibson's accounts show that, for the joust being held 4 and 5 June, William Mortimer, at a cost of £8, embroidered two half-bards* of russet velvet 'with knights on horseback, riding upon mountains of gold, with broken spears in their hands, and ladies coming out of clouds, casting darts at the knights'; the bare upper parts were decorated with clouds wrought in Venice gold and silver. He also embroidered two half-bases with hearts, ciphers and hands, clouds and sleeves and hands with darts, edged with Venice gold for £3 *6s*. After disarming and supper, a masque was performed.

Charles V made his state entry into London on Friday 6 June, in readiness to attend Whitsunday Mass at St Paul's. A rich tent was erected a mile from St George's Bar for the king and emperor

* A bard is body armour for horses.

to change their attire, while the heralds arranged the procession so that 'every man set forward in order, richly dressed in cloth of gold, tissue, silver, tinsel and velvet of all colours. There lacked no massive chains nor curious collars: an English man and a stranger rode together, matched according to their degrees. Before the emperor and king were borne two naked swords...' Equally matched henchmen wore velvet livery: the king's in purple, the emperor's in crimson. The crimson-attired Mayor of London and aldermen in scarlet melded into the procession.

A giant Hercules holding a mighty club stood on one side of the drawbridge at London Bridge; on the other Sampson with the jawbone of an ass. Mid-bridge was a crenellated castle made to appear built of white and black marble. Lady Medea, a pretty maid, stood in a tower guarded by her husband Jason, while to one side of him a dragon belched out fire. Another castle, with two great gates, was erected at the Conduit in Gracechurch Street where Charlemagne bore two swords: he gave the Sword of Justice to the emperor and the Sword of Triumphant Victory to the king. Overthwart the street leading to Bishopsgate, Italian merchants had constructed a tree with leafy branches, each leaf dropping sweet-smelling water. At the root was John of Gaunt and on each branch a picture of a king or queen and at its top pictures of Charles, Henry and Katherine.

The Cornhill Conduit, between embattled towers, had minstrels playing trumpets, shawms and sackbuts. Beneath the stage King Arthur sat at a round table. At the Stocks was an arbour full of roses, lilies, and other flowers, with birds, beasts and a pond full of fish; and round the arbour planets and stars moved. At the Great Conduit in Cheapside a four-towered quadrangular castle had galleries hung with cloth of gold and silver. In each tower was a lady (illustrating a cardinal virtue) and on the galleries sat children, men and women singing and playing instruments. A towered building set up at the Standard showed King Alphonse of Spain with a branch springing from his breast depicting the marriages which led to the emperor and king. At the Little Conduit a pageant was made to look like heaven, painted with clouds, stars and angels, while minstrels played and the angels sang. A lady issued out of a cloud and returned.

Hall wrote, 'Yet you must not forget for all the pageants how the citizens well apparelled stood within rails set on the left side of the streets and the clergy on the right side in rich copes, which censed the princes as they passed, and all the streets were richly hanged with cloths of gold, silver, velvet and arras, and in every house almost minstrels...' At the west end of St Paul's the two royals dismounted and stood under the canopy prepared for them, received by the Archbishop of Canterbury. They offered at the high altar and left, remounting their horses to ride to Blackfriars, where the emperor was to lodge, while his nobles stayed at the new palace of Bridewell.

On Saturday, emperor and king played tennis against the Prince of Orange and Marquis of Brandenburg. On Whitsunday, 8 June, emperor and king, in gowns and coats of white and cloth of silver, rode to St Pauls to hear Mass sung by Cardinal Wolsey. After a feast held at Bridewell, the two royals went by water to Westminster Abbey to hear Evensong. On Monday all dined in Southwark with the Duke of Suffolk and hunted in the park before lodging at Richmond Palace. The next day they went to Hampton Court and from there on Thursday to Windsor, hunting in the park Friday and Saturday. On Sunday they were entertained by a satire on King Francis as a proud horse which refused to be tamed or bridled was tamed by Force and bridled by Puissance.

Over the ensuing three days, council meetings were held in which it was agreed that war would be waged on Francis by land and sea, with the Earl of Surrey being appointed Lord Admiral of England. On Corpus Christi Day, all the Garter Knights (including Northumberland) rode to Windsor Chapel where the emperor sat in his own stall wearing his Garter mantle and gave the heralds 200 crowns. On 19 June, in Windsor Castle's chapel, the treaty against France was ratified; the Earl of Northumberland was one of the witnesses. On Friday the royals left Windsor and by easy journeying and hunting came to Winchester on 22 June. Meanwhile the Earl of Surrey had joined the navy at Southampton. On 1 July, the emperor's 180-strong navy sailed before Southampton. Taking leave of the king on 6 July, the emperor embarked and sailed, with Surrey's fleet as escort, to Spain, arriving ten days later. On his return, Surrey commenced 'a devastation of Normandy', and by the end of the month he had sacked and burned Morlaix.

During August, King Henry was informed the Duke of Albany was preparing to invade England with an army of Scots and Frenchmen. George, Earl of Shrewsbury was appointed by the king as his lieutenant general against the Scots (apparently to his dismay). He was instructed to travel to York, which he reached on 3 September. A commission gave him licence to obtain as much ordnance as he required out of Berwick Castle to be taken to Alnwick and a choice of Pontefract, Sheriff Hutton or Barnard Castle for a headquarters and residence.

Henry Percy also travelled to York, and along with his father was a member of Shrewsbury's privy council. Also in the council were Lords Dacre, Darcy, Latimer, Conyers and Sir William Bulmer, joined by Sir Richard Sacheverell (for his northern military experience), Thomas Magnus (paymaster and treasurer) and Sir Richard Rokesby (Wolsey's comptroller). Thomas Manners, Lord Roos had been appointed earlier in the year as Warden of the East and Middle Marches. Dacre sent news that Albany, after feigning an attack on the East Marches, was heading towards Carlisle. Shrewsbury sent him twenty thousand men to defend the city; he himself made plans to go east to 'fall in with the duke on his return to Edinburgh'.

Without authority, Lord Dacre met Albany at Solum Chapel on the border on 11 September and agreed a one-month truce. Defending his actions in a letter the day after, he said the truce was agreed at the behest of Queen Margaret, who wished to send a Scottish embassy to sue for peace; that the enemy army had been eighty thousand strong and well provided with victuals, arms and pieces of brass, while he had only sixteen thousand unwilling soldiers. He ended his letter: 'My lord, [if Lord] Percy would next month take the charge for the East and Middle Marches and himself for the West, he thinks it advisable for a survey of Berwick, Wark and Carlisle.' Wolsey communicated Dacre's letter to the king, expressing surprise Albany had dissolved an army of eighty thousand after being within 5 miles of Carlisle, which could not have resisted him. He wrote that Lord Dacre had made a truce without authority and the Lord Steward, advised of the truce, had on his own authority discharged the king's army and, for his disease and sickness, had 'returned home to his house'. Wolsey told the king he could, if he was so minded, pursue the war, the truce not being binding. But, he advised, if the lords of Scotland were minded for peace it meant they would not meddle on behalf of France; moreover, winter was fast approaching and if Henry accepted the truce he hoped the king would consider Dacre's presumption as *felix culpa*:

> Howbeit, to be plain, there hath been too much boldness on your folks' part, as well in taking truce and discharging your army without your knowledge; as in Albany's great folly in dissolving so great an army so sumptuously set forth, and advanced without doing any manner act or exploit, upon a bare abstinence of war concluded without any commission or authority.

Adding in Latin that they trembled with fear where there was no fear, he concluded that with the Scottish ambassadors pursuing peace, 'The Lords Dacre and Percy taking the charge of your east, west and middle Marches, such order must be taken for the discharging of your garrisons there, as shall be most expedient for your honour, surety of your borders and avoiding superfluous charges and expenses.'

Wolsey then wrote to Spinelli, the English ambassador to Emperor Charles, 'that albeit the duke of Albany had mustered four thousand Scots and marched to within four miles of Carlisle ... yet when they knew the Earl of Shrewsbury was appointed lieutenant general in the north, and had set forward with fifty thousand men to give them battle, remembering the fate of their king and nobles at their last invasion, they sent to Dacre to ask a month's truce'.

At the end of September, Surrey requested permission to break up the army in France. Two of his own household, nine Englishmen and forty-seven others had died, which had caused 'great alarm', and he was unable to keep the army together and could not blame the men for being afraid, 'for he that is whole and merry at noon is dead by midnight, and when they be dead their bodies as black as a coal'. His next letter was to report 'the weather has been so wet and cold that there are a great many men dead'. With Spaniards and Almains departing in great number, he had abandoned besieging Hedyn and was moving to Ardres. Given leave, he and the army arrived at Calais on 15 October, and the ships began transporting the army home. Notwithstanding rumours and Dacre's advocacy for Lord Percy becoming warden, the king was of a different mind: he appointed Surrey as Shrewsbury's replacement as lieutenant general of the army against Scotland – a sensible move bearing in mind his command experience and knowledge of the terrain – and appointed the Marquis of Dorset as Warden of the East and Middle Marches (with power to punish all offenders) to work with Lord Dacre, who continued in the post of Warden of the West Marches.

Sir Thomas Boleyn wrote from Laredo on 16 October saying their journey had not only been through very rough weather but had seen them attacked by Breton ships; his vessel had been rent open along the stern but they had finally arrived on the 11th to find Ambassador Spinelli had died.

During October, King Francis declined to hand command to his ablest general, Charles, Duc de Bourbon, who was also Constable of

France, and instead appointed his sister's husband, Duc d'Alencon. Snubbed, Bourbon brooded. When the king's mother claimed the estates of his deceased wife, his anger smouldered into rebellion and in March 1523 his chamberlain arrived in England to visit Wolsey, seeking to open communications between the duke and emperor; negotiations ensued over the next few months between all parties.

Dorset wrote to his king from Alnwick on 15 April, grateful for receiving his thanks and for being appointed to the king's Privy Chamber. He enclosed a list of gentlemen who had attended Dacre in his incursion or rode into Scotland and deserved thanks but whom Dacre had omitted to mention; these included Sir William Percy, Sir Henry and Thomas Clifford, his own brother John, 'who took the gout in the rode and never came out of his bed since', his brother Leonard, Sir William Lisle, Ralph Fenwick and William Heron and his kinsmen. Throughout April, Wolsey was inundated with letters from Surrey at Newcastle detailing the various excursions into the borders destroying villages, casting down fortresses and laying waste the countryside.

In London on 15 April, Henry Percy's father attended the first meeting of Parliament since 1515. For the ceremony, the king wore a long-trained gown of ermine-lined crimson with narrow sleeves over which he had a crimson mantle, open in front. The lawyers, in scarlet gowns and hoods and with white coifs on their heads, led the procession followed by various ambassadors, then black-clad abbots, bishops, barons, earls and dukes in scarlet gowns and mantles (the latter divided and open above the right shoulder). Cardinal Wolsey entered next with his usual retinue and last of all came the king, preceded by the elderly Norfolk carrying his sceptre and the Earls of Exeter and Devon carrying the sword and baton.

After mass at Bridewell, they all entered Blackfriars Hall, which had been prepared for Parliament with the placing of three rows of benches covered in red. For a fourth bench, in the centre, were placed four long woolsacks covered with red cloth. The royal throne had been placed on a dais four steps high at one end of the hall. The king seated himself; Wolsey sat on his right on a lower level. The cardinal being in poor health, Dr Tunstall, Bishop of London rose and made an oration, and so the ambassadors could understand it they were given interpreters.

On 18 April, the Commons presented Sir Thomas More to the king as their speaker. Subjects were varied and included agreement for a four-year subsidy to enable the war against France; the attainder of the Duke of Buckingham and touching upon Eleanor Percy, his wife; clothiers of Suffolk; incorporation of the physicians of London; creation of Sir Arthur Plantagenet as Viscount Lisle; and the death of Sir Edward Poynings. The latter had died in October 1521 at his Kent manor of Westenhanger and left no issue (except seven illegitimate children) and Northumberland was deemed his kinsman and heir and granted livery of his lands.

While the earl was in London, he attended the chapter meeting of the Garter Knights held by the king at Bridewell Palace, the first he had attended since 1510. At this chapter Sir Thomas Boleyn was elected a Garter Knight but, being still in Spain, his installation was appointed for August while the feast of the Garter Knights was appointed for 10 May at Windsor, for which Northumberland was excused. Worme's fragmentary accounts recorded: 'Betwixt breaking up of Parliament and my lord's coming up to London after Easter £301 19*s* 7¼*d*.'

A day earlier, Henry Percy's thirty-year-old brother-in-law Sir Henry Clifford had become the eleventh Lord Clifford after the death of his father, inheriting lands in Cumberland, Westmorland, Durham and Yorkshire. Clifford had been brought up with the king, and the two were close friends. But this had led to friction between Clifford father and son, for the tenth lord had complained bitterly of his son's 'ungodly and ungoodly disposition'. The younger Clifford had flouted his father's commands, threatened his servants and had struck and injured one of his old servitors; moreover, he clothed himself and his horse 'in cloth of gold and goldsmith's work more like a duke than a poor baron's son as he is'. The tenth lord had given him £40 to ignore the 'dangerous counsels of evilly-disposed young gentlemen', perhaps referring to October 1517, when the younger Clifford had been imprisoned for a fortnight in the Fleet and was said to be 'waxen a sad gentleman [*sic*]'.

During this last year, Lord Henry Percy had fallen deeply in love with the vivacious, sunny and witty young Anne Boleyn, who returned his love. Cavendish recorded that Lord Percy, 'who then attended upon the Lord Cardinal, and was also his servitor', would, when the cardinal repaired to court, 'resort for his pastime unto the queen's chamber, and there would fall in dalliance among the queen's maidens, being at the last more conversant with Mistress Anne Boleyn than with any other' and that there 'grew such a secret love' between them that at length 'they were ensured together, intending to marry'.

In these meetings did Anne and Henry share anecdotes of their different courts and childhoods? Did they laugh and gossip together about the event of the reign, the conference at the Val d'Or? Did they sing and dance together? Anne was an agile and graceful dancer, who invented new figures and steps to old dances. She was a talented singer and musician – playing flute, rebec, clavichords and virginals – and wrote her own songs, accompanying herself on the lute. Did they share a love of music and poetry? We only have those few bare words of Cavendish and must imagine the rest. Taking note of her intelligence, her gift of quick repartee, her free spirit and gaiety, we can try to see Henry Percy through her eyes and conclude he must himself have been intelligent, witty, serious and entertaining in conversation by turn, and likely played an instrument, danced well and was courtly in his demeanour.

Surrey was commanded to court by the king's letter of 3 June and appointed Dacre as his deputy for the two to three weeks he expected to be absent. On 5 June, Northumberland wrote to Dacre from Wressle, asking if he could borrow £100 until next Lady Day as he had been at great expense at the parliament in London and was summoned to return. He enclosed a warrant for its repayment by his receiver of Cumberland. On 14 June, Dacre begged to be excused from giving a loan because of his own high expenses.

It seems likely the two earls were summoned to be present at the state arrival on 15 June of the exiled King Christian II of Denmark and Sweden with his wife Queen Isabella (the sister of Charles V and thereby a niece of Queen Katherine). The royal couple were received at Dover by the Earl of Devon, Bishops of Exeter and Rochester and many knights and squires. They, their three children, four gentlewomen and a train of forty persons were brought to Greenwich, where they were received in the great hall by King Henry and Queen Katherine (under their cloths of estate) and all the nobles of the realm. The Danish king, with his family, had been exiled into the Netherlands by his council of state. They had offered his throne to his uncle Frederick, and he came seeking aid to be restored to a country he had ruled since 1513 (and, in the case of Sweden, since 1520). Hall recorded that the Danish royals were 'every day feasted at the court' and then conveyed to London to be lodged at Bath Place, not leaving until the first week of July.

While Surrey was in London, he and Dorset had debated Scottish affairs with the king in council. He wrote to Dacre to expect him at York on 2 July and at Newcastle two days later, where he would appoint a law session to deal with the 'notable thieves of Redesdale' on 6 July. He was, as a result, absent from the extraordinary and second chapter of the Garter held at Greenwich on 13 July, which Northumberland did attend, along with Dorset, the Dukes of Norfolk and Suffolk, Earls of Devon, Shrewsbury, Essex and Kent and Lords Abergavenny and Sir Richard Wingfield, and in which 'the brave Walter Devereux, Lord Ferrers' was chosen to join the order for his consistent gallantry. (He would be installed at a later date, being then overseas in France as captain of the English forces.)

Receiving orders from King Henry to make a 'rode' to burn Jedburgh, Surrey wrote to Wolsey on 14 August that he had long since written to him for 'twenty iron pieces of ordnance, eight lasts of gunpowder, some iron shot and 120 carts' which were still in London. 'If he had ever so great a power, he could do nothing without ordnance', he protested, confirming he administered such justice that he had frightened the country. A day later he wrote to Dacre to inform him they were unable to do anything until the ammunition, still on the Thames, arrived. He sent him the news the Duke of Suffolk was taking his army to Calais to await the Burgundians while the emperor was sending his army into Languedoc. Wolsey wrote to Surrey on 8 September saying the king wished him to remain in the north until after Hallowtide.

In his reply four days later, Surrey wrote he was 'glad to hear the Lord Percy will succeed him in command. If he marry my lord Steward's daughter, he will have great help from Dacre by reason of their alliance'. In other matters, he wrote that if the weather was fair and brought good tidings regarding the powder and shot, he intended to invade Scotland on Friday. A letter from Wolsey was sent immediately by Surrey to Dacre for him to read (and return and show no one), expressing gladness that 'Lord Percy will marry the lord steward's daughter; of which he is glad, and is sure Dacre will be also. The chief Baron is with the Earl of Northumberland to conclude the matter.'

The principals, of course, were having matters arranged without their knowledge. So far as Henry Percy was aware, his betrothal to Mary Talbot had been broken off years before. The 'alliance' spoken of by Surrey was that William, Lord Greystoke, son and heir of Lord Dacre, would be Henry's brother-in-law if he married Mary Talbot, for Greystoke had recently married Mary's sister Elizabeth. (Lord Thomas, it appeared, had also not allowed his son any choice in the matter, despite that he himself, when reaching his majority in 1488, had eloped with seventeen-year-old Elizabeth Greystoke, who stole out one night from Lord Clifford's castle of Brougham.)

Letters from Surrey to Wolsey kept him continually informed. On 27 September Regent Albany returned from France to Scotland, 'it is said with eight thousand men and six hundred horses', and Surrey had ridden to Berwick to inspect it, arriving 'at ten at night as weary as ever man was' and worrying about sickness in the town. On his way to Newcastle he had inspected Wark Castle and Wolsey's castle of Norham, strengthening both to sustain sieges of eight to ten days and 'trimming' the former with ordnance. He emphasised the need for money, gunners and men, saying Albany could gather 30,000 men while 'all Northumberland cannot make 2,500, some of whom will have to be put into garrison'. In a written postscript he again asked to be relieved at Allhallowtide and 'if my Lord Percy be not then ready to enter on the office of warden' that Dacre might be content to occupy for the time as his deputy, 'considering the near alliance they be now of. And though these country people be not the best content with him, I doubt not so it be known that my Lord Percy shall come shortly after, they will be content with him for the time. And since the king's pleasure and your Grace's is that my Lord Percy shall succeed me, I trust you will not command me any longer to remain here than Hallowtide.'

During September, Northumberland had visited his son-in-law at Craven to see his grandchildren (and brought back with him the Cliffords' clocksmith). On 30 September he wrote from Wressle thanking Clifford for 'my good cheer and costs I put you to' and reported that as William Worme had not come home yet, he could give no news other than that those who had not paid their money for the king's loan for the war were being chased. He sent Clifford his book of fines showing who had or had not paid, informing him that he would be content to take cattle or sheep to the value of what was owed by those who had not paid, so long as they were valued at reasonable prices.

Meanwhile, Surrey continued his stream of warnings that Albany was preparing to invade England and would head for Carlisle. He confirmed he had ordered beacons made and if the Scots came Sir William Bulmer was to 'see all the corn within

5 or 6 miles of the East Marches threshed and carried inland' and Sir Thomas Clifford, notwithstanding the sickness, was ordered to lie at Berwick with five hundred men and attend to the breaches in its walls. On 1 October, he begged that a hundred gunners be sent in haste, fearing Albany was about to do great mischief and foretold his entering perhaps 'between the eighteenth and twenty-eighth of this month ... If the King's army be only on their way when he enters, he will have returned before we shall be able to do any hurt to Scotland. Newcastle, Thursday, midnight.'

In another letter to Wolsey of the same date, Surrey begged 'to be discharged of his office' at Allhallowtide as promised, saying it was only a month away, by which time Albany would have done all he could; he reiterated that if Dacre deputised, the locals would put up with him for a time if they knew that Lord Percy was to be warden. Believing economics might win the argument, he wrote Dacre would be content with 40*s* a day while Surrey was paid £5 by the king 'much to his grace's charges, and nothing to Surrey's profit ... feels himself decayed in body, as well as worn out in purse, by these four years, during which he has been continually in the wars'. Despite Surrey's panicked agonising, the king's response from Woodstock, dated 5 October, was disheartening: after speaking with naval administrator William Gonson, he believed he could send only forty gunners and, though praising him for his vigilant eye, he did not think Albany would be in a position to invade the borders yet. As for the wardenry, he wrote, 'Surely, my lord, we have not as yet determined our pleasure upon any that should occupy that office.'

8

'DO YOUR DUTY'

Surrey had reported to Wolsey on 8 October 1523 that Albany intended to assemble the Scots–French forces on the 20th, and they were ordered to have thirty days' victuals; furthermore, he had brought from France 1,000 arquebusiers and crossbowmen, 3,000 long pikes and 600 horse, and 1,400 hundred mariners with pikes and crossbows plus artillery. Surrey reported he had therefore ordered all northern noblemen and gentlemen to be at Newcastle on the same day, noting the foul weather, 'yesterday with rain, and today with snow'. He gave the suggestion that Wolsey should send young southern noblemen and gentlemen to him, for if they were encouraged only to be 'dancers, dicers and carders, his grace will not be well served'. If the Scots were resisted now, he wrote, 'no man living will see them invade the realm again'. Albany was a man who took no man's counsel, he said, and was so passionate when thwarted that he would take his bonnet off his head and throw it in the fire: 'Dacre says he burned above a dozen bonnets when last in Scotland ... If he be such a man, with God's grace we shall speed the better with him.'

In the unwarranted postscript of a letter written on 10 October, Surrey complained that Northumberland would not come unless Wolsey wrote to him 'and so 1,500 of his men will tarry at home'. Yet, Northumberland dutifully arrived at Newcastle on 20 October and with him came eight chief captains, eight petty captains, Esperance pursuivant, two chaplains, two surgeons and 854 men (the cost of this 'northern journey', according to Worme's accounting, came in three tranches of £232 2*s* 5*d*, £124 2*s* 1*d* and £526 6*s* 2*d*). The same day saw the arrival of the Marquis of Dorset (bringing with him 'southern noblemen and gentlemen'), Lords Clifford, Latimer, Darcy and Scrope (and with them gentlemen from northern and midland shires) and all of Wolsey's northern retainers with his treasurer, Sir William Gascoigne. Surrey, with men enough 'the best willed he had ever seen', scribbled a note to Wolsey at 11 p.m. on 23 October asking him to 'favour his children in case he be killed. He has spent so much in the king's service that he should leave them the poorest nobleman's children that died in this realm these forty years.'

Northumberland and his troops moved to Alnwick, while Dorset took the vanguard (about six thousand or seven thousand men) to Berwick and Darcy went to Bamburgh. Surrey wrote to Wolsey on 28 October that Albany had been seen about Melrose and Dryburgh, and his company near the border the last week, but they 'have not burnt a house, or taken a prisoner, cow or sheep', and in the margin Wolsey wrote, 'A small occasion to raise the king's great power'. On 31 October, Surrey wrote to Henry VIII that Albany had been 'in a marvellous great fume ... because the axletrees of five or six of his great guns broke' but in the night spies revealed that Albany's 'great gun' had arrived and he now had 'eight cannons, two double cannons, twenty-four falcons and serpentines'. The following day he began attacking Wark Castle. Surrey moved to Holy Island, sending orders to all English companies to rendezvous at Barmer Wood on Monday 2 November. Then spies came and said Albany had retreated with his whole force.

Surrey wrote to Henry VIII that 'this morning [4 October], snow and sleet have fallen – the foulest and coldest weather he has seen', and that Albany, told of his approach, had 'clearly departed'. In a postscript he begged to be recalled, for if he remained during the winter it would 'cost him his life', writing that the letter was 'scribbled at Lowick the poor village, in my hall, my kitchen and my bedchamber all in one'. To Wolsey he wrote in similar vein with the addition of asking for letters of thanks to be sent to the nobles and gentlemen who 'never served with better will', ending with his desire to be discharged and 'Dacre to succeed him until Lord Percy come'. The king, inured to Surrey's complaining, wrote on 12 November that he could leave and Dacre take his place as soon as it was confirmed Albany had disbanded his army.

Dacre, receiving the king's commission to be Warden of the East and Middle Marches, was not ecstatic – he wrote to Wolsey on 18 November that he could not 'occupy the office to the King's profit, owing to his gout and his sore leg, and considering his expenses as Warden of the West Marches and Captain of Carlisle. The offices have never been united before; the greatest princes have held them separately.' He assured the cardinal he would hold it until Easter, there being none other to take the office, but preferred to be designated Surrey's deputy so as to cause greater fear.

During November, King Henry received a letter which accused Northumberland of having worn the Cross Keys, the badge belonging to Wolsey. The cardinal replied to the king on 26 November that his treasurer, Sir William Gascoigne, assured him (and was ready to attest upon oath to the king) 'that neither the Earl of Northumberland nor any of his retinue wore the Cross Keys' but the king's cognisance only and his own badge underneath. Backbiting between families meant there was always someone ready to sow discord.

From Naward Castle, Dacre wrote to Surrey that he was unable to meet him at Newcastle being 'sorely vexed with the gout', unable to stir even if 'fire should burn his bed'. Francis Talbot, newly married to Dacre's daughter Mary, wrote to his father-in-law for advice for Shrewsbury had said they were not to live in his house after Candlemas but at court. On 12 December, having managed to move to Morpeth, Lord Dacre replied that Lord Talbot should tell his father he would 'leave the ordering of himself and his wife wholly in his hands' but to show him how his feoffment would be insufficient to keep him at court and the dishonour to his father if he did not 'live according to his rank'; that he should attempt to come to an accommodation with his father, for absence would make the displeasure continue, thinking of the old saw, 'Far from the eye, far from the heart'.

Among his letters, Dacre had come across one from the Earl of Northumberland written from Leconfield on 24 November. He replied to the missive on 4 December saying he was unable to lend him the money he asked for, but it seems the earl had been unable to await a reply. His accounts show Esperance had received from Lord Clifford £100 and £20 in pledge of plate of twelve saucers on 3 December. The earl also borrowed £66 13*s* 4*d* from Alderman Semper (of York), which brought his borrowing for the year to £846 13*s* 4*d* (£100 of which had been borrowed of Master Amyes to pay the king's subsidy).

Two letters from Northumberland to Clifford show on this occasion he was not intending to make an immediate journey but was perhaps trying to cover a shortfall in funds for Christmastide and the New Year. They also reveal how well informed northerners were kept between themselves of national events. The first letter, written from Leconfield on 6 December, thanked his son-in-law for his kind and loving dealing in his 'necessity', and sent him news that Lord Sandys had gone to the king post-haste and Lord Mountjoy was leaving for France with men; a copy of the king's letter was enclosed. He asked Clifford to hasten his venison to court, ending the letter with his looking forward to seeing Margaret and Henry near the end of the festival season. The other letter, undated but written after 10 December, included news that Suffolk will be over in 'all haste' (already at Calais, he and the army sailed to England on 12 December) and that those who had been assessed and had not paid the king's loan had been given 'very rigorous words'. He also expressed his pride that his venison had arrived at the same time as the king at Wolsey's and had been marvellously well accepted.

On 17 December, from his house at Handsworth near Sheffield, Shrewsbury wrote to Dacre that he was looking forward to meeting him in London soon after Christmas and the bearer, his servant John Myres, would tell him what 'communication he has had with my lord of Northumberland about the marriage of his daughter Mary with lord Percy, which he trusts will take effect at the beginning of next term'. Despite plans being made between Shrewsbury and Northumberland, it appears no marriage took place at 'the beginning of next term', for Henry Percy remained single. Was it in the first few weeks of 1524 that the world came crashing in on Lord Percy and Anne Boleyn, crushing their hopes of marriage?

According to Cavendish, when the serious relationship between Henry Percy and Anne Boleyn came to the king's knowledge he was 'much offended'. He could no longer hide his secret affection for her, of which she was unaware, and revealed 'his secret intendment unto my Lord Cardinal in that behalf; and consulted with him to infringe the precontract between them'. Wolsey left the court and returned to York Place. Cavendish witnessed what followed:

> ... being in his gallery, called there before him the said Lord Percy unto his presence, and before us his servants of his chamber, saying thus unto him, 'I marvel not a little of thy peevish folly, that thou would tangle and ensure thyself with a foolish girl yonder in the court, I mean Anne Boleyn. Dost thou not consider the estate that God hath called thee unto in this world? For after the death of thy noble father, thou will inherit and possess one of the worthiest earldoms of this realm. Therefore it had been most meet and convenient for thee to have sued for the consent of thy father in that behalf – and

> also made the King's Highness privy thereto; requiring therein his princely favour, submitting all thy whole proceeding in all such matters unto his Highness, who would not only accept thankfully your submission, but would, I assure thee, advance you much more nobly, and have matched you according to your estate and honour, whereby ye might have grown so by your wisdom and honourable behaviour into the King's high estimation, that it should have been much to your increase of honour.'

The harangue continued. He was to behold what he had done through his wilfulness, having offended both his father and the king and 'matched yourself with one, such as neither the king, nor yet your father will be agreeable':

> And hereof I put you out of doubt: I will send for your father, and at his coming, he shall either break this unadvised engagement, or else disinherit thee for ever. The king will also complain to thy father, His Highness having intended to prefer her unto another person, with whom the king hath travailed already and being almost at a point with the same person, although she knows it not – although I am sure she will, when the king has informed her, be right glad and agreeable to the same.

Lord Percy then surprised Wolsey by standing up to him in a way that few did:

> Sir, I am sorry to have displeased the king not knowing his pleasure therein but I considered I was of good years, and sufficient, to take a wife where my fancy served me best, never doubting that my lord my father would have been right well persuaded. And though she be a simple maid, and having but a knight to her father, yet is she descended of right

> noble parentage: as by her mother she is nigh of the Norfolk blood; and of her father's side lineally descended of the Earl of Ormond, he being one of the earl's heirs general. Why should I then, sir, be anything scrupulous to match with her, whose estate of descent is equivalent with mine when I shall be in most dignity? Therefore I most humbly require your Grace of your especial favour herein; and also to entreat the King's most royal majesty most lowly on my behalf, for his princely benevolence in this matter, the which I cannot deny or forsake.

The cardinal looked at those assembled. 'Lo, sirs, ye may see what conformity or wisdom is in this wilful boy's head!'

Turning back to Lord Percy, he said he expected once he knew of the king's 'pleasure and travail' he would have 'wholly submitted' to the king's royal will and be fully 'disposed and ordered by his Grace's disposition'.

'Sir, so I would,' said Lord Percy, holding to his purpose, 'but in this matter I have gone so far, before so many worthy witnesses, that I know not how to avoid myself nor to discharge my conscience.'

'Why, thinkest thou that the king and I know not what we have to do in as weighty a matter as this? Yes, I warrant thee. Howbeit I can see in thee no submission to the purpose.'

'Forsooth, my Lord,' said Lord Percy, 'if it please your Grace, I will submit myself wholly to the king's majesty and grace in this matter, my conscience being discharged of the weighty burden of my promise.'

'Well, then,' responded the cardinal, 'I will send for your father and he and we shall take such order for the avoiding of your hasty folly as shall be by the king thought most expedient. Meanwhile, I charge thee, and in the King's name command thee, that thou not presume once to resort into her company, as thou intend to avoid the king's high indignation.'

At that the cardinal left the gallery. Northumberland, reported Cavendish, was sent for and 'at his first coming out of the north he made his first repair unto my Lord Cardinal', who explained the cause of his 'hasty sending'. They were long in 'secret communication' in the cardinal's gallery, after which the two drank some wine together before parting, the earl going to the gallery's end where 'he sat himself down upon a form that stood there for the waiters some time to take their ease'. Then he called his son, Lord Percy, to him:

> ... and said in our presence thus in effect: 'Son, thou hast always been a proud, presumptuous, disdainful and a very unthrifty waster, so hast thou now declared thyself. What joy, what comfort, what pleasure or solace should I conceive in thee, that thus without discretion and advisement hast misused thyself, having no manner of regard to me thy natural father, nor in especial unto thy sovereign lord, to whom all honest and loyal subjects bear faithful and humble obedience; nor yet to the wealth of thine own estate, but hath so unadvisedly ensured thyself to her for whom thou hast purchased thee the king's displeasure; intolerable for any subject to sustain! But that his Grace of his mere wisdom doth consider the lightness of thy head, and wilful qualities of thy person, his displeasure and indignation were sufficient to cast me and all my posterity into utter subversion and desolation.
>
> But, he being my special and singular good lord and favourable prince, and my Lord Cardinal, my good lord, hath and doth clearly excuse me in thy lewd fact, and doth rather lament thy lightness than malign the same; and hath devised an order to be taken for thee; to whom thou and I be more bound than we be able well to consider. I pray to God that this may be to thee a sufficient monition and warning to use thyself more wisely hereafter...'

He then threatened to disinherit his heir, 'for (praises be to God) I have more boys who, I trust, will prove themselves much better, and use them more like unto nobility, among whom I will choose and take the best and most likely to succeed me.'

Before departing the earl took leave of the cardinal's servants, turning last to his son, saying, 'Go your ways, and attend upon my lord's grace your master, and see that you do your duty.'

Cavendish reported that 'after long debating and consultation' the understanding between Anne and Lord Percy was 'infringed and dissolved ... whereof the former engagement was clearly undone. Wherewith Mistress Anne Boleyn was greatly offended, saying, that if it lay ever in her power, she would work the cardinal as much displeasure ... yet was he nothing to blame, for he practised nothing that matter, but it was the king's only device. And even as my Lord Percy was commanded to avoid her company, even so was she commanded to avoid the court, and sent home again to her father for a season; whereat she smoked: for all this while she knew nothing of the King's intended purpose.'

Was it Henry, Lord Percy's 'hasty folly' being resolved that prevented the proposed marriage taking place in the next quarter? Was it coincidental? Perhaps negotiations between the two earls were incomplete and the break-up occurred later in the year. In autumn 1524 Henry mentions being in disgrace with his father, which would bring it nearer to the time of the king's 'dart of love'. Although, besides Cavendish's cause and effect with twenty-four-year hindsight, there is nothing definite to connect any involvement by the king. Maybe the perceptive and shrewd Anne was correct in blaming Wolsey, who certainly would have not countenanced any interference in his plans. Cavendish's last statement on the destruction of the couple's hopes was: 'After that all these troublesome matters of my Lord Percy's were brought to a good stay, and all things finished that were before devised, Mistress Anne Boleyn was revoked unto the court, where she flourished after in great estimation and favour...'

On Trinity Sunday, 21 May, at Framlingham Castle in Norfolk, the second Duke of Norfolk died aged eighty-one years. He had served four sovereigns. Anne Boleyn's uncle Thomas was now third Duke of Norfolk; his eight-year-old son, Henry, took his place as Earl of Surrey. Around the same time, news came that the emperor had driven the French out of Italy; Bourbon was joining the emperor's troops with his own, and with Suffolk in France at the head of four thousand men, the French king was beset on two sides.

On the domestic front, Northumberland issued verbal orders from Petworth on 16 June that John Dent of Newcastle be fined 100*s* for breaking the arrest of various persons who had been arrested by Thomas Horsley, his constable at Warkworth. Informed that the new Duke of Norfolk was being ordered north to negotiate a truce with Scotland, he gave orders for repairs to be made at Warkworth Castle, having already arranged the conveyance of two thousand stones and the building of a limekiln near the castle. Horsley now contracted sawyers, carpenters and tilers to work on the great hall, the counting house, the brew house and draw well and had a new stair made. Plumber John Laycock received £6 7*s* 1*d* for covering the roofs of all the towers and other buildings. Edward Wharriour and Thomas Patenson cleared and 'ridded' the 'ground work' of the stone wall, and William Mason was paid the large sum of £6 6*s* 8*d* for mason work. Three loads of timber were brought from Shilbottle Wood to make window frames for the chapel in the keep.

Yet in the borders the killing continued. On 5 July, Dacre sent a party to burn a great town near Kelso and bring back cattle and plunder. They were spotted by Scotsmen of Teviotdale on their own way to make a raid and ambushed, with each side losing many to injury and taking prisoners. Two days later, Lord Maxwell, banners displayed, brought four thousand Scots over the West Marches by Carlisle and 'began burning on every side' until two thousand Englishmen assembled and set upon them.

Fighting took place for over an hour before the Scots fled, leaving behind three hundred prisoners. As Englishmen departed, taking away their captives, Maxwell saw the English were diminished and turned back to begin the fighting anew, releasing Scottish prisoners and capturing Englishmen in their stead.

In France that July, Anne Boleyn's gentle mistress, twenty-four-year-old Queen Claude, died in childbirth at the Chateau de Blois, having already borne Francis seven children. The Abbé de Brantome wrote of her that she was 'very good and very charitable, and very gentle to all, never doing any unkindness or harm to anyone either at her court or in the kingdom'.

On 4 October, Anne's brother George was contracted to marry Jane Parker. She was the daughter of Henry, Baron Morley and Alice St John, and her grandmother Alice had been married to Sir Edward Howard, brother of George's mother, Elizabeth. The most likely time for their marriage was between this time and advent or the early months of 1525 before Easter.

Despite being 'vexed with toothache and an imposthume in his mouth', on 6 October Norfolk, accompanied by Sir William Percy with a retinue of 133 soldiers, travelled to Berwick where, four days later, a treaty was concluded for a three-year peace between Scotland and England. On 25 October, Henry Percy's aunt Anne became the Countess of Arundel when her husband, William FitzAlan, became the eleventh Earl of Arundel on the death of his father, who was buried on 21 November at Arundel near his wife, Margaret Wydville, sister of Edward IV's queen. (Henry Percy's cousin Henry, when he became fifteen in 1527, requested to be placed in the king's house rather than Wolsey's and became a page at court.)

Leonard Grey, the younger brother of the Marquis of Dorset, was given royal permission to build a castle in Greenwich tiltyard. Preparations began on 6 November. On 19 November, Lord Percy wrote to his friend and brother Henry, Lord Clifford, telling him King Henry had 'for my advancement to honour' appointed him to be one of the courtiers to 'assault the Castle of Loyalty'. Realising he was likely to 'be not at a little cost' and 'to save his honour', he asked if he could borrow £100, for 'my father will do nothing for me but would be glad to have me put to lack'. He assured repayment, offering to have it bound by his uncle Alan (or another substantial person) as Clifford preferred. Did he ever feel aggrieved knowing how lavish his father had been in his spending in his younger days?

On 21 December, the brothers Lords Leonard and John Grey, Sir George Cobham (son of Lord Cobham), William Carey, Sir John Dudley, Thomas Wyatt, Francis Poyntz, Francis Sidney, Sir Anthony Browne, Sir Francis Bryan, Sir Edward Seymour, Oliver Manners, Percival Harte, Sebastian Nudigate and Thomas Calen, all Esquires of the King's Household, sent Windsor Herald 'into the queen's great chamber, the king being present, which herald had a coat of arms of red silk, beaten with a goodly castle of four turrets silver, and in every turret stood a fair well-dressed lady'. Blowing his trumpet, the herald made his announcement:

> Where the king of his bountiful goodness has given to four maidens of his court the Castle of Loyalty to dispose at their pleasure, they have given custody thereof to a captain and fifteen gentlemen with him, which captain sent forth me, Herald Chateau Blanche, to declare to all kings, princes and others of noble courage, that the captain will near to his castle raise a mount, on which shall stand a unicorn, supporting four fair shields. The first shield shall be White and whosoever touches that shield shall be answered six courses at the tilt by those of the castle with hosting harness and double pieces. The second shield, Red, betokening the Tournay and whosever touches that shield shall be answered ten strokes with sword, edge and point abated. The third shield, Yellow, signifying the Barriers and he that touches that shield shall be answered twelve strokes at the barriers with the sword, edge and point

> abated. The fourth shield, Blue, betokening the assault with such weapons as the captain of the castle shall occupy, that is, morris-pike, sword, target, point and edge abated.

The captain and company promised, said the herald, to defend the castle against all comers. No other weapon was to be used except those set up by Unicorn and no fire except matches for guns. Prisoners taken on either side were to pay a ransom of 4 yards of satin, and every captain taken 13 yards.

By December, the Scottish Parliament had removed Albany from his office of Governor of Scotland. On the 23rd, Scottish ambassadors who had arrived five days earlier seeking a peace treaty were taken to Greenwich by water and brought before the king and all his nobles. For their honour the king arranged a joust: six men of arms on horseback, armed at all points and with lances, came to the end of the tilt at Greenwich waiting any comers. 'Then suddenly entered into the field two ladies on two palfreys, in robes of purple damask, leading two ancient knights with beards of silver.' When the two knights came before the queen, they asked her leave to do feats of arms for, despite their advanced years, they still had courage and will to break lances. Consent given, they threw away their robes. King Henry and Charles, Duke of Suffolk revealed themselves, wearing gold embroidered with purple, silver and black. Out came the Earl of Devon, Lords Montague and Roos, Sir Nicholas Carew, Sir Francis Bryan, Henry Norris, Anthony Knevet and five others, everyone running eight courses, in which the king broke seven. The Scots praised the spectacle, especially the king's strength.

Once the knights disarmed, they went to supper and in the queen's chamber afterwards there was dancing. This was followed by a masque with sixteen men all dressed in gold and crimson, their shoes, caps and hoods all gold. The first two were King Henry and the Duke of Suffolk. The masquers partnered the ladies and danced a great while. Afterwards a void was brought in. When the Scots were conveyed to their lodgings, one of them asked if the king and lords were always so merry, for in their country there was but wailing and mourning in wartime. They were answered, 'The king and his court used them still all wartime as they do now for they set not by the French king one bean.' On 30 December, the Scottish ambassadors departed for home with peace agreed for three and a half years.

The foursquare Castle of Loyalty, made of strong timber fastened with iron, stood proudly in the tiltyard. It was 50 feet high with embattlements and loupes and 20 feet long on each side. Wherever men could enter, great rolls had been set which turned as soon as they were touched. On the north and south sides, two steep ditches had been dug to a depth of 15 feet, and between them and the castle was a pale with a steep and thick earthen rampart. The west side held a very steep bank. The castle was accessed by drawbridges. Many viewing it said they thought it could not be won in sport, only in earnest.

On 2 January, after long debate, Sir Francis Bryan and Francis Poyntz elected to defend the west side of the castle with pike target and sword point (edge abated) against Sir George Cobham, George Herbert, John Poyntz and William Knevet. At trumpets, the four gentlemen, pikes and swords at the ready, marched forward, crying, 'Harr, harr!' As they climbed up the bank, those within managed to beat them down, both sides thrusting, lashing and striking. They fought valiantly, but upon taking a breather they devised a new plan: George Herbert and William Knevet pinned down the two within so they could not put their heads over the bulwark, while Sir George Cobham and John Poyntz, using their swords, dug holes in the bank so they could climb up it. Before they had reached the top, however, Herbert and Knevet 'were fought out of breath' and the two within were free to fight the two climbing. Then John Poyntz managed to get on top of the bank and fought with his brother while a recovered Herbert protected him with his pike. Herbert then gained the bank but

1. Alnwick Castle. (Courtesy of Similitude via Pixabay)

2. Maud Herbert and Henry Percy, fourth Earl of Northumberland. (Image courtesy of York Museums Trust, Public Domain)

3. Warkworth Castle. (Courtesy of Dr Helen Kay via Pixabay)

4. Beverley Minster. (Author's collection)

5. Katheryne Spencer and Henry Percy, fifth Earl of Northumberland. (Image courtesy of York Museums Trust, Public Domain)

6. Wressle Castle. (Reconstruction, courtesy of Peter Brears)

Left: 7. Margaret Percy and Henry Clifford, Earl of Cumberland, Skipton. (Courtesy of the Heraldry Society)

Below: 8. The roll of arms for the Percy earls of Northumberland, from Sir Thomas Wriothesley's *Book of Standards* (*c.* 1525–34). (Courtesy of the Heraldry Society)

9. Hampton Court. (Courtesy of Waldo Miguez via Pixabay)

10. Le Champ de Drap d'Or – etching by James Basire. (Courtesy of the Yale Center for British Art, Yale University Art Gallery Collection)

Above left: 11. Henry Percy, sixth Earl of Northumberland, in a close-up from *The Register of the most noble Order of the Garter* (1724). (Courtesy of Newberry Library Staff, Chicago, LC:16004354)

Above right: 12. Queen Anne Boleyn – engraving by James Thomson from the original by Holbein. (Courtesy of Folger Shakespeare Library, Digital Collections)

Left: 13. *Wolsey Disgraced* by Richard Westall. (Courtesy of Folger Imaging Department, Folger Shakespeare Library)

Above: 14. Cawood Castle (Courtesy of the Landmark Trust)

Below: 15. The procession of the Knights of the Garter of 1534, depicted by contemporary Lucas Horenbout. (Courtesy of the Heraldry Society)

Above left: 16. King Henry VIII. (Courtesy of Folger Imaging Department, Folger Shakespeare Library)

Above right: 17. Thomas Cromwell. (Courtesy of the Indianapolis Museum of Art)

18. The beheading of Anne Boleyn. (Courtesy of the Rijksmuseum)

was overthrown. In the end, however, they all got over the pale. The two within fought valiantly but in the end were over-matched and the battle ended. 'There was never battle of pleasure better fought than this was,' Hall enthused.

Three days later, the knights of the Castle of Loyalty came to the barriers to challenge all men. 'Thither came the king, many lords and gentlemen who fought valiantly.' After another three days, the knights of the castle once again came into the field ready to answer all comers. The king came first, in base and bard of silver and ruffed black velvet beneath gold-embroidered purple velvet cut in knots or folds, fastened so it was curled. The king's band included nineteen others richly dressed. First to fight the king was challenger Sir Anthony Browne; both had their swords point and edge abated, but the king's strokes were so great that he still almost cut his opponent's shoulder plate. 'Then every man tourneyed as his course came and many a sword was broken and many a good stripe given, and when every man had struck their full number of twelve strokes, they parted and disarmed.'

On Saturday 11 March 1525, tidings arrived that on 24 February King Francis had been 'taken prisoner before the city of Pavia in Italy' by the emperor. Great fires were lit in the City of London and 'much wine was laid in many places so every man might drink'. On Tower Hill the Papal and Imperial ambassadors set up a goodly tent and had a great banquet with their counterparts from Flanders and Venice. On the following day the king, with all the ambassadors including those of Scotland (wearing mourning black, it was noted), Milan and Florence, rode in estate to St Paul's where Cardinal Wolsey sang a Mass with eleven prelates waiting upon him. Afterwards the choir sang the *Te Deum* with minstrels playing on all sides. The king returned to Bridewell to keep a solemn dinner.

On 21 March Henry Percy agreed an indenture between himself and John Coupland, merchant tailor of London, for 'goods supplied by him, to make over an estate of £10 a year for his use, his wife's and son's when he is married, in his father's lifetime; and when his father dies, an estate of £20 for their lives in place thereof. When this indenture is executed, and obligation of Henry Percy and Thomas Arundel for 200 marks will be cancelled.' On the indenture that was signed and sealed three days later, the wording was changed to read: 'For £100, if Percy, during the lifetime of his father, take a wife, he shall within twenty days after the marriage make an estate to John Coupland, Jane his wife and William their son of lands etc. of clear yearly value of £10 or after the death of his father, within a quarter of a year, of £20.' Clearly, young Henry had not yet married Mary Talbot.

9

'YOUNG LORD AND YOUNG MISTRESS'

In the summer of 1525, Lord Percy's father arrived in London to participate in the knighting and creation of the king's six-year-old son Henry FitzRoy as Earl of Nottingham and Duke of Richmond. In the ceremony making him Earl of Nottingham, which took place at Bridewell Palace on 18 June, Northumberland bore the sword that the king placed around his son's neck; at the second ceremony making him Duke of Richmond, he bore the ducal mantle. Making his son pre-eminent over all other dukes (unless he had legitimate issue), the king appointed Richmond Warden General of the Marches, keeper of Carlisle and castle and Admiral of England for life.

Standing in accordance with his new estate, Richmond watched the other creations: Henry Courtenay, Earl of Devon became Marquis of Exeter; two-year-old Henry Brandon (Suffolk's heir and King Henry's nephew) was created Earl of Lincoln; Sir Thomas Manners, Lord Roos was created Earl of Rutland; Henry Percy's brother-in-law Sir Henry Clifford was created Earl of Cumberland; and Sir Robert Ratcliffe and Sir Thomas Boleyn were created respectively Viscounts Egremont and Rochford (these latter having been officially notified on 17 March). In August, the Duke of

Richmond was given his own household at Pontefract and became the nominal head of the Council of the North.

On 8 September, peace between England and France was 'proclaimed solemnly' by trumpet throughout the City of London. Over the following month, news came from the north that heavy rains had destroyed crops and Lord Dacre had been killed after falling from his horse and was buried at Lanercost Priory, succeeded by his son William. During the autumn, King Henry, who had long coveted Hampton Court for its sophisticated kitchens, chambers, bowling greens, tennis courts and 60 acres of garden, received the lease from Wolsey. In return, Wolsey was licensed to lie at Richmond Palace at his pleasure. At Christmas there, the cardinal 'kept open household to lords, ladies and all other that would come, with plays and disguising in most royal manner'. Because of plague and 'great death' in London, the king kept Christmas at Eltham Palace with a small, select company (which became known as the Still Christmas).

Between 8 and 22 January 1526, Wolsey came to Eltham to compile a long book of ordinances, including items which may sound familiar. Accounts were to be viewed quarterly in the counting-house, and clerks were to attend daily and engross the expenses of the day before examination by the treasurer and comptroller between eight and nine in the morning. The first dinner on eating days would begin at ten o'clock and supper at four on work days; pages to rise at seven, make the fire and wake the Esquires of the King's Body so they could dress and be in the king's chamber at eight, with a yeoman usher keeping the door; in the great chamber, yeomen ushers and waiters must be present by eight in the morning, one of the waiters keeping the door.

To keep the royal Privy Chamber pure and clean and free from a great number of visitors 'who disturb the king's retirement, no one is to be allowed to enter it besides those he himself calls for', the exceptions being 'the Marquis of Exeter, which is the king's near kinsman, and hath been brought up of a child with his Grace in his chamber', six gentlemen waiters, two gentlemen ushers, four grooms, the king's barber, and a page. This was fifteen persons in all: gentlemen waiters Sir William Tyler, Sir Thomas Cheyne, Sir Anthony Browne, Sir John Russell, and Masters Norris (also Groom of the King's Stool) and Carey; gentlemen ushers Roger Radcliffe and Anthony Knevet; grooms William Brereton, Walter Walshe, John Carey and Urian Brereton; barber Penne and page Francis Weston.

Gentlemen of the Privy Chamber were to be ready by seven o'clock (or earlier if ordered) and must help dress the king, his garments being received by a groom at the Privy Chamber door from the yeoman of the wardrobe of robes. Two of the gentlemen were to lie overnight on the pallet within the Privy Chamber, prepared every night by the grooms, who were to make up the fires and lights before going to their lodgings. Privy Chamber personnel were to be friendly to each other. They were to keep secret all the things done there and not talk about the king's absence, his whereabouts or his pastimes, nor to press him with suits; indeed, the nearer someone was to his person, the humbler they were to show themselves. 'As hitherto, when the king has gone walking, hunting, or sporting, most of the nobles and gentlemen have gone with him, leaving the court deserted, and hindering the king in his sports, it is ordered that no one go with him at such times except those appointed by himself and warned by the gentlemen ushers.'

Whenever the king desired bread or drink, 'one of the gentlemen ushers of the Privy Chamber must command one of the grooms to warn the officers of the buttery, pantry, and cellar to bring it to the door of the Privy Chamber, where one of the ushers taking the assay shall receive it, bring it to the cupboard, and wait till one of the six gentlemen shall be discharged thereof. The same order to be observed at breakfast, and when the king is served for all night.' The barber was to be ready upon the king's rising with water, basin, knives, combs and scissors to trim his head and beard and he was to keep his own person and apparel clean and 'not go in company with vile persons or misguided women, on pain of losing his place'.

The yearly salary for grooms of the chamber was set at 40*s* a year, while the pages received 26*s* 8*d*. Wolsey appended a handwritten note to his ordnances: 'Young [George] Boleyn to have £20 yearly above' his normal salary (just over £33 *per annum*), and also 'to admit him to be one of the cupbearers when the king dineth out'. This addition will be of significance later.

Shrove Tuesday, 13 February, saw the king arranging the usual joust. He and his band's horses wore cloth-of-gold and silver bards with the bases richly embroidered with a man's heart in a press with flames about it, the accompanying motto in gold letters reading, 'Declare I dare not.' The Marquis of Exeter and his band entered wearing green velvet and crimson satin embroidered with burning hearts and over each a lady's hand descending from a cloud with a watering can dripping silvery drops. The crowd were thrilled at the many lances broken but, by a chance shivering of one lance, Sir Francis Bryan lost an eye and thereafter wore a patch.

At the end of the jousts the king had a costly banquet prepared at which he served the queen and her ladies himself. Is this the moment, as many people believe, when the king first showed covert signs he had fallen in love? Cavendish does mention that he loved Anne Boleyn for a long space without her knowledge. The king was thirty-four years old, still without an heir; Anne was eighteen.

On 4 March, Anne's sister Mary gave birth to a baby boy. She and William had him christened Henry. He joined his two-year-old sister, Katherine, in the nursery. These were also Lord Percy's first cousins once removed.

On 28 April, French ambassadors M. Brinon (President of Rouen) and Jean Joachim M. de Vaulx were brought to Greenwich. In the presence of the king and his great estates (and the Ambassadors of Rome, Venice and Florence) they humbly thanked him after a Latin oration which had detailed the horrors of the wars and how

Henry, while the French king was a prisoner, could have made conquest in France but had desisted for pity and compassion. On 6 May, the king hosted a banquet royal at Greenwich (at a cost of just under £163). Dishes of mutton, veal, oxtongue, eel, bream, carp, crane, heron, peacock, pheasant, capon, green goose (young, unhung and boiled), lamb, rabbit, chicken and pigeon, salmon and salad were served along with elaborate subtleties: a dungeon, a manor with a lake having swans and cygnets gliding on it, a tower set on a marchpane and two green-and-silver chessboards with gold-garnished chessmen.* In the same month, the king sent out commissioners to stop 'unlawful games' by the commons and 'in all places tables, dice, cards and bowls were taken and burnt'.

At the end of May, King Henry began his summer progress, going hunting early, returning after nine at night and eating supper with the queen in her chamber. In July, 'merry and in good health', the king visited Petworth, where Northumberland's officers presented him with six oxen and forty wethers. The king found 'good game and recreation, entertaining those gentlemen who resorted to him in familiar manner and with good words and presenting them with venison'. FitzWilliam informed Wolsey, 'There is not within 100 miles a properer and better cast house, more neatly kept, with fairer and pleasanter walks, except the king's houses and Wolsey's. Wishes Wolsey had seen the house, for there are sundry devices, which he has not seen elsewhere.'

On 3 August the king had moved onto Arundel – Lord Sandys wrote to Wolsey that the king liked the castle very much. Hall recorded in his chronicle that 'all this summer the king took his pastime in hunting and nothing happened worthy to be written of' except that it can be tentatively postulated that Henry was sending letters to Anne Boleyn. He writes of 'a buck killed late last night by my hand, hoping that when you eat of it, you will think on the

* Subtleties were essentially works of art made of food (usually desserts) served between courses.

hunter ... Written by the hand of your servant who often wishes you in stead of your brother. HR.' At the beginning of the letter he says it had not pleased her 'to remember the promise that you made me when I was last with you, which was that I should hear good news of you, and to have an answer to my last letter'.

Between September 1525 to September 1526, Northumberland's mutilated accounts show he borrowed £333 *6s 8d* from Richard Gresham, mercer of London, £20 on pledge of silver saucers and £50 from Sir Thomas Docwra, Lord of St John's among others, but the entry is incomplete. The sums might relate to extra expenses sustained through the king's Petworth visit, or perhaps pertain to the wedding of his son and Mary Talbot (or both), which appears to have taken place in late August – a scrap of an account for Lord Percy and his wife is dated from Saturday, 25 August 1526 (the day incorrectly written as the 23rd). That the two were married can be shown by John Hastings writing from Paris on 28 September to Burth at Aldgate, one of the earl's servants. He sent news of the fate of the King of Hungary, the insurrection at Rome and that King Francis was daily expected in Paris for the burial of Queen Claude at St Denis (her body having been moved from the chapel at Chateau de Blois), ending the letter with his wish 'to hear of my lord and lady, my young lord and my young mistress'.

Did Wolsey give Henry Percy the same lecture he had given to the twenty-four-year-old Earl of Oxford on his marriage in 1523? He had counselled that he should be loving and kind towards his wife so as to nourish 'perfect love, concord and unity' between them, bringing forth children to God's pleasure and 'like a nobleman shall cherish, love and entertain the countess with all gentleness and kindness to be used either to other'.

Lord Percy, still serving in Wolsey's household, wrote to his brother-in-law Cumberland on 16 October, thanking him for his loving letters and kind remembrance. He also related the singular pleasure he received from 'your fat pasties of a red deer', and the pleasure the cardinal had from those sent to him (notwithstanding his brother William Dacre having 'not long presented his grace with five pasties of a stag, but the accepting of them were not like his grace accepted yours'). He bemoaned that he and his father remained unreconciled, and claimed Northumberland had desired Wolsey to put no confidence in him, 'for you were all with my Lord of Norfolk. And this he said openly to my Lord, I standing by, with many more words than I can write; wherefore, my good lord and brother, I pray you keep this secret and be very wary, for if my lord my father means to do you any harm, you shall be assured of it.'

Percy then explained that the ten pasties Cumberland had sent for his father had arrived after he left and he had taken it upon himself to add two to the ten the cardinal had been sent, two to master chamberlain, two each to Mistress and Mr Hercy, and the other two he 'was so bold' as to give them to the Pope's ambassador. He concluded by writing that the king had arrived and was with the cardinal and had been given 'marvellous high cheer'. Clifford's brother Sir Thomas, who often acted as his brother's agent in London and at court, had delivered the pasties, for he wrote to his brother two days later saying that the king had come in all haste from Ampthill to Westminster to sit in council.

The reason for the king's hurry can be found in some other news related in the letter. On the Continent, the Great Turk had won all Hungary and slain their king, Louis II. Furthermore, the emperor's captains had entered Rome one night (19 September) with seven thousand horsemen and besieged the Pope in his palace. The pontiff had fled through a concealed way and was now hiding in Castel Sant'Angelo; the Neapolitans, spoiling the palace, had taken all the Pope's plate, money and other riches. French ambassadors had a long conference with Wolsey on 16 November, who told them he and the king had offered to be mediators between Francis and Charles so the armies could be turned against the Turk, and without delay regarding the danger; this was endorsed by Claude

Bouton, who had that day arrived by sea from Spain with the emperor's compromises.

On matters of love, during the autumn of 1526, King Henry sent a letter to Anne Boleyn telling her he was 'debating in my mind the contents of your last letters' and had put himself 'into great agony not knowing how you intend them', beseeching her with his whole heart 'to expressly certify to me your whole mind as to the love between us two. For necessity forces me to request an answer, having been for above a whole year struck with the dart of love, and not sure whether I shall fail or find a place in your heart and guarded affection...'

Anne's reply was a New Year gift. Her suitor thanked her for the beautiful '*etrenne*':

> ... not only for the fine diamond and the ship in which the solitary damsel is tossed about, but principally for the beautiful interpretation and the too humble submission which your kindness has used towards me in this case; for I well think it would be very difficult for me to find an occasion to deserve it ... and the demonstrations of your affection are such, the beautiful words of the letter so cordially couched, that I am obliged always forever to truly honour, love and serve you, imploring you to continue in the same firm and constant purpose, assuring you that, on my part, I will surpass it rather than make it reciprocal, if loyalty of heart and a desire to delight you, devoting my heart root to advance it. I pray also, if at any time before this I have in any way offended you, that you would give me the same absolution that you ask, assuring you, that henceforward my heart shall be dedicated to you alone.

He ends his letter '*H aultre AB ne cherche R*', with the 'AB' enclosed in a heart.

When Gabriel de Grammont, Bishop of Tarbes, Francis, Viscount Turenne (a gentleman of Francis's privy chamber), Antoine le

Viste (President of Paris) with Claude Dodieu arrived at Dover on 26 February 1527, they were escorted to London by Jean Joachim. Five days later all received an audience with the cardinal at Westminster. The bishop thanked Wolsey for his efforts towards both peace and freeing the French princes – Dauphin Francois and Henri, Duc d'Orleans – who had been taken hostage by the emperor in return for freeing Francis.

While the cardinal discussed serious business, King Henry arranged his Shrovetide joust. On Wednesday, 6 March, he was keen to try out 'a new harness all gilt, strangely made', and so he did alongside eight gentlemen who were all in cloth of gold embroidered with silver knots. The defenders, led by the Marquis of Exeter, wore blue velvet and white satin, made to resemble the waves and foam of the sea. In all 286 lances were broken, and after the disarming a costly banquet was set up in the queen's chamber.

It seems King Henry was deliberating sending Lord Percy northwards, for his father sent out orders from Wressle on 20 March to take musters of men, for his 'dearest son and heir Lord Percy shall lie and be abiding at my Castle of Alnwick for the defence of the borders'. His commissioners – Roger Lascelles, George Swinburne, Thomas Horseley and Thomas Erington – were to certify 'what number of sufficient persons be sufficiently horsed and harnessed to wait upon' his son to serve the king and how many were wielded bows, bills and demi-lances.

In London, Wolsey and the French ambassadors continued in conference. By 10 April, draft treaties – defensive and offensive – were drawn up for perpetual friendship and for marriage between Henri, Duc d'Orleans, the French king's second son, and Princess Mary. It was agreed that, after they were formally signed, two people would be sent to the emperor (one English and one French) to 'exhort him to universal peace' and restoration of Dauphin Francois and Duc Henri, who were then being held in Spain.

On 5 May at Greenwich, in the presence of ambassadors from Rome, Venice and Milan, the Bishop of London sang Mass (the cardinal being indisposed) and afterwards the king and French ambassadors swore the perpetual peace at the high altar. The Bishop of Tarbes and Viscount Turenne were afterward invited to dine with the king and Wolsey; President le Viste and Jean Joachim dined with the dukes, marquis and the ambassadors. On rising from the table, the king led them to the queen's apartment where, as the queen did not dance, by command of the king Turenne danced with their daughter Princess Mary (whom he thought very handsome but 'so thin, spare and small') while the king danced with Mistress Anne Boleyn, whom the ambassadors noted had served their late queen. After dinner they returned to their lodgings.

Next day, as the ambassadors discussed with Wolsey the conditions to be offered to the emperor, King Henry celebrated the peace with another joust. Dodging rain showers, the challengers sported bards and bases of purple velvet embroidered with knights riding upon mountains and ladies casting darts at them. The defenders' bards were covered on one side with gold-edged clouds and on the other side cloth-of-silver mountains full of gold olive branches, 'all moving'. As Wolsey returned to Westminster before the banquet, held later that night in the new banquet-house (erected on 15 April at one end of the lists), it cannot be known whether Henry Percy attended or whether his last vision of Anne, before both their lives changed, was seeing her dancing with the king on the previous day.

If Percy left with the cardinal he missed out on seeing the king, queens Katherine and Mary, two hundred damsels and the rest of the company enter through broad arches adorned with gargoyles and serpents, into a tapestried chamber brilliantly lit by hundreds of small white-wax candles, held in candlesticks shaped as lions, dragons and greyhounds. The purple brocade ceiling was decorated with roses and pomegranates. The royal table had a large canopy under which the king, his wife and sister sat. Two long tables were set up, the one on the right with the French and great estates pairing with a great lady and on the left the other table held the ambassadors and the other lords and ladies. Two cupboards, reaching from floor to roof, housed a display of gold plate. Dishes were in such abundance that the banquet lasted hours, musicians playing while people ate. A further two enormous cupboards housed the wine to be served at table. Rising from the table afterwards, they were organised into rank, then led through arches into another chamber with a lily-embroidered, silk-covered floor. On its ceiling was a map of the world with the zodiac and planets. Looking back, above the arches Hans Holbein had painted, in brilliant colours, the Siege of Thérouanne, for which he was paid the grand sum of £4 10*s*.

Three tiers of seating had been built on both chamber sides, each with a beam placed lengthwise for spectators to lean on. Gentlemen were seated on one side, ladies on the other. The Venetian ambassador, writing to his brother, said he was very surprised at the 'order, regularity and silence' of the methodical placement of the spectators. In the centre, at the front, the king sat on his royal throne; his wife and sister were seated below at his feet. Towards the centre of the hall was a freestanding arch, 5½ feet deep, decorated with figures. English songs were followed by Mercury, in sky-blue taffeta embroidered with eyes, giving a Latin oration. Cupid and Plutus followed, arguing as to whether wealth or love was the better, when three knights entered the hall in white armour. As they came abreast of the triumphal arch, a bar fell down. On the other side three knights appeared and the ensuing combat was so fierce that swords broke. Another bar fell down and the combatants stopped and withdrew. Suddenly, a painted curtain fell to the ground, revealing a tableau: eight lords sat around a cave upon a rocky mountain with rose and pomegranate trees, in which were 'eight damsels of rare beauty ... arrayed in cloth of gold', sleeves almost sweeping the ground.

Trumpets sounded and the ladies moved. Princess Mary emerged first, so bedecked with jewels that she dazzled onlookers. The ladies danced 'certain groups and figures' and when finished, they danced with the eight lords. Then six gentlemen, the king and Viscount Turenne among them, entered wearing silver and black, and as the king had hurt his left foot while playing tennis, all wore black slippers to disguise he was among them. They wore hoods in the fashion of Iceland, masks and silver beards. Each chose a lady to partner, the king presumably with Anne. After the dancing, all returned to the supper hall where the tables had been reset with confectionery. No one reached their bed until daybreak, with 'such sleepy eyes that the daylight could not keep them open'. On the morrow the Bishop of Tarbes and Sir Francis Poyntz departed for the emperor's court and Thomas, Viscount Rochford and Sir Anthony Browne departed for the French court.

An undated letter by Wolsey (most likely from the end of April) shows he gave Henry Percy permission to visit his 'somewhat acrased' godfather, taking the cardinal's messages with him, which were to tell the lord to be 'careful of his health' and to show him 'certain matters' to be advised of his 'further mind'. (As his godfather's name is not given there is no telling where Lord Percy travelled, although his letter to Thomas Arundel in June suggests it was in the far north of England, where he himself fell ill at the end of April.)

More importantly for Lord Percy, however, sometime between the sending of that letter and 13 May, his father died. We know this because on 15 May 1527 Northumberland's lawyer William Danby was commanded by the cardinal to make a book of the earl's documents, deeds and grants. One of the items listed was 'a debt of 2,500 marks by my Lord of Shrewsbury for the marriage of my Lord Percy', revealing that no dowry had been paid.

Although Cardinal Wolsey began judicial proceedings to examine the legality of the marriage between the King Henry and Queen Katherine at York Place on 17 May, he was not too busy to continue his interference in Henry Percy's affairs. On 25 May Cumberland and Brian Higdon, Dean of York wrote from Wressle to Thomas

Heneage, gentleman usher of Wolsey's chamber, confirming they had 'made a new proportion of expenses for the funeral of the fifth earl' as instructed. This they had arranged to take place on 4 June at Beverley Cathedral, but with Whitsunday being so near (9 June), they feared it made the time very short. Although they hoped not to exceed the sum Wolsey 'had assigned in his letters' but with the 'great resort of strangers' a heavy charge on the household, especially as 'neither beeves, muttons nor salt fish was left at my Lord's death, and only twenty marks in money, which is spent long ago, with much more, for which pledges have been given. More money must be borrowed before the funeral, else the house will break and sparple (disperse), which would be a dishonour while the body lies unburied. If it be broken up afterwards, the servants should have their wages at least for the past time and for this quarter. There are also many poor men to be paid for hand labour.' Although they would have found him useful, they also sent William Worme to the cardinal as he requested.

Meanwhile, a sorrowing Henry Percy wrote to his friend Arundel: 'Before Ambrose came unto me, I was going unto my house at Topcliffe toward the funeral of my late lord and father, whose soul Jesu pardon ... but seeing I know my Lord's Grace's pleasure contrary' he would not be attending the funeral at Beverley, 'the which to have been at I would have been very glad. Since the week after Easter I have been in jeopardy of my life [*circa* 28 April], not only by reason of an ague but also of mine old disease and the unhappy air of this north country; having none amendment until the time I came to Topcliffe, where something I now do amend.'

Cumberland and Higden wrote to Heneage from Wressle on 17 June, confirming they had, as Wolsey commanded, 'delivered to my Lord of St. Mary's Abbey in York, certain parcels of plate of my lord of Northumberland, late deceased, amounting to £666 6*s* 4*d*; which money they have received from the abbot, and therewith buried the said Lord. There were neither priests, scholars, poor folk, noblemen, nor gentlemen at the burial to the number they had prepared for, Whitsunday being so nigh, so that a good sum was reserved both of the money for the dole and for the housekeeping at the time of the burial.' They had thought to proportion the liveries with differing cloth quality but, time being too short to send to London, they had to use coarser cloth which had saved even more money. They confirmed the household had been discharged as per Wolsey's instructions in his letter of Thursday 11 June, which they received on Friday, and had paid them according to a book made by William Worme, but where it did not agree with the late earl's chequer-roll they had followed the latter. Both had viewed the earl's plate and jewels and attached an inventory.

As for Countess Katherine, they had suggested she go to stay with Cumberland, but she had said she felt too ill and weak to undertake the journey, notwithstanding Cumberland had offered her his house 'to be as chief lady and mistress of the same'. They thought she had declined moving to Skipton for the coldness of the air and that she 'would be glad to remain here or with Lady Pickering, being of kin to my lord her son, until otherwise provided for. She is willing to live poorly, and will be at pains to please Wolsey. My lord her son, and her children, go with my lord of Cumberland until Wolsey's pleasure be known.' Lady Pickering seems to have lived at Oswaldkirk, 20 miles north of York. The reference to 'kin' appears to be from a tradition that Thomas Percy, Baron Egremont had had a daughter called Margaret who married into the Pickering family in the 1400s. If 'her children' refers to Thomas and Ingram, they would be twenty-three and twenty-one years old respectively; the fifth earl appears to have done nothing to marry his two younger sons. Soon after his father's death, though, Sir Thomas married Eleanor Harbottle, the daughter of Guiscard Harbottle, sister of George; their first child, Thomas, was born in 1528.

10

'LITTLE EXPERIENCED IN ARMS'

On 18 June 1527, Henry Percy, sixth Earl of Northumberland, Lord of the Honour of Cockermouth and Petworth, Lord Percy, Poynings, FitzPayne and Brian received livery of his father's lands and was appointed, like his father before him, steward of the manor of Holderness with an annual rent of £20, witnessed by his uncle Alan. A day later Percy rewarded his Constable of Langley, Thomas Erington, by granting him a farmhold in Tyndale called Howden free of rent for life. He did this because Erington had tracked and killed the outlaw and rebel William Aberleton of Hillington, and a few days later he further rewarded him with a life annuity of 5 marks.

While Percy settled into his role, Cardinal Wolsey began preparations for his journey to France, ostensibly to negotiate a league between Henry, Charles, Francis and the Venetians; or an offensive league against the emperor; or one between Pope, France and Venice to defend Italy. Then news arrived from Italy, causing turmoil in Europe. In the first week of May, Bourbon's mutinous Imperial army had attacked Rome. Starving and destitute soldiers rampaged through the streets, raping and killing women, murdering anyone they came across no matter how young or old, pillaging houses and vandalising churches, using them as stables.

While the Swiss Guard gave their lives in a heroic rearguard action, the Pope had escaped by a secret path into the security of Castel Sant'Angelo, where he was effectively the prisoner of Emperor Charles V.

Henry Percy spent the next few weeks reaffirming various offices. Edward Edgore continued as auditor of castles and manors within Yorkshire, Northumberland and Cumberland; Attorney General Richard Lyster and his son Michael retained the offices of surveyor, receiver general and feodary of the Honour of Petworth and Poynings in Sussex; and Thomas Heneage remained feodary and steward for some Lincolnshire manors and bailiff for the Lincolnshire lordships of Burwell and Calceby. (Thomas later appointed one John Rudd to be his deputy; Henry Percy also granted John the office of surveyor with fees of 4 marks a year.) Percy's friend Thomas Arundel stayed on as receiver of all his manors in Somerset, Devon and Dorset, with the constableship of Stogursey Castle (and had a deputy called William Beld), and lastly, Sir William FitzWilliam (married to Cumberland's sister Mabel) had high stewardship of all the manors, lands and tenements in Kent, Surrey and Sussex, with an annual fee of £10 and the manor of Heyshott with appurtenances. His uncle William, as granted by his father, he confirmed as chief steward in Yorkshire (with special regard for Pocklington and Catton) and forester of Leconfield for which he received annual fees of £104 *6s 8d*.

My Lord of Northumberland, as Henry would now be styled, was at last freed from the cardinal's immediate presence at the beginning of July. Wolsey left his house at Westminster in his usual inimical style, accompanied by his great number of gentlemen 'three in a rank, in black velvet livery coats ... and great chains of gold about their necks. And all his yeomen, with noblemen's and gentlemen's servants following him in French tawny livery coats.' He rode on his mule, preceded by his two silver crosses and two pillars, the Great Seal, his cardinal's hat and a gentleman carrying his cloak bag. Cavendish was suspicious about the journey.

He believed the great estates were setting the cardinal in a 'snare' by getting him to travel overseas so they could, 'by the aid of their chief mistress, my Lady Anne [Boleyn] ... deprave him so unto the king in his absence that he should be rather in his high displeasure than in his accustomed favour'.

On his way to Dover, the cardinal had separate meetings with John Fisher, Bishop of Rochester and William Warham, Archbishop of Canterbury, discussing with them the 'king's secret matter'. Wolsey intimated that 'some inkling' of the matter had come to Queen Katherine, who had 'broken with his grace in a very displeasant manner', and that nothing was intended by the king except to discover the truth after the Bishop of Tarbes had raised his disquiet regarding the legality of the king's marriage and the legitimacy of his daughter, Princess Mary. The queen's 'inkling' had arisen after King Henry had told her they had been living in mortal sin all their marriage and should live apart. After she had burst into tears he had muttered that all would be fine, begging her to keep the matter secret between them. (Instead she had immediately sent one of her servants to Charles V in Spain, who was already in France returning with news that her nephew intended to entreat that the king's 'secret matter' be held at Rome and for Wolsey's legatine power to be revoked.)

From France, Wolsey informed the king he hoped to meet King Francis at Amiens on 26 July and had received an overture from the king's mother, Madame Louise, proposing that all free cardinals should gather together to govern the church as long as the Pope remained the emperor's prisoner.

Stretching his wings now that he was free of the cardinal, Northumberland on 7 July reappointed Sir Roger Lascelles, then in his mid-forties, to remain as steward with a fee of 20 marks, and on 22 July appointed him and his son Christopher as stewards of the manors of Spofforth and Topcliffe and master foresters of game at a fee of £13 *6s 8d*. Sir John Lamplugh was reaffirmed as lieutenant of Cockermouth and master forester in Wasdalehead and Eastdalehead. Thomas Kelke was retained as server of the board.

Northumberland then appears to have travelled to Petworth for on 16 July a land issue was heard in his court regarding his manor of Preston Poynings, and on 20 July he issued a lease with respect to his manor of Downhead – including meadows, pastures, common pasture and demesne lands and a licence to cut down woods – to Philip Horner, his wife Cecilia and their daughter Elizabeth for the term of their lives (and to the longest liver, giving them tenure for two generations) at an annual rent of £6, with a fine of £106 13*s* 4*d* to enter the lands. Providing leases covering more than one generation seems to have been a deliberate policy of his, for some of his later leases provide security of tenure for two – and in some cases three – generations.

In the north, two notorious outlaws, Sir William Lisle and his son Humphrey, broke out of Newcastle Prison and escaped into Scotland in July. From then and all through August they raided and burned places in Northumberland. Branded traitors for riding with the Scots, a reward was offered for their extradition and apprehension. Sir William was 'guilty of great extortion and wrong to his own mother and kinfolk' and, bearing a grudge against sheriff Sir William Ellerker, had stolen forty of his horses. Having driven the horses into Scotland, he had boasted by proclamation he was the 'captain of all thieves' of Scotland and England.

News of the king's progress, meanwhile, revealed he and the whole court were at Beaulieu and that the king went hunting daily and supped in his private chamber with the Dukes of Norfolk and Suffolk, Marquis of Exeter and Viscount Rochford. On 3 August, Mistress Anne at Beaulieu received 'a ring set with emeralds ... with numerous other presents of jewellery'.

On 11 August, Wolsey wrote from Amiens to King Henry informing him that Duchess Margaret had become aware of his intention to seek a divorce. Certain it would soon be known by the emperor, who would doubtless attempt to thwart him, Wolsey had written to the Pope requesting permission to convoke the cardinals. A week later Francis signed treaties of perpetual peace and marriage, in return for which King Henry withdrew his objection to Francis marrying Charles V's sister Eleanor, which was one of the emperor's stipulations. Only five days later, Spanish ambassador Mendoza wrote to Charles V from London: 'It is generally believed that if the king can obtain a divorce he will end by marrying a daughter of Mr Boleyn, once ambassador at the imperial court, now called Milord Rochford.' The secret was out.

Hearing that his mother had proposed to travel to Skipton Castle, Northumberland wrote to her on 21 August that he felt it would not stand to her honour after she had told the cardinal, when it was first proposed, that removing to Craven would have put her in jeopardy of her life. He felt if she moved at this time it would show 'marvellous inconstancy'. The letter is cited as being written at 'Ohelsan' – a misreading, for it seems he was probably writing from Chelsan (now Chelston), a manor house owned by the Carey family, and was probably visiting his aunt Margaret and her family while conducting his business in the south. Whether Henry's mother had moved to her dower house of Seamer by then is unknown, but it seems to have shortly become her main residence (her dower comprised fifteen manors in Yorkshire and included Pocklington, Catton, Hundmanby and Rawcliffe). Her son had the responsibility of paying her dower annuity of £413 *6s 8d*.

A fragmentary snapshot provides some insight into the lives and belongings of Percy and his wife Mary at this time. Running from August 1526 until August 1527, it lists the following: 'Board of Lady Percy *6s 8d* a week; board wages of two gentlewomen at 20*d* and 16*d* a week; board wages of a yeoman at 18*d* a week and [probably the groom at so much a week]. Board wages of Lord Percy ... him at such times as he ... said lady his wife by...' The wardrobe of Lady Percy was estimated to be worth £40. Of the two gentlewomen one had wages of 5 marks, the other 4 marks, and both were allowed 8 yards of cloth for their liveries. The wardrobe of Lord Percy comprised two gowns, one velvet furred with budge (lamb), the other lined with satin worth £19 13*s* 4*d*; two doublets of satin worth 4*s* 4*d* and 3*s* 4*d* respectively, the making and lining of each costing £4 13*s* 4*d*; six bonnets, two of velvet at 13*s* 4*d* and four French at 4*s* 4*d* each; ten shirts worth 100*s*; twelve pairs of hose, 6*s* a pair; four pairs of velvet shoes at 4*s* 4*d* each; and eight pairs of leather shoes at 12*d* each. Hats, girdles and points are listed but not priced. The value of Percy's clothes was a few pounds below that of his wife. Wages and liveries for his servants are not given but 8 yards of cloth for two long gowns for the yeoman and groom are listed as costing 4*s* a yard; 9 yards of cloth for three short liveries cost the same. Nine horses were hired at 2*d* each, 'one [and o]ther for the day and night'; over the year this cost £27 7*s* 6*d*.

From Wressle, Northumberland wrote to William Plumpton on 18 September regarding the matter between him and the tenants of Follifoot Poole in his lordship of Spofforth, saying that 'I have had and yet hath such business as I cannot attend it this time, wherefore I pray you be content to give sparing to the next head court at Spofforth at which time you shall have an end' and that if he did 'break out and make three or four gaps in Follifoot Field as you claim to do of custom yearly, I am content at this time so that you do make no more business therein.'

Returning from France, Wolsey arrived at Richmond on the last day of September to brief the king. A fortnight later Anne de Montmorency, Marshal of France and Jean du Bellay, Bishop of Bayonne arrived, being met on 20 October at Blackheath by the Marquis of Exeter, the Bishop of London, Viscount Rochford and Lord Mountjoy with five hundred men of honour and gentlemen. The French ambassadors were lodged in the bishop's palace. London citizens presented them with 'five fat oxen, twenty sheep, twelve swans, seven cranes, twelve pheasants, forty-eight partridges, twenty loaves of sugar, comfits and other spices plus wax and eight hogsheads of wine'. Two days later they were presented to the king, who stepped down from his throne and embraced them. For the occasion he was in black velvet lined with sable, his sleeves studded with diamonds.

Mid-October saw another letter of complaint winged to Wolsey from the north regarding outrages being committed by the Lisle family, who had united with the Armstrong clan. Both bands were proclaimed traitors. Letters written by the Duke of Richmond and his council to the Earl of Angus and King James (said to be guarded and kept constrained by Angus) were ignored. On 27 October, Wolsey received a missive from Sir William Eure, Sheriff of Northumberland and vice-warden and lieutenant of the Middle Marches. Writing from Harbottle, he asked Wolsey not to be miscontented with him, protesting that when he lay at Harbottle the Scots came down the River Tyne 16 miles away and although he did all he could to 'withstand their malice' and spared neither his body nor his goods, he could not be in two places at once.

On 3 November the Council of the North complained to Wolsey that, no matter what action was taken, the outlaws (numbering near a hundred and now including Fenwicks, Ogles and Shaftoes) continually robbed and spoilt the land; venturing as far as Hexham, they had taken twenty-four of the king's tenants. They had ordered Sir William Eure to lie at Felton instead of Harbottle but he had refused, desiring a specific order from the king or Wolsey. They complained he 'does not consider himself able to put good rule in the country; none of the gentlemen will do anything for him, for he does not trust them, and they bear no favour to him'. The only solution they could see, they advised Wolsey, was for 'some nobleman lying continually in Northumberland'. The explanation for all the robberies was revealed in the last line of the letter: 'There is great dearth of grain, and many poor people are likely to starve. Wheat is 24*s* a quarter and more likely to rise than fall.'

On Sunday 10 November at Greenwich, the French ambassadors presented King Henry with the Order of St Michael. He put on the cloth-of-silver robes embroidered with cockleshells and they placed around his neck the collar with an image of St Michael. After Mass, dinner and jousting, Hall wrote, 'the king brought the ambassadors to the new banquet chamber, which was hung with costly verdure all new, the ground thereof was all gold and the flowers were all of satin silver so that by the brightsomeness of the gold, the flowers appeared so fresh that they seemed as they were growing'. After supper there was a heraldic disguising in the great chamber. On either side of a fountain were silk trees, a hawthorn with white flowers and a mulberry tree full of berries, representing England and France:

> This fountain was all of white marble graven and chased, the bases were balls of gold supported by ramping beasts wound in leaves of gold. In the first work were gargoyles of gold fiercely faced with spouts running. The second with winged serpents all of gold ... on the summit or top was a fair lady out of whose breasts ran abundantly water of marvellous delicious savour. About this fountain were benches of rosemary fretted in braids laid on gold, all the sides set with roses in branches as they were growing about this fountain. On the benches sat eight fair ladies in strange attire, and so richly apparelled in cloth of gold embroidered and cut over silver that I cannot express the cunning workmanship thereof.

A play was staged which showed the captive Pope being brought to liberty by Cardinal Wolsey. Inevitably the king and his visitors danced with the ladies. We may assume Lady Anne danced with the king.

Although Northumberland is not mentioned, he was present, having been at Westminster on 17 October and for the Sunday ceremony. He remained at court, for on 2 December it becomes clear that the Council of the North had found their man. Percy received from the king a commission as Warden General of the East and Middle Marches towards Scotland and bailiff of Tynedale, with a salary of £1,000 per annum. He had power to array all men between the ages of sixteen and sixty in such places as 'Sir Henry Percy and Henry, late Earl of Northumberland, grandfather of the present earl, or any other warden of the marches'. English wardens were required to liaise with their Scottish counterparts, work with sheriffs and their own officers (two deputies, two serjeants, and others as required) to investigate murders, maimings, fire-raisings, violent thefts, animal rustling and land disputes, with authority to raise hue and cry, pursue with hound and horn and, in the warden courts, to determine all plaints and pleas, trying, sentencing and punishing offenders with or without assize judges present.

The earl wrote to Wolsey thanking him for the position, assuring him of his heart and service 'reserving my duty to the king'. In response to a list of questions regarding his role, he received the following instructions: make immediate proclamation where most necessary, assess Sir William Eure and Sir Ralph Fenwick, and if he suspected any inhabitant of 'burning, murder or robbery', have them brought in immediately to answer to the king's laws. He was provided with a list of men not retained in the king's service so that he could choose those he thought likely to favour justice and consider their potential abilities and qualities.

Leaving London, Percy travelled first to visit the Duke of Richmond and his council at Pontefract Castle, writing to Wolsey that he had been 'so well received that his dulled wit cannot disclose how much he was gratified with the duke's good qualities'. He also talked with and was advised by Thomas Magnus, once paymaster of Shrewsbury's privy council in the north. Northumberland stopped *en route* at Healaugh Park, writing from his manor there to William Plumpton on 17 December regarding a land issue William had with George Fulbarne in Little Ribston within his lordship of Spofforth, asking him to 'suffer the saving of it' until it could be better known to whom the 'right of the same belongeth'.

From there he travelled to Newcastle, arriving on 20 December to be met by Lord Dacre. He then sent out proclamations throughout

Northumberland, sending Sir William Eure to Redesdale and Thomas Erington to Tynedale for 'their coming in within eight days'. He arrived at Alnwick Castle on Christmas Eve. On St Stephen's Day, he wrote to Wolsey asking him to send thanks to Wolsey's chancellor Mr Gascoigne, Sir Thomas Tempest and Mr Bowes, who had remained with him 'studying what was to be done for the reformation of justice', and mentioned that he had not enclosed his book of fees for he had 'set every gentleman where they can do most annoyance to the king's outlaws' and would make the book once he saw how they acquitted themselves.

On the same day, Bishop du Bellay wrote from London to Montmorency back in France that as most of the noblemen were at home keeping order in the country, not many were about the king. 'The Earl of Northumberland has gone against this banished man who has done so much mischief. I fear he is terribly young, and little experienced in arms...'

11

'I WILL BE NO WARD'

Eight days into the New Year, Northumberland had already held a warden court at Alnwick and beheaded nine Felton outlaws for March treason and hanged five for felony, setting the country in 'fear and dread'. Informed a raid was about to take place, the earl sent a band of men under Roger Lascelles who, at midnight, captured all the miscreants. Northumberland had sent out proclamations that all outlaws should submit themselves to the king's mercy upon pain of 'the dreadful sentence of the church', adding if he had to arrest them he would 'hang them upon boughs', destroy their goods and houses and send their wives and children into strange regions.

On Saturday 11 January 1528, five hundred persons out of Tynedale came and submitted to Percy on their knees. He accepted pledges for good behaviour from eight principal persons. Of the four unmarried men who had fled to Sir William Lisle in Scotland, the earl ordered their houses and corn to be burnt and their livestock given to those they had most injured. He appointed Sir Ralf Fenwick as deputy over the area at an annual salary of £45. Similarly, four hundred men from Redesdale submitted; the earl took ten pledges. Sir William Eure was appointed over them at an annual salary of £44 13*s* 4*d*. Henry appointed his brother Sir Thomas his Lieutenant of the East Marches at an annual wage of £20, and Sir William Heron, Sir Roger Gray and Roger Lascelles as his deputies.

After rebels had entered the bishopric of Durham on 20 January, burning, robbing and taking a priest prisoner, Northumberland, aware the Tyne waters were high, ordered Heydon Bridge to be 'locked fast'. He sent Thomas Erington to direct a 'hot-trot' with his 'slot hound' (a sleuth hound bred to follow a trail for days). The rebels, unable to cross the Tyne, were caught at the bridge. In the struggle that followed William Charlton and James Noble were killed; Roger Armstrong and Archibald Dodd were captured. At the warden court held on 27 January, Northumberland ordered the two dead bodies to be hung in chains near Hexham and Heydon. The two captives were sentenced to be hanged in chains at Newcastle and Alnwick.

On the previous day, after the earl had attended Mass at Alnwick Church, he was stopped on his way by men kneeling in just their shirts with halters about their necks. It was Sir William Lisle and his son Humphrey, with Will Shaftoe and fifteen others, and they asked him to mediate for them and ask for the king's 'tender and piteous mercy'. The earl committed them to prison and wrote to the king for further instructions.

The earl received a New Year gift of plate from the king. At the same time, the king sent plate of varying weight to Cardinal Wolsey, Archbishop Warham, the Dukes of Norfolk and Suffolk, the Earl of Northumberland and Viscount Rochford. Most notably, however, Lady Anne received two bracelets set with diamonds and pearls, and, on 31 January, nineteen diamonds set in crown-gold trueloves and two borders of gold for her sleeves set with ten diamonds and eight pearls ordered from the king's goldsmith, Cornelius. Cavendish wrote, 'The long hid and secret love between the King and Mistress Anne Boleyn began to break out into every man's ears.'

Northumberland held a warden court on Thursday 6 February and sentenced Nicholas Lisle to death. The following day, on his way to Alnwick, he met with Sir George Hamilton, a Scotsman taking letters from King James to King Henry, who lodged for the night with him. He stayed to witness the execution on Saturday. Northumberland took the opportunity to ask Sir George to take a letter for him to Wolsey. In it, he wrote there had only been one 'spoliation' in the country since his arrival and that was 60 Scotsmen stealing 160 sheep belonging to Sir John Heron of Chipchase and that he had sent Dacre, after receiving complaints of his ills, six pieces of small artillery from the castle and offered, if the king approved, to go on 'a rode' with him.

News trickled from London: it was announced by Cardinal Wolsey in the Star Chamber on 13 February that the king 'not of his own seeking but rather against his will and intent' had entered into war with Charles V; Lord Piers Butler, travelling from Ireland, had at Windsor on Saturday 22 February been created Earl of Ossory, with the Ormond title agreed between him, Margaret Boleyn and Anne St Leger to be at the king's disposal. On that same Saturday, Henry's sister Margaret visited Alnwick with her husband to 'make merry' at Shrovetide. Lord Dacre (and presumably his wife) visited on 26 February and while all were together, Northumberland attempted to reconcile his two brothers-in-law. Grudgingly, Cumberland agreed not to pursue process against Dacre's tenants for riot or trespass and Dacre agreed he would not take action against the earl's tenants for hunting in his parks; both would in future refer all complaints to Northumberland.

Having received word from Wolsey that he and the king desired William Lisle and his son Humphrey and others to be attainted and executed so the king could claim their lands by forfeit, Northumberland replied on the same day requesting the justices of the York Assizes to be joined with him in the commission and meet with him at Newcastle after the Durham Assizes because he was not experienced in attainders. A sour letter came from Wolsey dated 17 March accusing him of using his ignorance of attainders and arraignments as an excuse not to execute the rebels, warning him he 'must not use such cautelous (wary) and colourable (pretence) dealing with him who has thus tenderly brought him up and set him forward, and by whose means the king has put him in such authority for he knows the whole ... and discourse of his privy suits and dealing and had not answered to Wolsey's expectations. If his suits had been just and reasonable, he would not have failed to set them forward. As for the sparing of Sir William Lisle's elder son he would rather he lives than dies (adding in Latin he did not desire the death of the sinner, but that he be converted and live) if it did not embolden others. The king therefore wishes him sent to the Tower and the execution of his father and the others to proceed with all diligence.'

Taken aback by this unwarranted admonishment, the earl made reply on 24 March that it was to his 'marvellous joy' that his Grace had of his great goodness warned him 'so graciously to be well aware of the thing that your Grace thought was in me; but on the other side your gracious letters have been as much to my heaviness as any thing that ever chanced unto me, seeing that anything should be done with my willing commandment or thought that should lead your Grace to think in me that which is written in your said letter. For, my good and gracious Lord, if ever I so much as thought in this matter of William Lisle and his fellows to make any labour to any person living but to your Grace, and by your means...'

He had, he said, merely written to the Bishop of London and Mr Tuke 'to move your Grace and none other to save some of their lives, which I take God to record, was for no particular profit or affection, but because I might be the more able to serve the King's Highness without danger', with William Lisle 'kinned and allied' with many in the borders 'to whom he must trust his life to do the king service'. He continued, 'For though I have little wit, and as little experience as any man, yet I am not I trust so mad or unhappy, but that I know how much your grace hath done for me, and in a much greater matter than this is, do trust I should not need to seek by-ways, as long as I have your good Grace to my help and chief comfort, next God and the King in this world...' Now he knew the truth, he said, he was sure his Grace would be sorry to 'shorten his days; the which, in very deed, I esteem not to be of very long continuance ... pondering that as I am most bounden next the king, I bear toward your Grace my heart and service, and ever shall, were I to die therefore, whatsoever malice shall report.' Northumberland then confirmed he had been at Newcastle since the first Monday of Lent with two hundred persons – and with the prisoners, whom he would execute on the coming of a judge.

Wolsey was angry that Northumberland had written to Brian Tuke about one of the sixteen, a son of Sir William who was no older than twelve or thirteen, and only with his father and his brother Humphrey for lack of food at home. Brian Tuke, in his turn, had written to Wolsey that although he knew nothing of the boy but had a son of similar age, he found, dwelling on that 'in my bed this night I could not forbear to water my plants, having in fresh remembrance what I knew in King Henry the seventh's days was considered and alleged touching the difference between the king's laws and an instinct or law that is in nature when Sir James Tyrrel and Sir John Wyndham were put to death and their sons pardoned. I thought convenient to advertise your Grace, what was showed me of the younger son, most humbly beseeching' to be pardoned for his 'boldness and simple pity'.

The earl wrote two letters on 2 April from Newcastle: one to King Henry expressing his gratefulness for the thanks he'd given him for his 'little service done in these parts ... according to his bounden duty'; the other to Wolsey that he had, with advice from the judge Sir Anthony FitzHerbert, and in accordance with the king's laws, justly proceeded against William Lisle and his accomplices, who had been attainted for treason and their lands forfeited. Now, having been hanged, drawn and quartered, their heads and quarters had been placed in conspicuous places as a 'terrible and dreadful example'. As directed, John Norton was taking Humphrey Lisle to London and he had kept by him the younger son of William Lisle to await the king's pleasure. He had also hanged six thieves of Tynedale for March treason.

Having compelled the men of Tynedale to submit, the earl adopted similar measures with Redesdale and on 21 April he hanged five Redesdale offenders at Alnwick while a great crowd of Redesdale men, in their shirts with halters about their necks, knelt on bare knees begging him to intercede for them with the king. In his report of events to the king, he mentioned he had followed orders to examine Cuthbert Harbottle, an 'idiot' whom some claimed was next heir to George. Although he had found the man lacking in discretion, Cuthbert had his living of Sir Ralph Fenwick and 'fulfils his trust wisely but he has no claim to Harbottle lands for they descend to George's heirs general, his two sisters'. News came from Scotland that Queen Margaret, her divorce pronounced at Rome on 11 March, had taken a third husband, Henry Stewart, who was promptly arrested after the marriage by her son, King James.

Northumberland kept his Maundy on Shere Thursday (9 April). On that day he received letters from Arundel and Wolsey. On Easter Day he fell ill 'both of his old disease and of a swelling at the stomach with extreme ague', and on 26 April he wrote to his friend that he 'expected he would never see him again', enclosing a chalice and sacring bell for a memorial in case 'God called him to his mercy'. With the letter, he enclosed one for Wolsey on the same date (with two leyers for a token) and 'a pot of green ginger for Tuke as he loves fasting'. (Henry VIII's Letters and Papers dates this event to the following year, but it surely fits here.) He wrote he had received Wolsey's handwritten letter and how of his great goodness he admonished him of his faults, assuring him that his 'poor heart cannot think, nor pen write, how much I esteem me bounden unto your Grace, whom I ever do and shall reckon my chief refuge, next God and the King'. He made a promise:

> I shall never write to no man of honour within the court of any matter, but I shall send unto your Grace the copy of the same letters, accounting myself now, by these your most gracious letters unto me, (notwithstanding I was so much bounden to your Grace afore for your gracious goodness showed unto me in my bringing up) so obliged, that I shall never be able to do your Grace the service that I am bounden to do ... but will spend my heart's blood in your service, of which, as he that is your Grace handiwork, your good grace shall be assured ... Most humbly beseeching your Grace to pardon me for not any (sooner) writing unto the same; for not only with mine old disease, but also with an extreme ague (as to all the country is not unknown), I was so vexed, that rather I was likely to die than live, and as yet but very hardly recovered as our Lord knoweth.

About this time, Thomas Arundel was appointed by Northumberland to be commissioner of his woods and forests in Somerset and Dorset, with a life annuity of £60 and a further one for £40 (and in the following year for £800 the earl conveyed to him the Devonshire manors of Slapton and Kingsdon with advowson of their churches).

In May, a somewhat recovered Northumberland gave Sir Thomas Wharton, his comptroller, the stewardship of Tadcaster and Healaugh (later adding an annuity of £20). Just as he rallied, sickness seemed to visit everybody else. On the last day of the month, Sir William Parr (one of the Duke of Richmond's councillors) wrote to Wolsey requesting a physician to be sent to them, 'there being none in these parts' and informed him six persons had died at Pontefract, 'first attacked with a great cold, next with a fervent heat and sweating'. With children also being sick of the pox, they had moved to

Ledston, a few miles north of Pontefract. In London, Bishop du Bellay reported to Montmorency that the king, after one of Anne Boleyn's maids had fallen sick, had 'in great haste, dislodged' and he had heard Anne had gone to her father in Kent:

> As yet the love has not abated. I know not if absence, and the difficulties of Rome, may effect anything. This sweat, which has made its appearance within these four days, is a most perilous disease. One has a little pain in the head and heart; suddenly a sweat begins; and a physician is useless, for whether you wrap yourself up much or little, in four hours, sometimes in two or three, you are despatched without languishing...

King Henry, having moved from Waltham to Hunsdon, wrote on 20 June to Anne that he had been 'troubled and distraught' until he had heard she was yet still well, assured it would spare her as it had him, and that her brother had fallen ill but was now quite well. And that since returning to Hunsdon he had been perfectly well and 'have not, at present, one sick person':

> I implore you, my entirely beloved, to have no fear, nor be too uneasy at our absence; for wherever I am, I am yours, and yet we must sometimes submit to our misfortunes, for whoever will struggle against fate is generally but so much the further from gaining his desires: wherefore comfort yourself, and take courage and avoid the pestilence as much as you can, and I hope shortly we will sing for joy of the return. No more at present, from lack of time, but that I wish you in my arms, that I might a little dispel your unreasonable thoughts. Written by the hand of him who is and always will be yours, Im HR mutable.

A day later the king was distraught after receiving in the night the 'most afflicting news'. He wrote to Anne he grieved 'to hear of the sickness of my mistress, whom I esteem more than all the world, and whose health I desire as I do my own, so that I would gladly bear half your illness to make you well'. He sent his physician and prayed her to be 'guided by his advice in your illness, by which doing I hope to see you again, which will be to me a greater comfort than all the precious jewels in the world. Written by that secretary, who is, and for ever will be, your loyal and most assured servant H (AB) R.' On the morning of Tuesday 23 June, the king had news that Anne and her father were both recovering from what was being called the Sweat. Not so William Carey, who had gone hunting in the morning and was dead before evening. The sweating sickness was particularly prevalent in Hull and York. Lord Darcy collected a range of recipes to protect himself and his household; one, as dangerous as the disease, suggested the use of nightshade leaves with other herbs.

During June, King James wrote to Northumberland deferring a justice day against border thieves as previously arranged because of a disturbance in his realm. Wolsey sent a letter dated 25 June which instructed Northumberland to deal with Liddesdale malefactors (the families of Armstrong, Crozier and Nixon) who, making an incursion in the West Marches, had slain eleven of Lord Dacre's servants. He moved to Prudhoe Castle, which gave easy access to Carlisle, Haltwhistle, Hexham and Alnwick. From there, Northumberland wrote to Wolsey on 2 July that his spies informed him sixteen-year-old King James had forbidden the Earl of Angus (his mother's ex-husband) or any Douglas to come within 7 miles of him. He accused them of keeping him constrained, spoiling the realm for their own profit and keeping no justice. He had passed attainders on them.

The following month, Northumberland opened his heart to Arundel concerning his troubles, having received his 'loving and kind advertisements, thereby not only well perceiving the true heart in old time which you have borne to me, but also your perseverant good mind of the same by which daily you do renew mine old bond of amity, which in heart cannot be more than it is, as it is bounden. Also I perceive some Judas about me, notwithstanding my goodness to all my servants, hath certified my Lord's Grace of my debts. I assure you, bedfellow, that which I do owe both for my lord my father and myself is but the sum of 6,000 marks, for which I trust I have taken such direction as is to mine honour, notwithstanding the practices of my servant thus to defame his master.' Asking Arundel if he was able to name the Judas, he asserted his 'house since my coming hither has been very costly (notwithstanding there is not a penny owing for the same) and specially by reason of dearness of corn, for every quarter will well cost 4*s*. And whereas that Judas wrote I could not serve the king if my Lord Cardinal did not take some order with me, I trust my lord, upon the information of such a light person, will not take nor follow no such ways as may pluck my poor heart from him, pondering what service I may do him…'.

The earl was 'troubled in heart' thinking of the falsehood of his own servants, and believed that there had been 'secret communication' between his treasurer and Wolsey, although he could not certify the truth of it and would have written more but 'sickness and my troubled mind will not suffer me'. He told Thomas in another letter that 'daily more and more it pleases God to visit me with mine old disease' and, being uncertain of his life, he fretted he had made no will 'for mine own soul or for the weal of those that will come after me'. He requested Thomas to request 'Mr Broke, Chief Baron of the Exchequer, after his term and his circuit finished, to take the pain to come down unto me for the perfecting of my Will; for I have written unto Mr Broke, desiring him for the same; and now have lain this sennight at my Castle of Prudhoe, within 5 miles of Tynedale, to see good order to be kept, the which now, thanks be to God, is well kept in this country'.

In his next missive to Arundel he expressed much surprise at the suggestion that but for the cardinal's illness he would have received loving letters from him, 'considering that in this country it is openly said that he loves me not, and will audit my stewards, Roger Lascelles and Thomas Johnson, so that all others will take example by theirs, and also put a governor to me, of which I would be very loath that his Grace should attempt any such things against me, pondering the heart and service I have borne ever unto him unfeignedly. But I put my trust in God, and less doth regard the surety of the world then ever I did ... And thus fare you well mine own bedfellow, and I pray God give my Lord Cardinal Grace that he make not all England speak of him and me.'

On 3 August Northumberland wrote again to Arundel, this time saying he had received his letters of 20 July which had been delivered to his servant that day at Newcastle expressing Wolsey's desire to have his father's chapel books. Agreeing he would send them even though he had trusted to set up his own chapel, he prayed 'God he may look better upon me than he doth', but felt he had lost 'very much' and was not 'better regarded' through the lies of his treasurer, the undeserved harsh words and 'by the news blown all over Yorkshire by Mr Manning that I am not regarded by the king or the cardinal, as he will tell me when I meet him in Yorkshire, which will be this month'. Those harsh words appear to be that he was accused of 'prodigality, sullenness, mistrust, disdain and making of parts'.

At last, Northumberland was finally moved to anger for he continued, 'I fear my word to Mr Manning will not please my lord, for I will be no ward.' Further, he hoped that, though the 'pains he takes and has taken' since he came north were not better regarded, both the flattering Bishop of Carlisle and 'that false Worme shall be brought to the misery and anxiety that I am in; and in such slanders'. He confirmed he would with all speed send four antiphonars,* 'such as I think were not seen a great while', five 'gralls', an orderly, a manual and eight 'professioners'.

* Antiphonars are books of antiphons or anthems sung or chanted at a liturgy.

He ended his letter with the wish that the cardinal would give him 'licence to put William Worme into a castle of mine at Alnwick in assurety until the time he has accounted for more money received than ever I received ... I shall give his grace £200 and a benefice of £100 for his College, with such other things reserved as his grace shall desire, but until such time as my auditors have taken account off him, wherein good bedfellow do your best, for else he shall put us to send myself, as at our meeting I shall show you...' There is a tradition at Alnwick that an auditor was confined in the dungeon under one of the towers until he made up his accounts to his lord's satisfaction. There was no further mention of Mr Manning in future correspondence, and during the year Northumberland granted to his physician, Stephen Thomason, for his service 'a lease of his lands, tenements, rents and buildings in the city and suburbs of York for twenty-one years at a rental of 5*s* and an annuity of five marks to William Bagthorpe, 'learned man in the law, in consideration of his discrete council'.

Northumberland's sorrows were to worsen. He wrote to Wolsey from Warkworth on 3 September that while he was absent from home, 'one Thirlkeld, servant to the Lord Dacre, was from him and his bedfellow [Lady Dacre and his wife's sister] with my wife, talking with her secretly a great space, after which her words against me might have been well amended, for which and other her former dealing, to your Grace not unknown...' This is seemingly a reference to a former letter in which his wife, at the urging of her sister, had vilified him. The letter continued:

> I have put Edward Edgore my auditor and Thomas Kelk with George Hodgson, my servants, to see her entertained a great deal better than she has deserved. Notwithstanding, I will not suffer her to speak with them, to contrive more malicious acts against me. Nevertheless Ralf Leche and one Sampson, a priest, was sent from my Lord of Shrewsbury to speak with her ... with whom I spoke, my Lord of Cumberland and Sir Thomas

> Clifford being present; and Ralf Leche using these words: that my master, hearing his daughter to be in some agony did send him and his fellow to bring her his blessing and to speak with her. To whom I answered that her malicious purpose, so manifestly known unto them by her letters, which they were privy unto, and contrived as did appear by the counsel of my lord her father, I could not be contented that he, or any from him, should speak to her to invent more malicious imaginations of untruth; being most sorry that my lord her father, therein regarding neither his own honour, nor the kindness of me, which took nothing with his daughter [i.e. no dowry], should set forward that which should touch both mine honour and life. And if my lord her father would make his excuse, that less he could not do, considering his duty to the king's highness.

He then told them that if Shrewsbury thought his daughter 'not so entertained as he would, and she being in fear of poisoning, would send for her', he would send his wife to him with a reasonable allowance and would never 'come in her company' as long as he lived. At this answer they left.

On the copy of the letter sent to Norfolk, there is a little further information. It appears Dacre had got Norfolk to enquire of Northumberland if his wife had the falling sickness (epilepsy) and, if he found she had not, he was urged 'to take her part'. On official matters, Norfolk was informed that Northumberland had put to death all the Scots of Teviotdale (a Douglas stronghold) that came to his hands (apparently referring to the Liddesdale action) except three (Sym, Laird of the Armstrongs and two others) and enclosed a letter for the king to show what was done. He also wrote that 'wardens have always hitherto had five hundred men; two hundred about their own person and three hundred in garrison', but he has but two hundred men appointed to him. He enclosed a copy of his proclamation which 'had been well observed in the Marches, appearing thereby unto me they dread more the pain of money than their lives'.

Despite domestic troubles and illness, Northumberland continued to conscientiously undertake his border duties. Edmund Noble, one of the chief outlaws, was captured and executed. From Topcliffe, Northumberland wrote to King James to arrange a justice day on the borders made 'unstable by the troublous affairs of Angus'. On 17 September he was given instructions he should receive Angus if he was driven out of Scotland into England; by return he enclosed letters from Angus and Roger Lascelles, who was keeping Wolsey's castle of Norham at Northumberland's request, expecting Angus to request lodging there. He asked for leave to visit the court for eight weeks to discuss border affairs and many other causes and bring with him Sir Thomas Tempest and Robert Bowes, who had given him counsel in all the king's affairs, ending with an assurance he would let king and cardinal know of the facts when he had 'perfect and true knowledge' of them.

Lascelles' letters, dated between 5 and 11 September, revealed ongoing events: Angus had been banished from Edinburgh and been attainted, his property forfeited. Requesting a safe-conduct to enter England, he asked for himself, his daughter Margaret and his two brothers to be allowed to lodge at Norham. After King James had gone to Stirling, Angus had sent eighty men to burn two towns to give the king 'light to rise by'. As he was residing at Coldingham Abbey, he expected an attack by King James (and perhaps on England too) and requested Northumberland to act as mediator for him. Lascelles added that the border thieves of both sides 'are stealing things fast reckoning there will be war and if there be not a stay soon I fear it shall be past redress ... for both sides spoil equally the tenants and friends of both'. Regarding a supposed threat against England, Northumberland assured Wolsey if James attempted such malice he would 'withstand his purpose as far as in me shall lie'. On 2 October King James, leading five hundred men, arrived at Coldingham Abbey only to find his prey had flown. Within a mile of the king, Angus waited with two hundred men (mostly border reivers) for James to leave the area and then pursued him 'so fast he drove him into Dunbar'. He sent his daughter Margaret Douglas to Norham, where Northumberland allowed her to remain.

In a moment of lightness the earl, according to a letter from Magnus to Wolsey on 7 October, had of late 'visited the Duke of Richmond' requesting to take him 'to see his house and manor of Topcliffe'. They journeyed together and the duke stayed one night whereupon Northumberland 'did unto him all the honour and pleasure he could in most goodly and humble manner'. Topcliffe was the earl's favourite residence as he enjoyed hunting and hawking in the fields and around the rivers. The manor was well stocked with game and fowl and both Little and Great Parks were well managed for coppice wood, timber and deer. In another, 'of late', Magnus mentioned Lord Dacre had also visited on his way to see the king and Wolsey because of the trouble between him and Cumberland. 'The grudges and displeasures do insurge and arise for the rule of town and castle of Carlisle', and his advice was to make them under one warden rather than divided between two.

Back at Newcastle, Northumberland observed Angus would be driven by necessity to enter England. He wrote to advise Wolsey he had been unable to obtain redress from King James for a raid by the Scots that had seen twenty-three men and sixteen cattle taken and that Sir William Ellerker, the king's keeper of Wark and Dunstanburgh, 'to the parlous example of all the country', had ridden into Scotland and returned with Mark Kerr and others to Wark Castle and hunted openly. With Ellerker being the king's servant, he desired advice on how to deal with the situation. On 10 October, by royal command, Northumberland sent out a proclamation from Alnwick for all men to be in readiness 'upon an hour's warning' to defend the borders (in case King James decided to raise an army to pursue Angus into England). He wrote to the king to confirm he would stay near the border and attend upon the king's commissioners, who were being sent north to negotiate a three-year peace with redress between England and

Scotland. He was also directed to 'let the people slip, if they will, with Angus'. He told Wolsey that Angus was so loved 'it would be very hard (even if he did his best) to withdraw the commons from riding with him to hurt or damage Scotland'.

The earl obviously distrusted Angus. He supplemented Lascelles' twenty men with ten of his own household servants and instructed him to allow only 'the earl, George and Archibald Douglas with three others' into the castle but to keep them in the outer ward to ensure they gained no knowledge of the inner wards. Angus informed Northumberland that King James had besieged his house at Tantallon on 18 October with twelve thousand Scots and French and artillery from Dunbar Castle, and that 'there was never so muckle pain, travail, expenses and diligence done and made for the winning of one house'. When James departed on 3 November to return to Edinburgh, a 'little after moon rising', Angus had set upon the men the king had left to transport away the artillery and slain their captain, the much-liked David Falconer. Not a way, it would seem, to endear oneself to one's king.

On 2 November, Northumberland wrote to Arundel that Sir William Ellerker was ill and thought unlikely to recover and so the earl wished, as previous wardens had, to have their keeping from the king, Wark being 'the stay and key of all this country'. His expressed hope was that, given the sacrifices he had made at Wolsey's desire for his wife's charges and his continuation as warden, he needed 'something to bear my charges and not always to undo myself and have no thanks, and put to these plagues and outbreaks'. Mary, as it transpired in a later letter, had left her husband, so he was at an additional charge of paying her a 'reasonable allowance'.

While English and Scottish commissioners met at Berwick for the peace negotiations, Northumberland returned to lodge at Alnwick. He was surprised on 16 November to be overtaken by Angus as he returned to the castle. He said he came to inform him James had sent John Campbell overseas to procure guns and gunpowder and William

Hamilton to Charles V for a peace treaty and a request to marry one of the emperor's sisters. Telling Arundel of the event four days later, he said Angus had asked for Arundel to be 'good to him in his affairs'. Arundel must have confirmed his visit, for Northumberland wrote he would 'bring up furniture for his house if Arundel will tell how much he requires'. Around this time, Northumberland obtained from the Abbot of St Mary at York his previous year's fee of 1,000 marks (just above £666). Wolsey had also given permission, if he wished, to redeem any portion of his plate 'at the value for which it lies to gage'. From a paper sent to Wolsey we can see that the earl's wage bill for his lieutenants, deputies and officers of the Marches totalled £486, so the sum allotted to him would not have covered all of the warden expenses, and it became obvious later he was remedying any deficiency through his own funds.

Back at Topcliffe, just before Christmas, the earl fell ill. On 20 December he wrote to Brian Tuke to thank him for the pains he had taken in his causes, and, advised by Tempest, he had asked Sir Ralph Fenwick to bring the captured Quentin and Sim Armstrong to Alnwick to speak with them for 'reformation of justice'. He had taxed Sim 'severely with his demerits towards God and his king'; he had replied he had thought never to see a Scottish king who did not keep justice and 'all set upon viciousness and his council of no stability', and that he and his adherents had laid waste 60 miles of Scottish territory 'and not a man in Scotland durst remedy the same', whatever the commissioners should conclude. Northumberland sent this declaration to the English commissioners and was informed by return they had 'concluded a peace' with an article for 'a right to invade Liddesdale and utterly destroy it if redress be refused'. To this Northumberland told Tuke, 'This is a mere brag for the Armstrongs muster three thousand horse.' He asked Sim to write articles to which he would be bound, which he had sent to Wolsey. His letter ended that he had 'been so sick of his old disease that he had all the rites of the Church administered to him, not expecting to live'.

12

'MY LORD, I ARREST YOU OF HIGH TREASON'

At the beginning of 1529 the borders were fairly peaceful, and Northumberland busied himself with gifts. He had sent a New Year gift of gold spoons to the Duke of Richmond, and on 11 January he granted Sir John Norton, who succeeded William Worme as the earl's treasurer, the lifetime lease of a corn mill at Topcliffe and made him master forester of all the forests, parks and chases in Yorkshire for a fee of £13 *6s 8d*, along with providing a gift of deer. (In July he also received an annuity of £20 out of the manor of Ribblesdale, which was later extended to include Richard, his son and the longest liver.) The following day saw the marriage he had arranged at Topcliffe between Thomas Johnson and Isabel, widow of the earl's lawyer Brian Palmes, who died during the winter of 1527. He gave them as a wedding gift the manor of Leathley (with land in Leathley and Castley), £200 to help them set up house and an annuity of £24 with rent from land in Ifield and arranged, at his own expense, to procure the wardship of Isabel's son Francis.

Thomas Cromwell, a senior member of Wolsey's personal council, made a note in February that Northumberland owed him two sums of £35 and £40 and that Master Norton at the earl's place in London had told his servant that the earl 'was disappointed of the money he expected at this time, but would see Cromwell paid shortly'.

In April, Northumberland wrote to Arundel that he had received word from his wife's father that she had been 'brought to bed of a child dead' and that Shrewsbury and those around her said, 'She looks for none other but death, and if she escape the physicians write plain she cannot continue.' Mary recovered but appears to have remained apart from her husband. Around this time the earl transferred some lands in his Devonshire manors of Slapton, Torbryan and Clifton Dartmouth-Hardness to George, Earl of Shrewsbury. Mary's father had initiated a Patent of Inspeximus regarding them, which would confirm the earl's right and title to them. During May, Northumberland appointed John Heron to be one of his gentlemen ushers of his chamber and 'bow-bearer in the lordship of Alnwick at 2*d* a day'.

During the spring months gossip had come from the south about the king's marriage with news that Blackfriars great hall had been set up to resemble a 'solemn court'. On 31 May Cardinal Campeggio (who had journeyed from Rome) and Cardinal Wolsey with notaries, clerics and others (including Thomas Arundel) opened proceedings regarding the legality of the king's marriage. On 18 June the king and queen were summoned to appear between nine and ten in the morning. On that day, Hall recorded, 'the king was called by name, for whom two proctors appeared, then the queen was called, which within short space, being accompanied with four bishops and other of her counsel and a great company of ladies and gentlewomen following her, came personally before the Legates, and after her obeisance, sadly and with great gravity done, she appealed from them, as Judges not competent for that cause, to the Court of Rome, and after that done she departed again'.

Cavendish reported that she never returned but the court continued, 'session to session, and day to day, insomuch that a certain day the king sent for my Lord at the breaking up one day of the court, to come to him into Bridewell and ... in communication in His Grace's Private Chamber from eleven until twelve of the clock and past at noon, my lord came out and departed from the king and took his barge at the Blackfriars stairs, and so went to his house at Westminster. The Bishop of Carlisle, being with him in his barge, said unto him (wiping the sweat from his face). "Sir, it is a very hot day." "Yes," quoth my Lord Cardinal, "If ye had been as well chafed as I have been within this hour, ye would say it were very hot."'

At the end of July, Campeggio declared 'in eloquent Latin' that papal courts suspended all causes at this time until 4 October, 'and if any cause be treated and judged in the mean season, that judgement to be clearly void'. When the king was informed Campeggio was returning to Italy, he was enraged. The Pope, he realised, meant to do nothing for him. Cavendish wrote, 'The king commanded the queen to be removed out of the court and sent unto another place. And his Highness rode in his progress with Mistress Anne in his company, all the grease season [August to mid-October].' Before departing he set the opening of Parliament for 3 November and sent out summons of attendance on 9 August.

Carlisle Herald arrived at Newcastle on Thursday 26 August, bringing a letter for Northumberland from Wolsey dated 14 August from Tittenhanger. He was directed to entertain the Earl of Angus, who was returning from court. He replied on 29 August that he had received Angus at Newcastle 'in as loving wise as could be', especially as all the gentlemen of Northumberland were assembled for the 'administration of justice on the borders' and had requested Angus to ensure his adherents kept good rule upon entering England. The previous day Northumberland, who had already granted his brother Sir Thomas Percy the manors of Kildale and Battersby in Yorkshire on his marriage to Eleanor Harbottle, granted him an annuity of 100 marks from the manors of Prudhoe, Corbridge and Langley.

This last may have been in response to a complicated land matter. Specifically, around this time Northumberland and his brother Thomas, for a consideration of 2,000 marks, concluded a legal action in respect of the Dorset manors of Durweston and

Okeford Fitzpaine (the latter having been given to Glastonbury Abbey by King Edmund Ironside in 1016) with messuages, land, pasture wood and moor, with £15 in rent. The querents were John Roo, William Walsingham of Gray's Inn (retained by Northumberland as a receiver, and who had been granted the Kent manor of Chelsfield by his father), Henry Whitereason (retained by Henry as a gentleman usher, and gifted £20 by him on his marriage) and Thomas Hereforde. (Later at Smithfield, on 25 November, the querents made homage to Richard Abbot of Glastonbury regarding the manor of Okeford Fitzpaine held of the abbey by knight's service for three knights' fees and suffered 'a recovery on Okeford Manor against Henry Percy, son and heir of the fifth earl, to the use of Thomas Kitson.) He also at this time gave his unmarried brother Sir Ingram an annuity of 100 marks.

Eustace Chapuys, a doctor of civil and canon law, arrived in London on 1 September to replace Mendoza as Emperor Charles's ambassador. Over the coming years, he will write letters that see only the good in Queen Katherine and only the bad in Anne Boleyn, reporting on every rumour or story (whether true or not) that put the latter in a poor light. Henceforward, Anne could not have a bad day, be irritable or snappy, happy or emotional without Chapuys putting the worst interpretation on it. Three days after his arrival, he informed Charles that 'the Dukes of Suffolk and Norfolk, and Milord Rochford, the father of the Lady Anne Boleyn, are the king's most favourite courtiers, and the nearest to his person. Now that the cardinal is absent from court it is they who transact all state business.'

Northumberland, visiting York, lodged with Mr Lawson for the night of 21 September. The council presented him with 20*d* worth of mayne bread and 3 pottles* of Hippocras. Two days later, the earl wrote to Wolsey that while sitting at the last assizes with Masters Fitzherbert and Spelman a supplication had been presented to him

* A pottle is half a gallon.

by John Erington. To save Wolsey's honour he had 'plucked it out' of Wolsey's liberty and into the king's court because the judges had told him the law was plainly in Erington's favour but they feared Lord Dacre, Wolsey's officer there, was not about to be impartial.

The earl was summoned to London in October. To supply wood for the royal household, he entered into a bond dated 16 October to the value of £66 13*s* 4*d* with Sir John Gage (Esquire of the King's Body) and Robert Fowler of Alciston in Sussex (yeoman) for them to have £50 worth of timber (wood and underwood) with 'right of entry to cut and carry for ten years' out of his Sussex manor of Waldron, reserving to himself 10 acres. Three days later he was in council debating the succession to Wolsey after he was deprived of the Great Seal, his star falling fast.

On 22 October the cardinal admitted to the king he was guilty of praemunire (meaning he had obeyed a foreign power other than the king under a royal statute of Richard II), which carried a penalty of perpetual imprisonment. He signed an indenture giving King Henry absolutely everything he owned and was ordered to remove to Esher Manor. There, he and his household 'continued the space of three or four weeks, without beds, sheets, tablecloths, cups and dishes to eat our meat, or to lie in. Howbeit there was good provision of all kind of victuals and of drink, both beer and wine' but he was compelled to borrow the dishes and vessels to eat and drink, and linen, from the Bishop of Carlisle and Thomas Arundel, and 'thus continued he in this strange state until the feast of All Hallows tide was past'.

On 25 October, Northumberland witnessed Sir Thomas More receive the Great Seal in the Privy Chamber at Greenwich. He remained in London for Parliament, at which Thomas Cromwell had managed to secure a seat and made good use of his eloquence, which he was noted for (along with speaking Latin, French and Italian). Thomas Audley was presented to the king as Speaker of the Commons. Many Acts were passed, including punishment for servants who stole their master's or mistress's jewels or goods which they held in trust; the rearing of calves to increase the number of cattle; limiting prices of imported woollen hats, bonnets and caps; and, at the last, that 'no person shall sustain any prejudice by means of the attainder of Thomas Lord Cardinal'. Cromwell had received a letter in which he was informed the cardinal was cast in praemunire for 'my lord Cardinal obtained his legacy and cardinalship without the king's licence ... and affects all who have received benefices from him'. The king appreciated the show of loyalty Cromwell had displayed towards Wolsey, and took him into his own service. Chapuys described Cromwell as living splendidly, being liberal with money and fair words, and enjoying pomp and ostentation in his household and his houses.

Back at Topcliffe, Northumberland wrote to King James on 25 November complaining that over a hundred Liddesdale men had invaded England at Birkshawes and seized all the cattle; that his servant Nicholas Ridley and eighteen others had pursued them like 'true men ought' but had been captured and four of them slain. He asked for 'immediate redress that it may not lead to a rupture, which would be much to the earl's discomfort, considering his proximity of blood to James'. On the November sheriff roll for Northumberland, his brother Ingram's name appeared alongside Thomas Erington. And Northumberland began looking forward to a visit by his sister and her husband during the Christmas festival.

Meanwhile at York Place (soon to be renamed Whitehall), Thomas, Viscount Rochford was created Earl of Wiltshire and Ormond on 8 December. His daughter and the king spent their time discussing plans for his new acquisition, which included adding new lodgings, a gallery overlooking a tiltyard, tennis courts, a cockpit and a new three-storey gatehouse connecting the east and west parts of the palace.

Wolsey, after perusing the list of his alleged misdoings, wrote to Cromwell assuring him they were mostly untrue and those true showed no malice to the king or realm, but he did take issue with one item. He was accused of having his cardinal's hat stamped under the king's arms on the groats issued at his York mint, and he said this was a 'malice' by Northumberland there being some disagreement 'betwixt him and me' – but it was more than likely it was alleged by Lord Darcy. He also requested to have Thomas Arundel with him. The king pardoned Wolsey on 12 February. Two days later he was restored to all the possessions belonging to the archbishopric of York (with the exception of York Place) and granted £3,000 in ready money, £1,753 3*s* 7½*d* worth of plate, and household apparel (hangings, bedding, napery etc) to the value of £800, horses, geldings and harness (£150), mules and harness for riding (£60) and six mules for carriage (£60). By estimation, he was allowed fish and salt worth £100, kitchenware (£80), fifty-two oxen (£80), seventy muttons (£12) and apparel for his body (£300). The whole totalled £6,374 3*s* 7½*d*. On top of that the king granted him a yearly pension of 1,000 marks. He was soon complaining it was not enough. Thomas Heneage was appointed steward and bailiff of the manor of Hampton Court and the town of Hampton for £6 13*s* 4*d* a year.

Northumberland's aunt Eleanor died on 13 February, having attained fifty-six years. After Buckingham's death she had married John Audley of Hodnill, and she asked in her will for her heart to be buried in London Greyfriars. On 1 April, Northumberland granted Sir Reynold Carnaby, gentleman of his chamber, a ninety-nine-year lease of the fishery at Ovingham for a yearly rent of £3 6*s* 8*d* (and said to give him a minimum £60 a year), a lease of the corn mill and granted the office of bailiff of Heydon Bridge. In the following month, Northumberland made his brother Sir Thomas steward of Tynedale at the usual fee of £6 13*s* 4*d*. The Marches were quiet. The Kerrs of Cessford and Ferniehirst had made peace with the Scots of Branxholme and others. They, agreeing to forgive all discord, had gone on pilgrimage to Scone, Dundee, Paisley and Melrose to say Masses for the souls of the dead.

Chapuys wrote to the emperor on 23 April explaining that Cardinal Wolsey had begun his journey northwards on 13 April and had set out with 'a train of more than 120 horses', and that the cardinal had sent his physician to him three times, 'offering his services to your Majesty, declaring that though no longer possessing any power, yet knowing so thoroughly as he does the nature of men and the condition of things in this country, he thought his advice might be of use'. On Trinity Sunday, 12 June, Northumberland had been summoned to court, and he was told to bring his seal. Chapuys, a constant news source, wrote to Charles that the peers had signed and sealed a letter to the Pope explaining the necessity for the king's divorce and remarriage. Did Northumberland recall that day how he had once thought to marry his first love? Did he ponder on the different paths they had taken? Queen Katherine had told Chapuys she was sure that if Anne was kept away from Henry for one month she could bring the king back to the right path.

When Arundel was granted wardship of Elizabeth Spelman during September, Henry sent him a warrant to take £100 'out of his woodfalls in his manors in Somerset and Dorset for Elizabeth' and also requested him to pay his debt to William Buttrey (probably for purchasing velvet, satin and sarcenet). Mid-October, King Henry decided all his clergy would be charged with treason and at the same time Cromwell was appointed to the Privy Council. Cardinal Wolsey moved from Southwell to Scrooby, from which place he sent two bucks (out of his park at Beverley) to Sir William Percy, with a letter saying he need have no fear of the king's displeasure for he had advised Northumberland and others he would not be dissatisfied with any who showed favour to Wolsey and treated him as his dignity required, ending, 'Howebeit I am right sorry that my lord your own beareth not unto you his good will which at my journey to these parts I shall be glad by all good means to know if you may attain.'

Reassured, Sir William escorted Wolsey with honour to Cawood Castle (probably from Bawtry) around 29 September. The manor house was a substantial residence fronting the River Ouse and was a favoured residence of previous archbishops. A three-storey gatehouse led to an outer courtyard. The inner courtyard had access to two moated gardens with roses, lavender and Star of Bethlehem, raised beds for fruit trees, a herb garden and five fishponds, and possibly a dovecote. There may have been a third garden along the river. Besides the gatehouse and Great Hall there was a gallery, library, a plate room (treasury), bedchambers and the usual offices of pantry, spicery, livery, great kitchen, brewhouse, bakehouse, butlery, chapels and stables. It was said he began renovations, employing up to three hundred workmen a day, with bricks and tiles being made on site as there was a good local supply of clay. After Dr Higden, Dean of York Minster and the head officers had welcomed him, Wolsey requested to see records and registers and decided his installation should take place in the Minster on 7 November.

During the autumn, Sir Thomas Wharton, Northumberland's comptroller (who undertook duties for Cumberland at times and was good friends with both men and trusted by both) was granted leases of certain Cumberland manors – Dean, Whinfell, Great and Little Broughton, Caldbeck Underfell and Birkby – at a rent of £72, from which he was to derive an annuity of £66 13*s* 4*d* (100 marks) with lands, tenements, fishing, a handful of mills and other profits. Northumberland also granted him a corn mill at Tadcaster, a coal mine in Northumbria and the manors of Healaugh (and the park) and Catterton in Yorkshire and appointed him Lieutenant of Cockermouth, with accustomed fees to him and his heirs, including fishing and herbage of the park. Thomas Kelke was appointed bailiff of Leconfield and keeper of the parks with an annuity of £10.

On 2 November Walter Walshe, a member of the Privy Chamber, arrived at Topcliffe. Two days later, Walshe and Northumberland, the former's two-hundred-strong retinue augmented by the earl's officers, set out for Cawood Castle, arriving just after dinner. After passing through the gates, the earl requested to keep the keys but was rebuffed by the porter, who explained, 'The keys were delivered to me by my master with a charge both by oath and command, and I ask your pardon for refusing your command. For whatsoever you command me to do that belongs to my office, I shall do with a right good will as justly as any of your servants.' The earl then asked him to swear he would 'keep well and truly the gates to the king our sovereign lord's use and do all such things as we shall command you in the king's name, being his Highness' commissioners, while we are here in this castle; and that you shall not let in or out at these gates any but such as you shall be commanded by us'. With this done, the earl returned the keys to the porter.

When Wolsey, about to rise from the table, was told by a servant on a landing mid-stair that the earl was in the hall below, he did not believe it at first. An usher, commanded to check, said it was indeed the earl. Sorry for having dined already and fearing he was unable to offer enough 'good fish' to make the earl a dinner, the cardinal mused he would have to have such as he had. Rising, he instructed, 'Let the table stand.' Before he could go downstairs, the earl had come upstairs. Wolsey, removing his cap, embraced him, saying, 'Although, my lord, I have often desired, and wished in my heart to see you in my house, yet if you had loved me as I do you, you would have sent me word before of your coming so I might have received you according to your honour and mine.' He would have such cheer as he could make, he said, trusting he would accept the same of him, 'as your very old and loving friend, hoping hereafter to see you often, when I shall be more able and better provided to receive you with better fare'.

Wolsey took the earl by the hand and led him further into the chamber and near the fire, saying, 'My lord, you shall go into my bedchamber where there is a good fire and may change your apparel, while a chamber is made ready for you.' He greeted the earl's servants and 'when he had taken them all by the hands, returned to the earl, and said, "Ah my lord, I see you have observed my old precepts and instructions which I gave you, when you were abiding with me in your youth, which was to cherish your father's old servants, whereof I see here present with you a great number."'

He then led the earl into his bedchamber, signalling Cavendish to keep the door. The two stood at a window by the chimney. Once they were alone, the earl, in a faint and soft voice, said to the cardinal, laying his hand upon his arm, 'My lord, I arrest you of high treason.'

The cardinal was so astonished he stood still and silent for a long space. At last he said, 'What moveth you; by what authority do you this?'

'For truth, my lord, I have a commission to warrant me and my doings.'

'Where is your commission? Let me see it.'

'Nay, sir, that you may not,' said the earl.

'Well, then, I will not obey your arrest: For there has been between some of your predecessors and mine... an ancient grudge, which may succeed in you... So, unless I see your authority and commission, I will not obey you.'

Walshe entered the room and, removing his hood, was stopped by the cardinal from kneeling before him. 'Sir, here my Lord of Northumberland has arrested me of treason but by what authority or commission he shows me not although he says he has one. If you be privy thereto, or be joined with him therein, I pray you show me.'

'Indeed, my lord, if it please Your Grace, it is true that he has one.' He beseeched Wolsey to hold them excused, there being 'annexed unto our commission certain instructions you may not be privy to'.

Asking why he could not see them, the cardinal said if he read them he could better help them perform their duty, having been 'privy and of counsel in weighty matters' and would 'prove and clear himself' despite his enemies, having 'an understanding whereupon all this matter grows'.

Turning to Walshe he said, 'I am content to yield unto you ... but not to my Lord of Northumberland without I see his commission.' He handed over the keys to all his coffers and Northumberland assigned two grooms to attend upon the cardinal for the night. His own gentlemen stayed in the outer chamber and about the house. Dr Augustine, Wolsey's physician, was despatched with all speed to London.

Despite intending to leave on Saturday morning, their departure was deferred until Sunday and by the time the earl had ensured all was in good order within the castle it was drawing fast to night. Cavendish related that the earl assigned to attend upon Wolsey...

> '... five of us, his own servants, and no more; that is to say I, one chaplain, his barber, and two grooms of his chamber, and when he should go down the stairs out of the great chamber, my lord demanded for the rest of his servants.'
>
> The earl answered that they were not far for he had enclosed them within the chapel so as not to disquiet his departure.
>
> 'Sir, I pray you,' quoth my lord, 'let me see them ere I depart, or else I will never go out of this house.'
>
> 'Alack, my lord,' quoth the earl, 'they should trouble you; therefore I beseech you to content yourself.'
>
> 'Well,' quoth my lord, 'then will I not depart out of this house, but I will see them, and take my leave of them in this chamber.'

The earl gave leave for the servants to be released from the chapel. Wolsey took his leave of them. In the inner court he mounted his mule. Beyond the outer gate, three thousand persons, said Cavendish, waited outside to lament his departure, crying out,

'God save your grace.' As they rode onwards, Wolsey asked Cavendish where he thought they would lodge him that night. When Cavendish told him it would be Pontefract, the cardinal was dismayed. 'Alas,' quoth he, 'shall I go to the castle and lie there and die like a beast?' Cavendish rode forward to Sir Roger Lascelles and returned to tell the cardinal he was to be lodged within Pontefract Abbey. Northumberland remained behind at Cawood, seeing to 'the despatch of the household and to establish all the stuff in some surety within the same'. The goods and plate, which took six days to transport to London, was weighed at the Tower, taking two men three days.

The earl also travelled to London, for after hearing agreement had been reached for a marriage between his friend Sir Thomas Arundel and fifteen-year-old Margaret Howard, the daughter of Lord Edmund and his second wife Jocasta Culpepper, he wrote from his house of Canonbury on 20 November to Sir John saying his son Thomas was repairing to him on his way to be married and praised his 'weighty good qualities and faithful assuredness'. He also took the decision to help the burgesses of Alnwick develop trade at Alnmouth port by providing wood to enable them to construct a harbour and he would formally confirm 'all such liberties as his noble ancestors had aforetime given unto the burgesses of Alnwick and Alnmouth'.

Sir Roger Lascelles faithfully delivered the cardinal to the care of the Earl of Shrewsbury at Sheffield. Falling sick there, Wolsey remained for three weeks. Although still very sick, he then travelled to Leicester Abbey where on his arrival he told the abbot he had come to leave his bones among them, which he did, dying on 29 November. Perhaps the cardinal's death resonated with the earl, for he at the end of the year granted the chantry in Topcliffe chapel to his priest, William Coppam, 'in consideration of his virtuous disposition', to pray for the souls of his ancestors and especially his father's.

13

'VALIANT COURAGE AND GLAD HEART'

Parliament opened on 16 January 1531 and Northumberland attended all the sessions. On 28 February, King Henry attended in person, remaining for two hours in the House of Lords giving a speech on justice, defence of the realm and the liberties of the church. He introduced a new Act of Poisoning, prompted by the events of 18 February when the Bishop of Rochester's cook had made a pottage which had killed two servants and sickened everyone who ate it, including some poor people. The cook confessed he had thrown in powder to give people the runs as a prank. For the 'prank' he was boiled alive in hot water at Smithfield. Other Acts passed included one in which the clergy were pardoned for praemunire and fined £100,000.

Henry Whitereason received on his master's behalf the earl's one-quarter fee of £150 and advance of £250 for the next quarter, due in June. At the same time, the earl's wife Mary appears to have been persuaded to return to him. On 1 April she, with her husband and his brother Ingram, alienated the Kentish 'manors of Westwood, Easthall, Rokesley (Ruxley), Horsmondon, Tirlingham, Northcray, Newington Bertram and twenty messuages, along with many acres of land, meadow, pasture, wood and 100*s* rent in the manors and moiety of the Hundred of Folkestone to

Sir William FitzWilliam, Sir Thomas Cheney, John Baker, Thomas Wharton, Henry White (under-sheriff of London) and William Walsingham to hold to them and the heirs of William Walsingham for ever'. (These were part of the Poynings inheritance, and the transfer either did not go ahead or he defaulted, for he was in debt when he died in 1534.)

On St George's Day at Greenwich, Henry Percy was by unanimous vote elected to become a Knight of the Garter, receiving his Garter and St George 'with the greatest joy'. His installation was appointed for 6 May at Windsor Castle and on that day, at two o'clock in the afternoon, the habited Garter Knights rode to St George's Chapel from the castle. Dismounting, they entered the chapter house. Black Rod kept the door. Sir Thomas Wriothesley, Garter King of Arms called out, 'Lord Henry Percy, Earl of Northumberland.' Viscount Lisle and Lord Sandys met him at the chapter door and escorted him to the king's deputy, Robert Ratcliffe, Earl of Sussex, who presented him with the order's gown and hood, which he donned. Garter King of Arms delivered his mantle to a herald of arms who held it 'lying overthwart both his arms'. The earl, still escorted, passed down the body of the church and through the door by the king's stall, followed by the knights. Passing into the choir, the knights made reverence to the altar and then the king's stall. Northumberland stood outside his own designated stall where he made his oath to the registrar and was then given the mantle by the herald, put on him by his two escorts. Setting him in his stall they said, 'God give to you great honour long to continue to the pleasure of Almighty God, and to the honour of this Noble Order, and to the increase of your honour.'

Newly elevated, Northumberland was ordered by the king to be one of the thirty-strong delegation sent to Queen Katherine at about eight or nine o'clock on the night of 5 June. Norfolk, in hectoring tone, told her King Henry was displeased and grieved that by her means he had been 'cited by a public edict to appear' at Rome personally, this being neither reasonable nor honourable as the king was entirely sovereign in his kingdom. To his statement she should be content with a place and judges chosen by common accord, Katherine replied she would have no other judge than the Pope and she had more 'cause for lamentation and regret' for the Pope had shown more favour to the king than herself. She turned to the group and said 'they should admonish' those who had put the king on the course he was on. Dr Lee, when he tried to dispute with her, was told he could go and discuss his arguments in Rome. The queen cut short the Bishop of Lincoln's oration by saying she was the king's true and lawful wife and as for her 'knowing' Prince Arthur, the proofs spoken of were false and forged, 'as she could say boldly, knowing the truth better than anybody in the world. Gardiner attacked this last point, citing 'that the presumption of the law would suffice' and would be credited against her, considering also that she had lived some time with Prince Arthur, and they had slept together. He was told he too could go and vent his presumptions and laws at Rome with the others.

The king anxiously awaited their return. After Norfolk had finished 'dressing up' his report, Suffolk baldly told the king the queen was ready to obey him in all things but there were two others she must first obey: 'God was the first and her conscience the other.'

On the regional front, rather than continue a lawsuit which had been ongoing since 1466, Northumberland entered an agreement on 12 June whereby Thomas Perrot and his heirs received the leasehold of the Welsh lordships of Laugharne and Walwyn, for an annual rent of £80, on condition Perrot surrendered his unfounded claim to Brian estates in Devon and Dorset. Then on 7 July, like many peers had before him, Northumberland agreed to act as guarantor to a loan King Henry had entered into with Anglo-Italian banker Antonio Bonvisi for £8,062 *9s 6d*, pledging the Honour of Cockermouth and its castle and all his estates in Cumberland. Cromwell made himself a note that the earl was to enter into a recognisance for £10,000 (later recorded as 20,000 marks).

A day later the earl, in return for Henry Pole, Lord Montague surrendering a life annuity of £40 out of Petworth, granted to him in tail male the manor of Staple Fitzpaine in Somerset.

For the rest of the year Northumberland was in the north. He thanked Cromwell from Newcastle on 13 August for his 'manifold kindness' and for help in a cause which seemed to involve an unnamed ward. At Alnwick, the friars of St Mary of Mount Carmel of Hulne were granted 'the whole of the manse there together with annual alms of 20 marks with the fishery horsebote, heybote, firebote and full ingress and egress of the port, with honey and wax out of the park, pasture for eight oxen, two horses, twenty-five cows and one bull, given to the friars by the earl's ancestors with additional pasture for eight oxen, sixteen cows and two horses'.

In September, Northumberland moved to Warkworth in response to the resumption of nightly depredations by the Kerrs of Ferniehirst and Cessford. He sent officers to attend to prisoner-exchanges. While sending on letters found through stop-and-searches conducted on Scotsmen passing through England to France, Northumberland reported to King Henry he was meeting with express refusals for redress. In the following month, Northumberland appointed his brother Thomas and his infant nephews Thomas and Henry to the offices of constable and steward of Prudhoe Castle and demesnes without charging any rent. To his brother Ingram he gave an extra £76 13*s* 4*d* out of the estates towards the cost of his house and appointed him steward and master forester in Northumberland for a yearly fee of 50 marks (on top of his 100-mark annuity). This brought the support Northumberland was paying out for his brothers, uncle, mother and wife to around £1,128 yearly; this did not include the consequent loss of revenue from the manors they held of him.

His thoughts turned again to prayers for the dead. On 3 December, Northumberland gave into the keeping of George Lancaster, his chaplain, for his diligent service and his virtuous disposition, the hermitage 'builded in a rock of stone within Warkworth Park' on the banks of the River Coquet for saying a weekly Requiem Mass, with a yearly stipend of 20 marks and with 'right of occupation of the little gres-ground called Coney Garts; also the garden and orchard belonging to the hermitage, with pasture in the park for twelve kine, one bull, two horses and a draft of fish every Monday and twenty loads of firewood'. The chapel was carved by expert masons into the sandstone cliff in the 1400s.

In response to letters of complaint from King James, who declared he could get no redress from Northumberland and Dacre, King Henry sent Carlisle Herald in November to announce, in the presence of his envoy Thomas Scott, that he found the redress offered to be so favourable that had James known of it he would have wondered how his commissioners could say nay and 'neither hastiness, want of redress, or slackness may be imputed to our wardens ... whereof one, the Earl of Northumberland was altogether absent' and Dacre, the other, 'clearly discharged from blame'.

On 21 December 1531, as instructed by the king, Northumberland met with the Scottish Earl of Bothwell at Dilston. He was aggrieved at King James, having been imprisoned for six months and threatened with execution, his lands given to the Teviotdale Kerrs. He told Northumberland if King Henry made war upon Scotland, he would support him with one thousand gentlemen and six thousand commoners, and see him crowned at Edinburgh. And King James would deserve being deposed after his treatment of his nobles: Angus banished, Crawford wrongfully disinherited, Argyll imprisoned and Moray, Lord Maxwell and Sir James Hamilton disregarded. Northumberland found Bothwell witty, learned and well mannered, and 'of his years as goodly a gentleman as ever I saw in my life'.

The king sent his usual New Year gift of plate to Northumberland. In return he sent King Henry an 8-ounce gold trencher. On 7 January 1532 the earl appointed Robert Horsley keeper of the gates and steward of Warkworth Castle for life (at a combined annual salary of £6 *6s 16d*) and superintendent of the park at 13*s* 4*d* (as his father Thomas had been before him); Cuthbert Carnaby at the same time was appointed constable of the castle for life at £10 a year.

The earl travelled from Warkworth to London in preparation for attending Parliament, due to open on 15 January. He had left orders for his officers – Robert Ogle, John Weddryngton and Roger Grey – to summon all who had complaints to a warden court to be held at Morpeth on Monday 8 January and that his two brothers would 'come and occupy the room' in his absence to redress 'enormities' committed by Redesdale and Tynedale men. It was not long before Northumberland received a complaint from his officers, who wrote that three poor men had come to them at Morpeth on 9 January saying their neighbours, true commons on the Tyne, had risen only to avenge themselves on men of Redesdale and Tynedale for spoiling their goods. They had since been told that Redesdale had put in pledges to John Heron, and that Redesdale and Tynedale were bound to his brothers since the meeting at Rothbury; had they known they were authorised they would have laid their pledges with them. On their return on Saturday 13 January they learned 'they were only at command of Sir Thomas, Sir Ingram Percy and John Heron'. His brothers had waxed indignant at them for trying to obey his orders.

At the beginning of March, after receiving a complaint from King James that Northumberland had inflicted injuries on his subjects, the king again summoned the earl to examine matters. He wrote to King James that he had found, according to the law, a ship at Tynemouth 'stopped for payment of customs' and that the Sheriff of Northumberland – and not the earl – had arrested the Scotsmen near Warkworth because they carried no safe-conduct. Mentioning that open-day forays were made into England by James's subjects, the king said he was sending Carlisle Herald to James. The herald was to appoint a justice-day and to request the

Scots-held English ship be allowed to sail to Berwick for delivery to Sir Thomas Clifford.

Between parliamentary sessions, the earl stayed at his newly acquired manor in Hackney, just outside London. Sir Thomas Neville had exchanged the manor for some of the earl's lands in Sussex, which gave him a base. The earl had already exchanged his Aldgate house for property in Cumberland and had leased out the Percy Inn in Aldersgate (in his family since 1343) to William Paget, a clerk of the king's signet, although he had reserved several rooms 'for his own private lodging'. Hackney Manor was surrounded by countryside and, situated on a hill, had a panoramic view of London. The manor had an outer and inner courtyard and was large enough to have a hall, gallery, library, great chamber, dining chamber, bedchambers and chapel, plus the usual offices and large gardens. From there, on 26 March, he signed a release cancelling an obligation by the abbot and convent of Alnwick to maintain a chantry priest at Warkworth Castle (imposed on them in 1427 by his ancestor the second earl) and pardoned them of any penalties incurred for not having done so during his life, his father's or his grandfather's.

Although Parliament was still in session, the Chapter of Garter Knights was kept at Greenwich. The king gave Northumberland a letter to excuse him from attending the Windsor Garter feast appointed for 12 May. While he was at Greenwich, the king said he intended to make the earl Sheriff of Northumberland for life, only having to pay the Exchequer £40 annually 'without making any further account'.

Northumberland was at Alnwick on 18 May for, on that Saturday, he wrote to his sister Margaret thanking her for her kindness and pains she had taken with him at his house and noting he was looking forward to seeing her and Henry at Craven before Trinity Sunday (26 May). His plans were altered abruptly for, at a summons by the king, he was at Greenwich two days later. At four o'clock he was present to witness Thomas Audley being knighted by the king before being presented with the Great Seal creating him Lord Chancellor in place of Sir Thomas More, who had resigned. The earl remained in London for a few days.

For unknown financial reasons, on 27 May, Northumberland granted Henry Pole, Lord Montague, son of Margaret Plantagenet, and three others (unnamed) various lordships with advowsons in Somerset 'to hold to use of Henry, Marquis of Exeter £520 per annum'. And on 8 July he entered into an indenture of sale between himself and Sir Edward Seymour for £1,600 in respect of his Sussex manors of Poynings, Perchinge, Preston Poynings, Ashcombe, Waldren, Chinting and Pengeden. It is clear he did not intend to lose these latter manors for on the following day the two agreed an indenture that if Northumberland repaid the money to Sir Edward at Michaelmas 1533 at the font in St Paul's in London the sale would be void; but if the earl defaulted, Sir Edward would be able to enjoy the premises. Another record, dated 10 July 1532, named it a sealed mortgage.

In a letter dated 10 July from Westminster Henry Percy thanked his sister for the present she had sent him (through a bearer named Shires) and gave her his 'right hearty thanks' By 12 July he had travelled to Prudhoe Castle, and via Jake (a friend of the earl and bearer of the Cliffords) he sent a letter to Margaret and Henry that he had been looking forward to seeing them at Topcliffe:

> ... assuring you that the kindness thereof is not a little to my comfort, for the king excepted, you be the persons in the world I would fainest see, and that my comfort doth rest in. And for the certainty thereof as that by reason of this troublesome world is unknown, as by my letters unto the King's Highness you shall perceive, the copies whereof I sent you, thinking never so long to I speak with you, in whom, as I have said, I have my most confidence. And concerning my going up, I send herewith the copies of my letters I received from the King's Highness and Mr Cromwell.

Again his plans were suddenly changed, for a grant reveals he was back at Hackney on 16 July. (The grant was drafted in Cromwell's handwriting and Northumberland agreed that Robert Hogan, the king's master cook, had licence for his friend and fellow Richard Hill, serjeant of the cellar, to hunt in the great and little parks and coneygarth of Petworth and send him any venison he requires.)

While the king was at Ampthill between 16 and 23 July as part of his summer progress, between those dates Norfolk returned to London. A letter by Chapuys dated 22 July related Northumberland had been summoned to London on a serious matter: he was to be questioned regarding an alleged precontract between himself and Anne Boleyn. Mary Talbot told her father that 'for the previous two years he had abstained from her company and in a quarrel at her complaining at his behaviour, he replied he was not her husband, that he had long ago been betrothed to Anne Boleyn ... the countess sought freedom by writing to her father to give an account of the quarrel and asking him to lay it before the king'.

It is possible in the light of Mary's previous behaviour that she had exaggerated what was said; perhaps Percy had merely said he had wished they had never married and he had been able to marry Anne. Whatever the truth, Shrewsbury immediately wrote to Norfolk, who himself immediately conveyed the development to Anne. She took it to the king and desired him to investigate the matter. Thus, in the presence of the Privy Council, Northumberland denied there had ever been a precontract between himself and Lady Anne, swearing an oath on the Blessed Sacrament in front of Norfolk, the archbishops and the king's canon lawyers. The earl had returned north by 6 August, presumably on his way to Topcliffe, for on that day he was visiting or lodging for the night at York, where he was gifted two great pikes, 3 gallons of Gascony wine and 2*s* in mayne bread. Possibly in response to his own abhorrence of his wife and a certainty their marriage would remain childless, Northumberland decided if he died without issue, the reversion of the Percy Fee in Craven should pass to his nephew Henry Clifford (although he reserved to his heirs the rents and jurisdictions). The Percy Fee was land immediately north to his brother-in-law's own Honour of Skipton.

The August weather was hot and dry and at sunrise on Monday 19 August 1532, a great number of Rutherfords, Kerrs and Davisons (and others) entered Tynedale after riding through the night to make a foray at Haltwhistle. Thomas Erington, with six-score of the townsfolk, battled them, managing to wound over a hundred and take twelve prisoners. Those twelve appeared at the earl's warden court, held at Hexham on the Friday, and were executed on Sunday. In his letter to the king, the earl observed, 'The shout and cry came to Bewcastledale and Gillesland before it reached Langley but no-one came to the rescue.' It would be revealed later that Dacre had deliberately ignored the cry. Northumberland, at his warden court held in Newcastle, sentenced to death one Hector and Andrew Armstrong, who had been intercepted by Sir Ralph Fenwick before they burned one of the earl's towns on the Tyne. He respited the former when he offered sureties to keep good rule among the Scots.

In obedience to the king's instructions, he ordered all Newcastle gentlemen to lie at their own houses to keep watch. When Dan and Mark Kerr with seven hundred men 'ran an open-day foray into Norhamshire', the earl reported to the king the country had risen at his command to the rescue; however, as he had complained to King James, the Scots had murdered three and taken several men captive. The East and Middle Marches were put on a war footing and Northumberland ordered men to be in readiness at Newcastle for 18 September and appointed Roger Lascelles as their captain. Dacre was told to be in readiness on the West Marches. On 3 August, he reminded Cromwell of the king's promise to make him Sheriff of Northumberland for then the country would 'perceive the love his Grace bears unto me, and for my service in ministering of justice', which latter statement he knew would be supported by the justices. Knowing war was likely to ensue, he also asked for his warden's fee in advance. (Other letters of the time reveal payments were often hard to come by: Sir Arthur Darcy wrote to Cromwell from the borders on the same day that he had 'not had a penny of his Grace for three years, nor of his father for four ... and has been the king's servant fourteen years'.)

News wended north that eighty-three-year-old William Warham, Archbishop of Canterbury had died on 22 August while visiting his nephew. At Windsor on 1 September Anne Boleyn, Lady Rochford (styled as such since her father's earldom), 'one of the daughters and heirs of Thomas Earl of Wiltshire and Ormond', was created Marquis of Pembroke, granted £1,000 a year. The poet Robert Whittington described her as 'Anna, the shining jewel, her beauty unrivalled'. On 8 September, Northumberland's uncle Joscelin died, alleged by his brother William to have been poisoned by three of his servants and a maidservant who had pilfered his goods. He wrote to Cromwell on 19 September that the poisoners had been sheltered by Sir Richard Tempest, Thomas Walterton and his friends at the inquest at York. He requested Cromwell to help him gain wardship of Jocelin's son and heir, Edward, who was nine years old and been married to a Walterton – 'a sorry bargain, his blood considered'.

Because of the potential war with Scotland, Northumberland remained at Warkworth. He purchased seventeen loads of hay for his horses (at 2*s* 4*d* a load), twelve wagonloads of grain and four loads of slates for reroofing some of the buildings. He received royal instructions to entertain Angus and his brother George and to secretly 'let slip' Redesdale and Tynedale men to ally with Liddesdale to annoy Scotland. Dacre, hostile to Northumberland, continued being obstructive, insisting prisoners taken in the east had been taken in the west and allowing prisoners to escape. (Routinely interfering with Northumberland's jurisdiction ensured paybacks, ransoms and fines went into his coffers.)

Lancelot Kerr, leading three hundred horsemen, burnt Northumberland's town of Alenam on 3 October, and a day later his town of Newstead. During the forays Lance stole hundreds of cattle, captured twenty-six prisoners and murdered two children, the elder not yet fifteen years old. On Sunday 13 October, a hundred light horse came by night and plundered the earl's town of Lowerbotell. On Monday, spies informed Northumberland that King James had appointed James Stewart, Earl of Moray as Warden of the Scottish East and Middle Marches and promised him three thousand men and Coldingham Abbey for his residence. Moray, from Edinburgh, ordered Mark Kerr to burn any place near Warkworth at midnight to give Northumberland light by which to put on his clothes.

Although strict watch was kept at the threat, on Thursday 17 October, thirty light horsemen managed to reach Whitell on Shilbottle Moor, intending to burn it. When they found they had nothing with which to light a fire (and hearth fires were not kept at night), they seized a pregnant woman and stabbed her in the head and side. Despite the lighting of beacons, the Scots escaped. In retaliation, Northumberland and Clifford ordered five hundred horsemen of Glendale and Berwick to join George Douglas on a rode the next morning. At dawn they burned Coldingham (leaving only the abbey standing) and £2,000 worth of corn, taking eight Scottish prisoners, sixty horses and two hundred cattle. On 22 October, from Warkworth, Northumberland reported to the king all occurrences that had passed and that he and Clifford had devised a plan to burn Kelso, requesting to be allowed twenty light pieces of ordnance.

On 29 October the earl wrote to Cumberland to say that while Moray remained in Edinburgh he had acted the steward and made a fire to warm him. He then proffered his usual invite for Margaret and Henry to come to him for Christmas, confirming he had admitted Lancelot Marton as his bow bearer with 'fermehold' in Langestrothe in Wharfedale, as they had both desired. On

14 November, adding to his grant of 4 October making Sir Reynold Carnaby (with his brother Thomas to cover absences) Constable of Langley Castle, he also granted them the forestership of the park for life and made them receivers of the Langley lordship. Along the edge of the Cheviots on Wednesday, 20 November, the three Teviotdale families with lairdship – the Kerrs of Ferniehirst, Kerrs of Cessford and the Buccleuch – displayed their standards and brought three thousand reivers into the Middle March, vowing to show their hatred of Northumberland by setting fire to Alnwick Castle. They ran three forays which resulted in the seizure of a great number of prisoners, horse, sheep and cattle.

Five days later Sir Thomas Wharton sent a letter to Cumberland from Warkworth thanking him for sending Jake with venison and wildfowl, which had given the earl much pleasure, especially as he was suffering a little from his old disease. He explained that letters from Cumberland always revived the earl when he was ill, as did the 'good mirth' he received from Jake. The king, via Wharton, sent instructions for Cumberland to ensure his garrison had 2,500 men and for Sir Thomas Clifford, at the king's charge, to increase the 1,000-strong garrison at Berwick by 1,500 and send 200 well-armed men to Newcastle for 5 December.

Receiving royal orders to 'destroy, waste and burn corn and towns' in Scotland, Northumberland, aware 'sundry of the Merse' had moved their goods, corn and cattle around Donglas (3 miles from Dunbar), and despite a 'frost so sore', invaded Scotland at eleven o'clock on the night of Wednesday, 11 December. Taking the whole garrison and his own Northumberland men, he first burnt Raynton, leaving no pele,* gentleman's house nor grange intact. On their return to Berwick, the force burnt and destroyed ten towns, taking many Scotsmen, two thousand cattle and four thousand sheep, arriving back as night fell with no dead or injured.

* A pele is a type of small, square defensive tower commonly seen on the Scottish border.

He had also, at daybreak, sent a separate party led by George and Archibald Douglas to burn and destroy five towns and others in Donglas with all the corn.

Sending a letter to the king regarding the exploits, the earl desired 'thanks to be given to Sir Thomas Clifford, Sir Arthur Darcy, Sir Richard Tempest and others' on a list he enclosed, ending with a request for their elevation, having been informed by those around him it had been customary for wardens 'in their rodes' to advance the order of knighthood to those deserving it for 'it would encourage the hearts of gentlemen to serve me the better to serve your Highness'. Cromwell, having received news of the rode from many sources, wrote to Northumberland to congratulate him on the success of his 'prosperous fortune and victory' against the Scots, which had shown his 'valiant courage and glad heart and mind' to serve the king. His service, Cromwell said, was regarded well by the king and 'lovingly accepted'.

The king once again sent a New Year gift of plate to Northumberland, and his service was extended; on 1 January 1533 he received the king's commission to levy as many subjects as he thought proper to defend or annoy the Scots, with power to array the lieges in east and north Yorkshire, leading them during the king's pleasure against the Scots. Sir George Lawson, the royal treasurer, wrote to Cromwell on 2 January praising Sir Thomas Wharton for the experienced and wise counsel he gave to Northumberland. Sir Thomas himself was much pleased at seeing John Gage, a friend of the earl, arrive to visit his master at this time. Lawson wrote again on 9 January from Warkworth with the darker news that Scotsmen had come as near to the castle as they had dared, killing five people and capturing six others. He confirmed he had paid the garrison's wages but said more money would be necessary to cover the expenditure for conveying artillery. This letter revealed that Northumberland had been paying for carriage of ordnance out of his own money.

Ten days into the New Year, Moray arrived at Melrose Abbey with two thousand men. On the morning of Saturday, 11 January, Dand Kerr of Ferniehirst led three hundred or four hundred of Moray's men into England, burning houses and corn stacks at Brankstone, Learmouth, Cornell, New Etall and Heaton. On Sunday, Northumberland, Angus and his brothers, intending to reciprocate, were thwarted by swollen rivers but a rode was made by Clifford, Darcy, Tempest and Eure on the night of Thursday, 16 January. Lawson arrived at Newcastle after visiting Berwick and wrote to Cromwell that Northumberland had moved to Alnwick. The earl was 'of good courage and has the best will to do the king service', he said, and in order to protect corn shipments was sending a ship out to sea at his own expense (perhaps justifying the monies requested – all given for loyal service to the king). He also said he intended to advise the king to make a staple at York or Newcastle for 'Cromwell can understand what pain and cost it is to ride so often from Berwick to York on short warning'.

On 3 February, Northumberland, with captains Sir Thomas Wharton, Sir Reynold Carnaby, Lord Conyers and Sir Ralph Fenwick and four hundred men, led a 'rode into Teviotdale'. They entered at nightfall and attacked Branxholme, where Lord Buccleuch resided. Although they did not find him at home, they seized his servants and left no house, stack or sheaf of corn unburnt outside his gates and in his towns. They returned around midday having lost no men, and brought with them four hundred cattle, forty prisoners and above sixty horses and mares. The earl, writing to the king, asked him to send thanks to those whose names he enclosed 'and to remember the painful and diligent service of my poor servant Wharton'. Two days later, coming to pay 'wages and coats', Lawson arrived at Warkworth and reported to Cromwell that the last rode was to be 'greatly commended'. By 21 February, although the Scots threatened invasion and had two thousand men lying around Jedburgh and Kelso (and more expected by the full moon), they had done nothing. From Alnwick on 22 March, Sir George Lawson offered Cromwell further assurances:

> My lord warden doth the best he can to have good espials, and takes as much pain as maybe, to his great cost and charges to serve the king ... and is as ready as any man to leap on horseback ... for the defence of these borders and has a right good order for the keeping and continuance of the watches of the fells, fords and straits to give warning in time and has caused part of the fords to be casten ... to stop the Scots entering.

With fighting and rodes intermittent, there were peaceful times between which allowed the Cumberlands and Northumberland to visit each other. On 2 March, Sir Thomas Wharton, in a letter which showed he held great affection for Northumberland, wrote personally to Cumberland to inform him how much comfort the earl derived from his and Margaret's visits. He also asked if they would give him six or seven days' warning of their coming so he could order provisions for their servants and horses. During this calm, on 8 March, Northumberland agreed a lease with John, the son of Sir John Heron of Chipchase, for land called Carreyhouses which adjoined his forest of Birtley Wood (with a few other parcels of land) for a yearly rent of 6*s*. (This was still leased by the Herons in 1606 at a rent of £20 per annum.) Perusing the rents of Northumberland's estates, although prices were rising at that time, the earl did not endeavour to raise rents or leases, nor did he make enclosures like other landowners in the area. Whether this was because he was a sympathetic landlord or simply lacked the necessary business acumen will remain unknown.

To Northumberland's surprise, a French envoy, a Monsieur de Beauvois, arrived at Alnwick on Friday 19 April. He had been given consent by King Henry to travel to Scotland on a mission to negotiate peace between England and Scotland. Continuing to follow royal orders, on Saturday night Northumberland sent a hundred men of the garrison to burn Blackburn-in-the-Marsh before daybreak, taking away a hundred cattle, three hundred sheep and eight nags. He sent another party, numbering sixty men, to Coldingham Abbey but they were intercepted. When their warning made it to the earl at Berwick, he raised the alarm and sent the rest of the garrison under Sir Thomas Clifford. They regained most of the sheep, cattle and nags the Scots had retaken, and also took twenty of the ambushers.

In response, Beauvois complained from Coldstream that he was 'surprised that the English invaded Scotland ... pondering he was come to make a peace'. Moray, meanwhile, issued proclamations at Jedburgh forbidding invasions of England. Beauvois continued his journey to Edinburgh. On the morning of Saturday, 26 April, 'after the daystar was up', Lance Kerr and two hundred Scots came in at Coquetdale, burning Prenwick and Alenham but were prevented from taking prisoners or goods by the beacons being lit. Northumberland, assuring the king he would annoy the Scots when 'light served to ride', sent Sir Ralph Ellerker, Sir Thomas Wharton and his brothers, with Robert Bowes, John Horsely and George Fenwick to foray in Scotland while he himself followed with men to burn and harry much of the area between the waters, taking prisoners and cattle. Despite King James offering to enter amity and peace with a truce for six months, Sir Thomas Clifford wrote on 4 May from Greenwich that King Henry intended to keep the garrisons in readiness, although they were 'not to do anything unless the Scots first attempt any exploit' whereupon they could 'revenge the same'.

On the same day, the earl received news that may have made him pensive. Dr Fox wrote from Greenwich to Cumberland (and by extension informed Northumberland) that King Henry had married Anne Boleyn. Moreover, the king so appreciated their doings on the border that Cumberland might not be invited to the queen's coronation. (Cumberland and Margaret were in fact invited to attend Queen Anne's coronation, to be held on Whitsunday

1 June.) Henry Percy replied to Cumberland, thanking him for the copies of the king's letter and his own loving letter with the news his sixteen-year-old nephew Henry was to be made a Knight of the Bath (as was Henry Percy's friend Thomas Arundel).

For his part, the earl wrote, he had not yet learned whether or not he was attending the coronation but his friends at court were soliciting for him to attend, especially with peace likely on the borders. As a 'grand estate' and Knight of the Garter, Northumberland could expect to attend. Assuming he would, he and Cumberland swapped notes on liveries: Henry thought he would take with him 140 horse with his gentlemen in tawny with broad black velvet gardes (like they have at court) and his yeomen in plain tawny with red caps and black feathers. He asked whether they should meet at Skipton to ride together, or at Topcliffe. Either way, he looked forward to seeing them.

There is no mention of Northumberland at the coronation of the woman he once loved, but this does not preclude his presence. His barge may or may not have been one of those which clustered around Anne's barge on Thursday 29 May when she was rowed on the Thames from Greenwich to the Tower of London. All the barges and small boats were hung with banners and pennons to make a colourful and shining display in the summer sunshine. With music provided by flutes, drums and trumpet, with shooting of cannon, 'it was a right sumptuous and triumphant sight to see and hear all the way as they passed upon the water' according to one onlooker. At the Tower landing, the people made 'a long lane' to the king's bridge and tower entrance, where she made her way to the king, who kissed her.

On Saturday, wearing a dress in the French fashion, Anne mounted a gold-canopied litter covered in white satin for her conveyance to Westminster. On Sunday, between eight and nine in the morning, she came into Westminster Hall to go in procession to the abbey. Preceding her, the Marquis of Dorset bore her gold sceptre, the Earl of Arundel the ivory rod with the dove and the Earl of Oxford her crown, while the Knights of the Garter – who may well have included Northumberland – are described in the records as walking in front of her. Queen Anne wore a surcoat and ermine-furred purple velvet robe. Once he had anointed her, Thomas Cranmer, Archbishop of Canterbury set the crown of St Edward on Anne's head. He then placed the gold sceptre into her right hand and the rod and dove into her left. He removed the heavy crown after the *Te Deum* and placed her own lighter one in its stead. After Mass, offering, taking the holy sacrament and having a little repose, Anne left the cathedral, her right hand held by her father and her left hand by Lord Talbot, deputising for Shrewsbury.

The earl was at Warkworth on 9 June for he wrote to the king enclosing letters from Beauvois and King James, mentioning that 'sixty broken men did run at certain nags of the garrison at Norham but were chased back into Scotland, four of them being taken prisoner and twelve others with forty cattle and sixty sheep' and two ships, holding Scotsmen's goods, were being retained at Newcastle. As a result of Beauvois' efforts, the commissioners – Magnus, Clifford, Sir Ralph Ellerker the younger and Sir Thomas Wharton – moved to Newcastle for July, as did the earl. On 15 July Sir George Lawson advised Cromwell that Clifford was writing to Mr FitzWilliam that if the king was 'disposed to make overtures to have the earl's lands in Northumberland they will be most valuable and always make his warden strong and more able to serve with less wages'. Was Clifford hoping to replace the earl?

With peace negotiations held up by arguments over Cawmills, on 26 July Northumberland advised the king he would do better to raze it to the foundation, it being 'so ruinous none can keep it'. The discussions continued. On 23 August Northumberland wrote from Newcastle to the Cumberlands with 'true and steadfast heart' saying that war with Scotland was still possible but he thought personally it would be peace. They would all soon receive the news that Queen Anne, on Sunday 7 September, was brought to bed of a fair daughter at Greenwich at three in the afternoon. On the following Wednesday, she was christened Elizabeth.

14

'SORE ACCRASED OF MINE OLD DISEASE'

Still on duty in the north with the commissioners, Northumberland was prevented from meeting Sir Edward Seymour at St Paul's as they had arranged. Writing from Newcastle on 27 September 1533, the earl thanked Cromwell for moving the king to ensure Sir Edward did not take his 'advantage'. To the intimation the king desired to purchase his Petworth estates, he said he would discuss it with Cromwell at his next attendance and would gladly follow his advice. In fact, Cromwell had paid the £1,604 owed to Seymour – and he ensured it appeared regularly in his remembrances.

Tuke, now clerking for Cromwell, listed Northumberland's debts at this time: the £8,000-plus Bonvisi loan for which he was guarantor; the redemption of the aforementioned £1,604; £66 13*s* 4*d*, dated 10 May 1527, regarding the wardship and marriage of a daughter of Sir John Thwaytes arranged by his father; the 1527 fee for Henry's livery of £316 13*s* 4*d*; and a debt to Castelyn for £120 (which Northumberland believed paid). Tuke also noted a sixty-nine-year lease on Poynings made on 2 July 1523 for £144 11*s* annually. With regard to the Bonvisi loan, Henry VIII had written to Tuke that payments were to be made in June and September 1535 until 1539, although if any were willing to be bound to those sums, mortgages could be arranged for twenty years' purchase.

A one-year truce between England and Scotland was announced on 1 October 1533, and, desiring to save the king money, Northumberland arranged to disband the garrison, using his own money to pay their wages. The Scottish commissioners had for a time lodged at Warkworth and the earl arranged for the beer supplies to be replenished: William Fynche, the miller, delivered 68 gallons of beer (at 3*d* a gallon) to Robert Erington and purchased '2 vats and 12 hogsheads' from Edward Baxster of Newcastle and a cooling vat from Thomas Weghtman to enable the castle to brew its own. He employed Blayerde, a master mason, to take down and rebuild the fireplace in the great chamber (presumably because of any resultant mess, 'divers tables, portraits and saints' pictures' were removed from Warkworth and taken by Robert Hayle to Topcliffe).

During the year, the earl's physician Dr Thomas Wendy was granted Sutton and Duncton in Sussex and he retained a lawyer of Grey's Inn – William Stapleton of Wighill – at a fee of £10 a year, making him his feodary in Yorkshire. William and Sir Thomas Wharton got on and had often worked closely together. They were also kin: William was married to Thomas's sister. In November, Northumberland received his patent making him Sheriff of Northumberland, with all the rents, services, royalties, profits and so on belonging to the office, for a term of seven years at an annual fee of £40 so long as he 'duly, truly and diligently' served and executed all manner of the king's process. At the end of seven years he was to deliver an account on parchment into the Exchequer, with an option to renew the position for a further term of seven years, and so on as long as he should live.

Sir Thomas Wharton wrote from London in December with the news that on the day Henry, Duke of Richmond married Norfolk's daughter Mary Howard, Queen Anne danced with the bridegroom and the king with the bride. Afterwards, the queen had danced with Northumberland's nephew Henry, Lord Clifford. After Christmastide Northumberland travelled to London, staying at Hackney, ready to attend the parliament due to open on 15 January 1534.

Ten days later Northumberland signed a book of inventory compiled by Stephen Stamforth and Edward Carnaby of his 'stuff at his place at Hackney': a sparver (bed canopy) of cloth of gold and blue velvet with yellow and blue sarcenet curtains fringed with yellow and blue silk; a counterpoint of cloth of gold and blue velvet; a down bed and other bedding; two down beds and eighteen feather beds with bolsters; nine trussing beds (one of cloth of tissue and tawny velvet, embroidered with the earl's arms and cognisance) and sixteen small quilts for the trussing beds; four silk quilts (two red and two yellow); a blue cloth of estate with gold baudekin; fifteen pairs of fustians with fifteen down pillows and cases; twenty pairs of fine sheets and eleven pairs of coarse; eighteen counterpoints of verders and tapestry; three chairs covered in cloth of gold damask and blue-and-gold baudekin; three small pieces of fine arras and seven counterfeit with the Story of Atlanta, six pieces of the Story of Venus, six of Aeneas and twenty-six pieces with fine verdure, park work and roses, eleven not so good with beasts and birds; three fine carpets in yellow and blue, ten coucher carpets and seventeen cupboard carpets; ten window carpets of yellow, russet and tawny Bruges satin lined with buckram; and seventeen cushions, some in tawny velvet, some blue with baudekin and verders.

Chapuys repeated a fanciful anecdote in his letter of 11 February to the emperor: he had been informed Northumberland had remarked Queen Anne was determined to poison Princess Mary. Upon being told by another gentleman that Anne had instructed her father's sister not to allow Mary to breakfast privately in her chamber, and seeing the earl was familiar and had credit with Anne, he had warned Mary to be on her guard against poisoning.

Cromwell unearthed further debts on 21 February which he laid against Northumberland: firstly of Henry's father, unpaid by William Worme (delivered to Cromwell by Robert Ormeston, servant of Sir Thomas Neville), a bond of John Lamplugh of Cockermouth and Gilbert Weddell dated 9 December 1519 of £152 10*s*; William Worme and William Burgh of a bill of 2 December 1525 for use of plate worth £64 13*s* 10*d*; and another by William Burgh of a bill sealed on 21 August 1525 for £35 14*s*. Another document was 'delivered to Burgh': two gilt pots, two flagons (worth £48 2*s* 10*d*), ale and water pots to Henry Whitereason and a gilt cup for the christening of Lord FitzWalter to John Spence and two caps of assay to William Burgh, totalling £76 14*s* 2*d*. As the only birth which seems feasible is that of Thomas, son of Henry Radcliffe, in 1525 this must also be a sum owed by the fifth earl. As for Henry's own debts, there was a bill dated 3 December 1528 for £52 19*s* 2*d* (presumably for when Arundel visited) and another to Henry Whitereason of 12 December 1529 for £189 3*s* 8*d* (and maybe relates to the Christmas visit by his sister and her husband).

In all, his father's debt came to £329 12*s* and his own £242 14*s* 10*d* for a total of £571 14*s* 10*d*. This may be why Henry Percy took out a bond for payment of 1,000 marks with Audley and Cromwell in this year. During February, Northumberland decided to appoint Cuthbert Carnaby (Reynold's brother) receiver for Northumberland at a fee of £13 6*s* 8*d* and constable (jointly with Sir John Heron) of Warkworth Castle at a fee of £10.

On Monday 23 March 1534, Northumberland with his own retinue of sixty horse conducted three Scottish ambassadors – the Bishop of Aberdeen, Abbot of Kinloss and Adam Otterburn – through London to Taylors' Hall, where they were to lodge. Two days later, the ambassadors were brought to Westminster for an audience with the king. On Thursday the bishop was feasted by Norfolk and the Privy Council at Westminster. Talking after dinner, he relayed news King James was marrying the French king's daughter Magdalene.

On 30 March, the king was present for Parliament's passing of the Act of Succession. It declared Henry and Katherine's marriage as void, Mary a bastard with no claim to the throne and the king's marriage 'to his beloved wife' Queen Anne as valid, with succession to the throne settled on their children, making Elizabeth heir apparent. While the king watched, Chancellor Audley, Archbishop Cranmer and the dukes of Norfolk and Suffolk ensured that 'every lord, burgess and all other, were sworn to the Act of Succession and subscribed their hands to a parchment fixed to the oath'. Parliament was then prorogued until November while 'commissions were sent over all England to take the oath of all men and women at which few repined, except Dr John Fisher and Sir Thomas More'. Despite Cranmer's attempts to persuade them not to stand 'against all the realm in their opinion', their insistence saw them imprisoned in the Tower of London.

Northumberland remained active. While he was at Greenwich on 9 April, he instructed the master forester of Westward in Cumbria to deliver 'one buck in season in summer, one doe in season in winter yearly' from the forest to Edward Aglionby, Constable of Penrith Castle (and a gentleman usher of the king's chamber). During April, Sir William Gorynge wrote to Cromwell that he had heard Northumberland was selling his Sussex manor of Duncton (worth £18 *6s 8d* yearly) in Petworth, which adjoined his house and lands, and offered Cromwell £40 if he acquired it for him on a twenty-year lease; this was part of the property the earl had granted to his physician. A chapter of the Order of the Garter was held at Greenwich on 23 April and Northumberland attended. The Windsor feast was appointed for 17 May and the king arranged for the Duke of Richmond to stand in his place, to be assisted by the Duke of Norfolk, Marquis of Exeter, Earl of Northumberland and Lord Abergavenny.

Construction continued at Warkworth over the next few months. Six masons and eight labourers removed and rebuilt the stone wall between the gateway and Montague Tower, and Sly, the smith, got *2d* for mending the key to the great gate. Robert Mylne made a new drawbridge at a cost of *6s 8d* with timber from Acklington

Park, in which the earl's six nags, two horses belonging to Sir Thomas Wharton and thirty-three horses belonging to the earl's servants and his trumpets were 'allowed to run'. The armoury was renovated and a new forge sited. The earl had a double door made and hung for his chamber and a freestone (a cool countertop) was set up in the larder. A bed and writing board were made for the comptroller's clerk. The roofs of the great barn, keep, hay-house and house where the tents lay were repaired. Lastly, 'Robert Wharriour and William Patenson were absent fourteen days riding to Topcliffe with disguising stuff'. (A hint of merriment during spring with the Cumberlands?)

London was set in a stir when William, Lord Dacre was seen being committed to the Tower on 15 May. Sir William Musgrave, a knight of the body, had accused Dacre and his uncle Christopher of treasonously deceiving the king, conspiring with the Scots in November 1532 to have Musgrave and his tenants slain and seeking the destruction of Henry, Earl of Northumberland. Six days later commissions were sent to Henry, Earl of Northumberland, Ralph, Earl of Westmoreland, Henry, Earl of Cumberland, Sir Thomas Clifford, Sir Thomas Wharton, serjeant-at-law Thomas Fairfax and Robert Chaloner to enquire into treasons by Lord Dacre. They were also directed to take inventories at Naworth, Greystoke, Morpeth and Kirkoswald and Sir Christopher Dacre's houses at Carlisle and Crogling.

At Naworth, the treasure house was found to contain three bags of ready money (2,640 marks 12*s* 6*d*), another 300 marks and plate. The latter included two gold standing cups (one with a rose and the other with Douglas arms), two great silver standing cups (a lion holding the Arms of Scotland on both their covers), a pair of silver pots (with roses around H and K on their tops), a great parcel-gilt standard pot (a Scottish lion on its top) and three little bowls with Adam and Eve engraved on their bottoms. In a letter to the king of 17 May he was told they had 'found little of importance' even though they had repaired to the places with great secrecy, going different ways to avoid suspicion 'and with less company than would have been expedient in such wild country had not Lady Dacre showed herself conformable'.

Sir William Musgrave wrote from Penrith to Cromwell on 12 June 1534:

> [A]ccording to your directions, the day and time of every indictment shall be perfectly known ... This service to the King will, however, be chargeable to me, and you and I shall specially bear the blame in this matter touching the lord Dacre and Sir Christopher his uncle. Therefore stand stiffly upon it, that I may have your aid; for divers of this country, and especially those that are bound for the lord Dacre's goods to the King, will in nowise trust that he shall have any overthrow ... For the country has been so overlaid with him that they thought here was no other king. Notwithstanding, I am confident everything shall be so substantially set forth on my behalf that what I have alleged cannot be denied.

Northumberland sent Sir Thomas Wharton to take all the inventories to Cromwell. He wrote from Morpeth on 29 June, referring to the last talk they had together, requesting that at that time he did not make Wharton Warden of the West Marches, 'seeing as you know he is mine one hand and I cannot forbear him from me ... being right sore accrased of mine old disease'.

Despite the rock-solid allegations, when Lord Dacre was arraigned at Westminster on 9 July he answered the indictment 'manly, wittily and directly confuted his accusers'. Chapuys wrote Dacre had 'defended his cause so well for seven hours that he was declared innocent by twenty-four lords unanimously and acquitted by twelve judges', a novel thing not heard of for one hundred years, 'for no one ever knew a man come to the point he had done and escape'.

As a result of the March discussions with the Scottish ambassadors, a peace treaty was signed at the Blackfriars in

Guildford by Northumberland, Audley, Winchester, Norfolk, Cumberland and Cromwell. The occasion was celebrated by, as John Husee wrote to Lord Lisle, 'a wrestling as has never before been seen; for which purpose some have come out of Cornwall and Devonshire to show their cunning'. Notwithstanding Dacre's acquittal, Cumberland was appointed in August the new Warden of the West Marches and Governor of Carlisle – city and castle – and provided with twenty-three soldiers (twenty horsemen and three porters of the keys of the city). He also was granted the office of Steward of Penrith along with others manors and lordships. At the beginning of Michaelmas term, Thomas Cromwell was made Master of the Rolls.

Around 8 September, the Nativity of the Virgin Mary, Mary Talbot, the earl's wife, appears to have left the matrimonial home for good to live with her father. Whether she told her husband she was never returning or whether she left him to find out is unknown.

The Talbots did not favour the new reforms, although they toed the line. Of Northumberland's religious sympathies there may be a hint in a letter Chapuys wrote to Charles V on 30 September reporting a conversation he held with Lord Darcy, who 'considered himself as one of the most loyal vassals the king had in matters which did not injure his conscience and honour' and had told the ambassador many were of his opinion, although he dared only to declare himself to one or two, saying nothing even to his two sons, 'as valiant in arms as any in the kingdom ... With the assistance of your majesty he would raise the banner of the Crucifix together with yours, and among the first things he would do would be to seize some lords who favoured these follies, such as the earl of Northumberland and some others', and with assistance from the emperor in arranging for King James to invade England, and 'that you should send some small force to the mouth of the Thames to give fight to those hereabout. It would be necessary also to bring a small number of harquebus men to the North, with harness and other munitions of war, and some money for poor gentlemen who lack means to equip themselves, lest they should be gained by the king; for in the North there were great lords, but they had no money to advance to others.' Two he named were the Earl of Derby and Lord Dacre.

On 2 October, Northumberland attended the wedding of Agnes Wharton and Henry Curwen at Topcliffe Chapel; the proceedings were conducted by his dean. Just before leaving Wressle for Parliament, which was due to return on 3 November, the earl appointed his brother Sir Ingram vice-warden and lieutenant of the East Marches and undersheriff of Northumberland, requesting him to 'take some pain to see good rule established on the borders'. The Archbishop of York, Edward Lee, appointed Sir Reynold Carnaby as his bailiff, chief steward and receiver of Hexhamshire. Dacre, detained in London by the king, confessed some fault and threw himself on the royal mercy – the king's mercy was to fine him 10,000 marks and order him not to move beyond 10 miles of London.

The earl, while in London, decided on 13 December to lease the manor of Corbridge to Sir Reynold Carnaby, his heirs, executors and assigns for a term of ninety-nine years at an annual rent of £26, and made him steward and forester of Rothbury. (Sir Reynold's father, William, had been bailiff of Corbridge at 2*d* a day.)

When Parliament ended on 18 December, the Act of Supremacy had been passed. King Henry was now entitled Supreme Head of the Church of England and held full authority to reform all its supposed errors, heresies and abuses. He was granted the first fruits and tenths of all spiritual dignities and promotions. The Treasons Act was brought in at the same time, making it treason to deprive the king of his name, dignity or title. The day before Parliament ended Northumberland wrote from Mile End to Cromwell that he was too ill to attend to the unfinished 'great matter between the king and him', but trusted 'Cromwell to offer to the king the bargain' as Cromwell knew both the value of the lands and 'what had been offered by others for them'; that he would 'do as the king pleases, for his physicians tell him he must not remain here'.

The 'great matter' seems to refer to the 'bargain and sale' between Northumberland and King Henry of certain of his manors. By 18 January 1535 it had been agreed the earl would sell to the king, via his council, his Honour of Petworth and the Sussex manors of Poynings, Perchinge, Preston Poynings, Pengeden, Ashcombe, Waldren and Chinting, his manor of Hackney in Middlesex (evidently for Cromwell as the king formally signed it over to him on 24 September 1535), all his Lincolnshire manors (already earmarked to be exchanged for certain manors of the Duke of Suffolk that the king desired to own) and his Welsh properties and everything pertaining to them including 'lands, tenements, rents, reversions, meadows, pastures, woods, advowsons, churches, chapels, fishing waters, forests, parks, chases, warrens, fairs, markets, tolls, lets, views of frankpledge and all other hereditaments', with notice of all leases and rents to remain in force. In return he was to be cleared of any financial liabilities. Within the indenture were provisos for a certain parcel of land Dame Jane St John owned by inheritance and one for Mary, Countess of Northumberland 'concerning such right and title of dower as to the same countess shall or may come or fall by or after the death of the earl her husband' as she may 'lawfully demand'.

Chapuys, ever ready to promulgate any incident showing Anne in a bad light, had written to the Emperor on New Year's Day that he would 'be delighted to know that the earl of Northumberland is no longer such a friend of this king and of his ministers as he used to be, for the earl's physician informed me two days ago his master had lately complained to him of certain wrongs and injuries received at the hands of members of this government, and had declared that those who had so behaved towards him would soon have to repent of their ill-doings', and that the earl had charged Queen Anne 'with arrogance and wickedness, saying, among other things, that a few days ago she had heaped more injuries on the Duke of Norfolk than on a dog, so much so, the duke was obliged to quit the royal chamber'. (In a letter of 28 January, Chapuys said his friend – presumably Lord Darcy – had 'sent to warn me that perhaps the Earl of Northumberland was sending to tell me some things, and that I should consider what was possible and not trust him too much, for he was very light and hasty'.)

Lord William Howard left on 15 January to travel to King James with the news he was to be elected to the Order of the Garter. Northumberland sent him an apology that he would not be in Yorkshire nor Northumberland 'to have shown you such rude pleasures as be in those parts. But I beg you to use my park and other my pleasures as your own'. The earl must have been somewhat recovered for he attended the special Garter chapter at Westminster on 20 January in which King James was formally elected to the order. Thomas Wall was ordered to follow Howard, taking with him a book of the order that was being specially made: the vellum for it cost 5*s*, illumination of the arms and letters 10*s* and other writing 20*s* and the binding and gilding 2*s* 8*d*. The cover had purple velvet and crimson satin (each half-yard at 7*s*), purple silk for laces (4*d*), white and green silk for the seals (12*d*), red silk for strings and garnishing the bag (12*s*) with a half-ounce of Venice gold (5*s* 2*s*). For the bag: shaping, making and garnishing cost 3*s* 4*d*, red sarcenet for lining was 1*s* 4*d* and the box cost 8*d*. He departed with book, collar and habit on 27 January.

Despite overseeing all the reports by officers sent to hold general visitations of all churches, monasteries and clergy in England, Cromwell found the time to attend to the engrossment of the indenture made between Northumberland, Suffolk and the king dated 3 February. In the interim, Northumberland must have travelled to Topcliffe for on 24 January he wrote from his lodge to Cromwell thanking him for his 'gentle and kind letter from the Rolls of 11 January', in which he was apparently accused of not making due execution of justice upon the East and Middle

Marches and had 'a sword borne before him from Topcliffe to York'. He confirmed justice days had already been arranged between himself and King James for 3 February on the East Marches and two days later for the Middle March and counsel and officers of both sides had been summoned to be in attendance. As for the other matter, which occurred during a commission in which officers were sent to assess grain stocks and pricing, he said they had met at York and a sword had been 'borne afore him as doth belong to the office ... and used of late days by the Earl of Rutland. Good master Secretary, if that same were taken by the king of me to be done in pomp and pride of myself, without his most gracious authority which I have for the same, it should be unfeignedly to my discomfort.' He suggested the complaint came from the 'great enmity borne against him by many' as Cromwell 'well knew'. The letter ended by saying Cromwell would be pleased to hear of 'the coming up now of my friend Sir Reynold Carnaby, whose sad conversation and good qualities I need not to write'. He asked Cromwell to give 'firm credence to my friend Sir Thomas Wharton, with whom it may please you to communicate, such as shall stand with our pleasure in mine affairs and causes'.

Additions were made to the 3 February indenture: Northumberland and Dr Thomas Wendy 'bargained and sold' the manors of Duncton and Sutton, leaving the king holding all the Percy properties in Sussex. For a further £460 the earl also sold to the king his manor of Oxnall and all his possessions in Gloucestershire. On 25 March, Northumberland granted Dr Wendy (with his son John) a sixty-year indenture at a rent of 6*s* 8*d* for Buckden and Starbotten, two adjoining Yorkshire manors valued at £41 4*s* a year, together with an annuity of £40. As always, the earl is revealed to have an inherent sense of fairness and justice.

It appears (from a letter the earl wrote in the beginning of 1536) that Northumberland returned to London in spring 1535 and met with the king at Hackney. (He was reported as being there on

Thursday and Friday, 8 and 9 April before joining Queen Anne at Hampton Court on the Saturday.) They apparently discussed the earl's personal circumstances and whom he could name as heir. One of the earl's projects bore fruit: the new harbour at Alnmouth had increased the port's revenue to such a degree he assigned an annual fee of £5 8*s* 4*d* to his servant George Clarkson on 18 April. Although he remained in the south, Northumberland did not attend the Garter ceremony held at Greenwich on 23 April (perhaps feeling too ill to attend), although a sealed letter confirmed he had observed a Mass for the souls of the dead. He was granted by the king on 4 June a special licence to 'appoint three of his servants to shoot with cross-bows and handguns at any fowl, deer, or other game, either in his own grounds or any other man's in any part of the kingdom north of the Trent'.

On 17 June John Fisher, Bishop of Rochester was arraigned at Westminster for high treason. Five days later he was beheaded at Tower Hill and his head set on London Bridge. On Thursday 1 July, Sir Thomas More was similarly arraigned at Westminster. He was executed on 6 July.

Northumberland had not been present; he had returned to Topcliffe, where he received news concerning unrest occurring in Craven in response to recent enclosures of moors and wastes. On 5 July he wrote to King Henry that he and Ralph, Earl of Westmorland had fully intended to be at 'the sessions' but the summons sent by Sir Richard Tempest came 'by a foot fellow' which had given them only one day's notice. As for the insurrection, Sir Marmaduke Constable senior had been at Topcliffe with him and had ridden through the night, taking the earl's order to Stephen Hamerton to assist in apprehending malefactors. This duly occurred and eighty-two persons had been arrested, although more – women and children – had taken part. Nineteen of the most notable offenders had been imprisoned in the castles at Skipton, Sandal and Wressle. He reported that the only other occurrences – a dispute between the Fenwicks over a land title, and another between Shaftoe and Waddington – had been pacified through surety by his brother Sir Ingram.

Sir Richard Tempest, also writing on 5 July, complained to Cromwell that 'My Lord of Northumberland received Cromwell's letter but was so sick that he could not act', so he had only Robert Challoner to muster a company and none of the king's commissioners to suppress disorder. On the same day, Stephen Hamerton wrote to Cromwell that although 'not in the commission but by the command' of his master he had been put in readiness to assist both Constable and Tempest.

In between, on 4 July, Northumberland received a letter from the king dated 29 June in which he learned the Sheriff of Yorkshire, William Fairfax, was accusing his treasurer, Sir Thomas Johnson, and Thomas Middleton, his bailiff of Spofforth, of stopping him doing his duty. Ordered to send them to London, on 10 July the earl replied he was sending them even though neither had the 'rule nor meddling in the lordships where they are complained of', which belonged to Sir Thomas Wharton. The earl informed the king that among the untruths the sheriff had told him was that three hundred of his tenants had impeded him in executing his duty, yet he was unable to 'make a hundred men there'. Referring to another miscreant named in the letter, he protested he had no officer called William Smyth, who was 'a light person sent upon malice pretenced to disturb the laws and break the peace'. He wrote to Cromwell on the same day that 'the sheriff makes pretence to some ground belonging to a chantry of the earl's in the lordship of Tadcaster', and had sued out *latitats** to attach a number of his tenants, who procured *supersedeas*,† and put in sureties. As for Smyth, he was upheld by the sheriff to 'molest the earl's tenants at Tadcaster. Sometimes he has been so drunk that he knew not what he did, and had to be carried out of the town. It is

* A *latitat* is a writ summoning to court a person who is believed to be in hiding.
† A *supersedeas* is a writ delaying legal proceedings.

true the earl, as justice, on the complaint of his tenants, kept him prisoner at Topcliffe, but had released him before the king's letter came', as the clerk of his courts could personally testify.

Another example of northern backbiting occurred when the earl, on his way into Northumberland to 'do justice on offenders', received information on 12 July that one Anthony Heron and two brethren of Mountgrace had asked to go into Scotland; upon being refused, the two priests had run away before being brought back and warded. At Darlington on 14 July, Northumberland reported the incident to the king, saying he had ordered a watch for Heron (who had gone to St Albans for the abbot) and would send him when he was taken, otherwise commending the prior and monks as being 'conformable to the things passed in Parliament'. In his letter to Cromwell he made apology for not reaching Newcastle yet, meaning to have been but for the 'sickness he has been so long troubled with'. Sir Francis Bigod wrote to Cromwell from Middleham asking if he or the king had given leave for Northumberland 'to keep with him daily two of the obstinate friars ... There lieth a great matter on knowledge of that.'

At the warden court Northumberland held at Newcastle on 28 July, seven persons were arraigned and six of them condemned for March treason. In his report to the king he mentioned 'Sir Humphrey Lisle of Felton and Alex Shaftoe were indicted for treasonous doings in the East and Middle Marches', and after they had fled from persons sent to arrest them he had issued proclamations against them. He announced he would remain at Newcastle until the justices arrived and would 'proceed further in ministering justice'.

On 30 July, Sir Thomas Clifford wrote from Newcastle to King Henry, Norfolk and Cromwell accusing Northumberland of being 'out of ill-will towards the writer for speaking to the king' on behalf of the earl's brother, Sir Thomas. And because of it the earl had 'caused certain gentlemen to be indicted, by a packed jury' at the warden court and had 'forbidden his servants to speak with him'. He begged for the earl to be forbidden to 'meddle with him and that the matters be submitted to an indifferent judge'.

Sir Thomas Percy sent his own complaint to the king, accusing his brother of having neglected to fulfil the provisions of his father's will until he was on the eve of marriage, when he made him a deed of gift of certain lands to a yearly value of 100 marks out of Prudhoe, Langley and Corbridge (not mentioning the other manors he had been given). Furthermore, he claimed the earl promised 'to make him dispend 300 marks a year in fees and offices' and how with great labour he had defended this from the Scots but his brother had granted the lordship of Corbridge to Sir Reynold Carnaby in fee farm at a much lower rent than its accustomed value. Having refused to give up possession of Corbridge to Sir Reynold, he had gone to speak to his brother who had rudely turned him out of his house. He requested the king to make an injunction against the earl to allow him to enjoy his lands, to not alienate them further and to remove Sir Reynold and his brothers from the earl's company 'as they have caused division between the earl and his wife, his brothers and nearest friends', ending with his desire to become the king's servant.

By the time Northumberland had received the king's letter (from Berkley Herons) detailing the accusations made against him by Clifford and his brother, justices Christopher Jenney and Mr Spelman had completed the assizes in Northumberland and departed. Conscious the justices would corroborate his actions, Northumberland followed the king's secondary instruction and immediately commissioned Sir William Eure, Sir Robert Ellerker, Robert Colinwood, Lionel Gray and Christopher Mitford to investigate the allegations. Responding to other accusations made against him, Northumberland wrote from Brancepeth to King Henry on 15 September that, regarding delivering malefactors to Clifford, the king's letter of 8 July had not reached him until 14 August so he had no knowledge of the request until then. The direction to commit the Craven rioters to Wressle had also come too late, but he had sent Sir Thomas Johnson to remove some from York Castle to Wressle (affirmed by a different letter of complaint about Sir Thomas removing them). He said he had been 'accompanied by the most substantial persons of Northumberland and taken bonds of all the headsmen of Tynedale' at Hexham and enclosed both the bonds and a certificate in which the commissioners confirmed they had examined indictments, witness depositions 'from freeholders of the country' and the verdict given at Newcastle and had found 'no ground for the allegations' that the indictments had been procured by Sir Reynold Carnaby.

While Northumberland was at Newcastle he had sent to Cromwell, at his request, a copy of the indictment made against Walter Scot, Laird of Buccleuch at the eyre held at Jedburgh for his 'treasonable intercommoning with the Dacres', ending his letter that he trusted aways to Cromwell's 'mediation, and especially now, as he has some enemies of late, owing to what he has done according to justice'.

Mid-August Cromwell received information that Sir Reynold Carnaby had good land in Kent worth nearly £200 a year with four or five benefices and was desirous of selling some of it. The informants decided Cromwell should be advised so he could inform Northumberland 'because they think the land was had from him'. The result was Cromwell communicated his own wish to Sir Reynold to purchase the manors in Kent for himself for the sum of £200. (There is no record of how Sir Reynold obtained these Kent lands.) By September, Northumberland had returned to Topcliffe, welcoming a visit from the Cumberlands. On 20 September he made Reynold's brother Lionel bailiff of his manor of Byker. On 17 October Cuthbert Carnaby, gentleman of his chamber, was granted a lease of pannage and herbage in Newsham Park for a term of sixty years for 3*s* 4*d* and to 'have, hold and enjoy the manor of Newburn' for £23 13*s* 4*d*. On 2 November, the earl granted Sir Thomas Johnson the stewardship of Spofforth and park, with the usual fees of the office (£13 6*s* 8*d*), and keepership of the Little Park at Topcliffe, with herbage and pannage of both parks for ninety years to him and his son at a rent of £6 13*s* 4*d*. (Earlier in the year, he had made him a grant in fee of the manors of Waltonhead near Spofforth with six messuages and Arrow in the Yorkshire Wolds.)

Three men seem particularly favoured by the earl (and Cromwell) as shown by his grants: Sir Thomas Wharton, Sir Thomas Johnson and Sir Reynold Carnaby. All were fairly young men, experienced in border affairs and warfare. He trusted them and they appear to have served him (and the king) loyally. Other grants show a general care for his servants. On 3 November he wrote to Cromwell from Topcliffe asking for aid for his servant Roland Bradforth (who had done good service in the Scottish wars) after his father had been arrested by Lord Mordaunt because of a dispute over land between them. He also mentioned Sir Thomas Clifford was 'daily worsening in his illness'. Sir George Lawson described Clifford as being 'marvellously vexed with palsy'. Writing three days later from Topcliffe, Northumberland thanked Cromwell for the goodness shown to him after their conversation in his garden at Canonbury, especially concerning Berwick, and that Sir Thomas Clifford was so ill he had lost speech and was unlikely to recover. He offered Cromwell 1,000 marks if, by his means, he gained the captainship of Berwick.

Sir Reynold wrote from Topcliffe on 28 November to Stapleton and Whitereason that he had received a letter from his cousin, Christopher Wharton. He had decided, although unable to bring Lord Mordaunt lower than £665 despite the decay of his land, to direct his cousin to conclude the bargain and give preference to Mr Say if he desired to buy any of his Kent lands. The stewardship of the honour or manor of Petworth was granted by the king on 10 December to Sir William FitzWilliam (previously the earl's high steward) and made him master of the hunt of deer in the parks and keeper of the great and little parks with herbage and pannage, and keeper of the warren with all the usual fees and offices. On the same day the Duke of Suffolk was granted the Lincolnshire manors that had lately belonged to the earl and his uncle Sir William. On the same day, Suffolk was pardoned of all the debts he and his deceased wife Mary owed to the king.

As Christmas drew in, Northumberland held a court at Topcliffe on 16 December to enquire into an alleged riot in Gawtres forest. He requested a 'pardon of license from the Parliament' that was due to commence on 4 February 1536.

15

'THESE BLOODY DAYS HAVE BROKEN MY HEART'

Around two o'clock on the afternoon of Friday, 7 January 1536, Katherine of Aragon died at Kimbolton Castle. Within an hour of her passing Cromwell was sent a letter informing him that 'the groom of the chamber here can cere her',* and they had sent for a plumber to enclose her body in lead. Instructions followed for them to have her interred at Peterborough Cathedral. From Greenwich on 11 January, Ralph Sadler wrote to Cromwell that after he had asked the king about a hearse 'to be had at Paul's', like his sister had had, the king responded that 'she was a queen'; a hearse was not required for the princess dowager.

From Topcliffe Sir Reynold Carnaby wrote to Cromwell on 21 January that since his last letter to him, as devised with Stapleton, he understood Cromwell had written to the earl asking for his attendance and would have gladly complied and satisfied him 'concerning the parting with my poor lands in Kent, yet all would not serve that I should come up without some displeasure to my old master, to whom I am so much bound'. He said Sir Thomas Wharton would explain to him when he arrived in London, and would bring with him a letter for the king from the earl. The letter,

* To cere a body is to wrap it in waxcloth.

dated the following day, referred to the 'words had betwixt us at Hackney' and his proposal of making the king his heir of all his lands and possessions for, 'now being unfeignedly sick and having no issue of his own body', he wished 'to provide such as may be most expedient for the furtherance' of the matter. 'It is not the debility of my blood which forces me to this, but the love I bear to your Majesty, as a true subject and one of the poorest of your blood and who has truly served your Majesty.' He sent with Thomas Wharton a bill of articles signed by his hand. This was apparently a petition for 'recompense and surety of and for delivery of ready possession of all his lands to the king's highness' in return for lands to the value of £500 for life, 'to be made sure for eight years after for performance of his will. The further sum which the king will assign him for the residue of his lands to be paid quarterly from the customs of London.'

Running at the lists on 25 January, King Henry frightened the spectators after he and the great horse he was riding 'both fell so heavily that everyone thought it a miracle he was not killed, but he sustained no injury'. A few days later Queen Anne lost the child she was carrying, 'delivered of a man child as it was said, afore her time, for she said she had reckoned herself at that time but fifteen weeks gone with child; it was said she took a fright for the king ran that time at the ring and had a fall from his horse...' George Wyatt wrote of the incident: 'She waxing great again and not so fit for dalliance, the time was taken to steal the king's affection from her, when most of all she was to have been cherished.' That after the miscarriage, 'the king came to her, and bewailing and complaining unto her the loss of his boy, some words were heard break out of the inward feeling of her heart's dolours, laying the fault upon unkindness, which the king more than was cause (her case at this time considered)'. He took this harder than he might have done had he not been 'overcome with grief ... he was then heard to say to her, he would have no boys by her'. Chapuys reported that Anne had given two causes for her miscarriage to the king: one was the fall from his horse and the other that she loved him so greatly and vehemently 'that whenever she hears of his loving another woman but her, she is broken hearted'. All the court was aware by this time of 'Mistress Seymour, to whom, as many say' the king has lately made 'great presents'.

From Topcliffe, Northumberland explained to Cromwell on 2 February 1536 that because of his recurrent sickness he and his wife would likely not come together. As he knew, it had pleased the king...

> more of his goodness than of my deserts, to give me licence (having none issue of mine own body) to denominate and make mine heir which of my blood I will (bearing the name of Percy) of all such lands as be comprehended in the indentures betwixt his Majesty and me; perceiving the debility and unnaturalness in those of my name, and for the great and most gracious goodness that I have always found in his Majesty and for the natural love that I bear to his Grace (which I would he knew as well as God doth), being most unworthy of his blood, have determined finally (as you shall perceive by the copies of my letters sent unto his Majesty at this time) to make his Grace mine heir of all my lands aforesaid, I having none issue of mine own body lawfully begotten. The occasion of the haste hereof is only by reason of my continual sickness and that my wife is a young woman and likely to continue, that if God shall call me shortly I might be sure his Grace shall prove my true and steadfast heart...

He then enclosed all the letters and articles, ending,

> Good Master Secretary, as him to whom I account myself most bounden next my master, doth in this cause commit all things to you and your order, whether it shall please you to take the delivery of my letters with declaration of mine

> articles yourself, or else to appoint Sir Thomas Wharton to fulfil the same. And thus, Master Secretary, as in him whom rests my chief confidence next the King, I betake this, with all other my poor affairs to the order of you, as our Lord knows, who have you ever in his keeping with long life.

Twenty days later he wrote again to Cromwell, saying that although he could not express all his obligations he hoped one day he had it in his power to show his gratitude. Finding Cromwell had twice written for Sir Reynold, whom he could not well spare, and understanding he wished to speak with him about the lands in Kent, he had given the man leave. He also desired credence regarding certain matters in respect of his brother Sir Thomas Percy. On 26 February, after receiving letters from King Henry and Cromwell desiring him to repair to the king with all 'convenient haste', Northumberland replied he had 'been very sick for a whole year, and has long kept his chamber, but will come with what speed he can'.

In response to the earl's request, the king appears to have first made a proposal on 9 March:

> [The earl] to have a pension of £1,000 out of the Exchequer beginning at Midsummer with £1,000 in hand for payment of his debts to be put in the hands of discrete persons as the king appoints. £1,000 was to be secured by patent to the earl's executors for his funeral and legacies. A sum of 500 marks or £500 to be given him in hand towards the setting up of his household and two mansion houses to dwell in with a park to feed his beefs, muttons and geldings and to hunt in. A warrant dormant to be delivered to him for two stags in summer and two hinds in winter for life in a forest (left blank) and other warrants for bucks and does. The king to appoint some discrete person to have the order of the earl's household and give the earl a general pardon, and grant an annuity to his wife for her dower.

On Saturday 11 March, in Parliament with its carefully predetermined agenda, the king personally presented the bill for the dissolution of all lesser monastic houses of the value of 300 marks and under. Cromwell was busy setting up his Court of Augmentations to record the revenues arising from his visitations and closures, appointing himself High Steward of all lands lying north of the River Trent for an annual fee of £100. He also brought Northumberland's scattered lands in Yorkshire, Northumberland and Cumberland (with a yearly value of £3,876) under the jurisdiction of this court. The southern lands now held by the king had been valued at around £3,266 yearly (an income apparently higher than his father's and despite the grants by which he had been accused of diminishing his inheritance).

Making his way slowly to London, Northumberland wrote from Stamford to Cromwell on 21 March asking that northern abbeys of his foundation and others not be granted until he had spoken with the king. (The priories of Merton and Hornby had already surrendered, as had Fountains Abbey the previous month, with others following.) He enclosed with his letter an instrument of notary, begging Cromwell's advice and assistance. It appears that, while he was lodging in the Queen's Chamber in the dwelling house of Richard Lucas at the Sign of the White Hart in Newark the day before, the earl had signed, sealed and countersealed a 'notarial instrument' of arrangements between himself and the king which involved the earl entirely surrendering all his property (as from 5 February 1535) to the king except for lands worth £500, to grant a jointure for life to any wife of a yearly value of 500 marks, plus liberty to grant annuities worth in total £100 and his land sales, leases and annuities to be confirmed by statute in Parliament.

The king appears to have done this in response to letters sent by Shrewsbury of 12 and 13 March: the first, addressed to the king, saw him express his disquiet at the knowledge Northumberland 'has sold to the king and others a good parcel of his lands, and if any Act should pass in this Parliament about it' then his daughter was in danger of losing her living; he therefore requested the king to not give his assent to the Act until his daughter was provided for. In his second letter, addressed to Cromwell, he said that as his daughter was married to the earl she was 'therefore by law entitled to dower of all his lands at the time of espousal' and, hearing Acts are to pass in Parliament, he is worried 'his daughter shall be defeated of her dower in the lands to her utter undoing, as she has no jointure or other living and begs Cromwell's favour that she may be provided for'.

On Good Friday, 14 April, Thomas and Elizabeth Boleyn were in court when it was noted that the countess was 'sore diseased with the cough'. Her son, George, Lord Rochford, was busy at Greenwich handling the details of his sister's intended visit to Calais with the king, organising provisions to be ready at Dover. At Westminster on 15 April, with regard to the Poynings manors in Kent, Sir Richard (an alias of Sir Reynold Carnaby) and his wife Dorothy were given licence to alienate the manors of Tirlingham, Newington Bertram, Rokesley and Westwood by Cromwell who then purchased them. Sir Reynold used the monies to purchase Lord Mordaunt's (Northumbrian) manors of Brunton and Newton-by-the-Sea and a third part of the manor of Jesmond in South Tynedale ('seized into the king's hands by Henry Earl of Northumberland' for the non-accounting of John Middleton when Sheriff of Northumberland). From Richard Beaumont he purchased the manors of North Charlton and Ditchburn and from others he bought the manors of Fallodon, Newton-hall and Bearl, building up a tidy estate for himself.

On 23 April, Northumberland attended the chapter of the Order of the Garter at Greenwich. With him in attendance were the Dukes of Richmond and Norfolk, the Earls of Westmorland, Wiltshire, Sussex, Rutland and Oxford, Lord Sandys and Sir William FitzWilliam; the determination was made to hold the usual Windsor feast on 21 May, with Northumberland taking the king's place. Westmorland was admonished to be present unless he could be excused due to urgent affairs of business. After Mass for the dead the following day, the king, making a survey of the votes, elected Sir Nicholas Carew to the Order 'by reason of his many excellent and glorious exploits', which was greeted by applause.

The following day – the last day of Parliament – the king signed patents for various offices of the Court of Augmentations and his own private 'Act Concerning the Assurance of the Possessions of the Earl of Northumberland to King Henry and His Heirs'. Through this Act it was established that Northumberland, for 'the tender and fervent zeal love and affection he bore to the king for default of issue of his body', wished all his property after his death to 'come unto the king and to his heirs and successors for ever, for the augmentation and increase of his imperial crown'. Clauses stipulated the earl could not alienate any of his property and Thomas Cromwell received an annual fee of £20. There were many provisos: they covered grants and leases he had made (as detailed earlier) to Lord Montague, Sir John Norton, Sir Thomas Percy, Sir Thomas Arundel, Sir Thomas Johnson, Sir William Percy, Sir Thomas Wharton and Sir Reynold Carnaby (and the rest of his family), plus one to cover Christopher Hales for the lands Sir Reynold Carnaby had sold to him. The list goes on as it appears the earl had attempted to ensure all his servants received their annuities, offices and grants: Thomas Kelke, Christopher Wharton, Gilbert Weddell, Nicasius Heron, Henry Whitereason, Stephen Stamforth, William Stapleton and many others.

Other clauses concerned Sir William FitzWilliam, Richard Gresham, Northumberland's nephew Henry Clifford, Sir Humphrey and Robert Ratcliffe and the Marquis of Exeter. A clause safeguarded his mother's jointure and for his wife, if he wished, a jointure of 500 marks. He was empowered to make a will of 'lands, tenements and hereditaments to the clear yearly value of £500 over all charges for term of eight years next after his decease ... where he shall die seized of estate of inheritance in fee simple or fee tail ... for the due payment of debts, legacies, bequests and funeral expenses of the earl after his decease'. He was left power to make certain leases for terms of twenty years or less and to provide rents and grants not to exceed in all the clear yearly sum of £100 (and for the term of their lives only) and to 'by his sufficient writing and deed under his seal and sign manual give and grant all manner of offices and their fees which have been used and accustomed to be exercised and used for offices' as in the time of his father and himself currently.

This same day, whether by the king (who had not signed it) or Cromwell and Audley, two commissions of oyer and terminer (to hear and determine) were sent out, usually issued only after the arrest of a person accused of misprision, treason, rebellion, felonies, murder, homicide, rioting, plotting, insurrection, extortion, oppression, contempt, concealment, ignorance, negligence, falsities, deception, conspiracy or being an accessory. They were to enquire into 'every kind of treason, by whomsoever committed' in the counties of Middlesex and Kent. It seems a wide net was being cast.

On 30 April Mark Smeaton, a court musician, was invited to dine at Cromwell's house in Stepney. Early in the morning of 2 May he arrived at the Tower and was put in irons. He was shortly joined by Henry Norris and in mid-afternoon by Anne's brother, George. About five o'clock in the afternoon, Queen Anne was brought 'in full daylight' to the Tower of London by Norfolk, Chancellor Audley, Cromwell and Sir William Kingston, Constable of the Tower. She fell on her knees at the gate, beseeching God to help her as she was not guilty of what she was accused. Rumours soon spread: she was accused of adultery 'in which she has long continued, with a player on the spinet of her chamber' and Norris had been arrested for 'not revealing the matter'. William Brereton, Sir Francis Weston and Masters Page and Wyatt were also committed to the Tower. At Hampton Court, on the evening of 11 May, Sir William Paulet wrote to Cromwell that Norfolk, although he was Lord High Steward, 'had no knowledge that the indictment was found and asked me whether the parties should proceed to their trial or not. I told him I knew not. As to commissioners he said he knew not how many were required, nor whether they ought to be barons or not so he could not tell whom to name, and if he knew, yet he would name none till he learned the king's pleasure and so he will me to advertise you.'

Wriothesley summarised the dramatic events of Friday 12 May:

> There were arraigned at Westminster, Sir Francis Weston, knight, Mr Henry Norris, Brereton and Mark, being all four of the king's privy chamber and there condemned of high treason against the king for using fornication with Queen Anne, wife to the king, and also for conspiracy of the king's death, and there judged to be hanged, drawn and quartered, their members cut off and burnt before them, their heads cut off and quartered; my Lord Chancellor being the highest Commissioner he giving their judgement ... And the morrow after, being Saturday, 13 May, Master Fitzwilliam, Treasurer of the King's House and Mr Comptroller deposed and broke up the Queen's household at Greenwich and so discharged all her servants of their offices clearly.

During Saturday, Cromwell sent Sir Reynold Carnaby to Northumberland at Newington Green regarding a 'supposed precontract' between him and Queen Anne. The earl wrote to Cromwell that he had not only been 'heretofore examined upon my oath before the Archbishops of Canterbury and York, but also received the blessed sacrament upon the same before the Duke of Norfolk' and others of the king's council who were learned in the spiritual law and he assured Cromwell that 'by the said oath and blessed body which afore I received and hereafter intend to receive, that the same may be to my damnation, if ever there were any contract or promise of marriage between her and me'.

Of the events of Monday 15 May, Wriothesley wrote: 'There was a great scaffold made in the king's hall within the Tower of London, and there were made benches and seats for the lords, my Lord of Norfolk sitting under the cloth of estate ... he holding a long white staff in his hand, and the Earl of Surrey, his son and heir, sitting at his feet before him holding the golden staff' of the duke's office as Earl Marshal of England; Lord Audley sat on his right hand and the Duke of Suffolk on his left, then all the twenty-six peers (out of fifty-three) in their degrees. 'And first the king's commission was read, and then the Constable of the Tower and the Lieutenant of the Tower brought forth the queen to the bar, where was made a chair for her to sit down in.'

According to Crispin, a French gentleman who witnessed the trial, after Anne was seated she had looked at all her judges with a 'cheerful countenance'. Her indictment was read out. She, 'having an excellent quick wit and being a ready speaker, did so answer to all objections, that had the peers given in their verdict according to the expectation of the assembly, she had been acquitted'. Returning to Wriothesley, 'then were twenty-six of the greatest peers there present chosen to pass on her, the Duke of Suffolk being highest, and, after they had communed together, the youngest lord of the said inquest was called first to give verdict, who said guilty, and so every lord and earl after their degrees said guilty to the last and so condemned her'. Except it is likely the Earl of Northumberland did not utter the word, being taken ill and carried out of the chamber. 'Norfolk, bound to proceed according to the verdict of the Peers, condemned her to death, either by being burned within the Tower on the green or beheaded, as his Majesty in his pleasure should think fit.' The court arose and she was returned to her chamber.

Burnet cited Crispin as recording that 'all who saw or heard her, believed her innocent. Both the magistrates of London and several others who were there said they saw no evidence against her.' Chapuys wrote that 'when the sentence was read to her, she received it quite calmly, and said she was prepared to die, but was extremely sorry to hear that others, who were innocent and the king's loyal subjects, should share her fate and die through her'. She ended by begging that some time should be allowed for her to prepare her soul for death. Chapuys continued: 'A few find fault and grumble at the manner in which the proceedings against her have been conducted, and the condemnation of her and the rest, which is generally thought strange enough. People speak variously about the king, and certainly the slander will not cease when they hear of what passed and is passing between him and his new mistress, Jane Seymour...' The public were not impressed that he daily dined with ladies, remaining until after midnight, returning by river with music and singing. Nor were they fooled by his trying to hide his affection for Jane Seymour by lodging her 7 miles away in the house of Sir Nicholas Carew.

Of George's trial Wriothesley wrote, 'Her brother was arraigned for treason which was for knowing the queen, his sister, carnally, most detestable against the law of God and nature, treason to his prince and also for conspiracy of the king's death: Whereunto he made answer so prudently and wisely to all articles laid against him, that marvel it was to hear, and never would confess anything, but made himself as clear as though he had never offended.' In his letter to the emperor, Chapuys was firm on the matter of George:

> No proof of his guilt was produced except that of his having once passed many hours in her company, and other little follies. He answered so well that many who were present at the trial, and heard what he said, had no difficulty in waging two to one that he would be acquitted, the more so that no witnesses were called to give evidence against him, or against her, as is customary in such cases when the accused denies the charge brought against him. I cannot omit another charge in the indictment, namely, that the concubine, his sister, had said to his wife that the King was impotent. This, however, was not read in public; it was given to him in writing, under

> protest that he was only to say yes or no, without reading aloud the accusation; but to the great annoyance of Cromwell and others, George read it out aloud…

On 17 May, the accused men were beheaded at Tower Hill. 'Their bodies with their heads were buried within the Tower of London, Lord Rochford's body and head within the Chapel of the Tower, Mr Weston and Norris in the churchyard in one grave, Mr Brereton and Mark in another grave in the same church yard within the Tower of London. And the same day, in the afternoon, at a solemn court kept at Lambeth, the Lord Archbishop of Canterbury and the doctors of the law' nullified the marriage between Anne and King Henry 'and so she was discharged, and was never lawful Queen of England'. Crispin said of the men that her brother was executed first and 'with him, all the rest suffered a death, which they had no way deserved. Mark Smeaton only confessed he has deserved well to die.' When the queen heard how her brother and the other gentlemen had suffered and had sealed her innocence with their own blood, but that Mark had confessed he deserved to die, she broke out into some passion and said, 'Has he not then cleared me of that public shame he has brought me to?'

Wyatt, being in the Bell Tower, witnessed their executions and wrote his poem '*circa Regna tonat*',* in part of which he says:

> These bloody days have broken my heart.
> My lust, my youth did then depart,
> And blind desire of estate.
> Who hastes to climb seeks to revert.
> Of truth, *circa Regna tonat.*
>
> The Bell Tower showed me such sight
> That in my head sticks day and night.

* '*Circa Regna tonat*' roughly translates to 'thunder rolls around the throne'.

There did I learn out of a grate,
For all favour, glory, or might,
That yet *circa Regna tonat.*

By proof, I say, there did I learn;
Wit helpeth not defence too iron,
Of innocency to plead or prate,
Bear low, therefore, give God the stern,
For sure, *circa Regna tonat.*

Of his friends, Wyatt wrote another poem, giving each an elegy:

In Mourning wise since daily I increase,
Thus should I cloak the cause of all my grief...
The cause is great of all my doleful cheer
For those that were, and now be dead and gone.

Of Anne's brother he wrote:

Some say, 'Rochford, haddest thou been not so proud,
For thy great wit each man would thee bemoan,
Since as it is so, many cry aloud,
It is great loss that thou art dead and gone.'

The poem ends:

And thus farewell each one in hearty wise!
The axe is home, your heads be in the street;
The trickling tears doth fall so from my eyes
I scarce may write, my paper is so wet.
But what can hope when death hath played his part,
Though nature's course will thus lament and moan?
Leave sobs therefore, and every Christian heart
Pray for the souls of those be dead and gone.

About this time Anne is said to have written her own poem:

> Defiled is my name full sore
> Through cruel spite and false report,
> That I may say for evermore,
> Farewell, my joy! Adieu comfort!
> For wrongfully ye judge of me
> Unto my fame a mortal wound,
> Say what ye list, it will not be,
> Ye seek for that can not be found.

Queen Anne was executed on 19 May 1536, a day later than she had expected (the swordsman-executioner of St Omer, summoned on 9 or 10 May, was delayed). A scaffold of four or five steps was set up on the green within the Tower of London, by the great White Tower. Moving gracefully, the queen came out of the Tower around eight o'clock in the morning, accompanied by four ladies. She wore a robe of black damask over a red damask skirt and a netted coif over her hair. She mounted the scaffold, watched by the Mayor of London, aldermen and sheriffs, as well as the Lord Chancellor, Dukes of Richmond and Suffolk, the king's council and earls, lords and nobles present. Queen Anne spoke briefly 'with a goodly smiling countenance':

> Masters, I here humbly submit me to the law as the law hath judged me, and as for mine offences, I here accuse no man, God knoweth them, I remit them to God, beseeching him to have mercy on my soul, and I beseech Jesu save my sovereign and master the King, the most godly, noble and gentle Prince that is, and long to reign over you.

Crispin said she had 'never appeared more beautiful'. With her own hands she removed her hairnet and replaced it with a little linen cap. She knelt down upon both knees, arranging her skirts while one of her ladies covered her eyes with a bandage. They moved a little away. The queen prayed and at her last said, 'To Jesu Christ, I commend my soul.' The executioner smote off her head at a stroke; she was 'not yet twenty-nine years of age'.

Alexander Ales, who was attending on Cromwell at that time, wrote a long time after that, having been unable to sleep in the early hours of 19 May, he had crossed the River Thames at Lambeth and entered the archbishop's garden where he found Cranmer weeping with grief. Later that day, at his lodgings, Ales listened to the talk of the people around him: their verdicts were that it was no new thing for gentlemen of the king's chamber to dance with the ladies and it was customary for young women to write to their near relatives to tell them they had become pregnant and receive their congratulations.

On 20 May, at nine in the morning, Jane Seymour and Henry VIII were betrothed. The king thought it would be kept secret but it was no secret for Chapuys wrote that 'yesterday the king, immediately on receiving news of the decapitation of the *putain* entered his barge and went to the said Seymour, whom he has lodged a mile from him, in a house by the river'.

It soon became widely known that the night before Anne was beheaded she had jested that no one would find it hard to invent a name for her, saying with a laugh they would call her '*la Reine Anne sans tete*'.

16

'LET THEM STRIKE OFF MY HEAD'

Two days after Anne's execution, Northumberland was at Windsor to deputise for the king at the Garter feast. Although he would not have been present at her death, he would have been unable to avoid hearing about it. And possibly while at Windsor there was talk among the peers about her 'good end'. Was this why Northumberland was seized by 'an unseasonable dizziness of the head and a faintness all over his body'? They feared that if he was not present at divine service the rest of the ceremonies could not go ahead. But as always with Henry Percy, duty kicked in and he recovered enough to fulfil his role.

Sir Nicholas Carew, well known for facilitating the king's courtship of Jane Seymour, was duly installed. On 30 May 1536 the king married Jane in the Queen's Closet at York Place. Five days later, Whitsunday, she was proclaimed queen at Greenwich, going in procession after the king with a great train of ladies, her household having been completely assembled by that date. On Whitsun Eve Chapuys had met with Cromwell, who told him that 'he had planned and brought about the whole affair' and ironically went on 'to extol beyond measure the sense, the wit and the courage' of Anne and her brother. Within eight days of his marriage, the king was overheard to say upon seeing two beautiful young ladies that he was 'somewhat sorry that he had not seen them before he was married'.

King Henry and Queen Jane left Greenwich on 7 June, travelling in the royal barge by water to York Place, every lord in his own craft going before them. The ships on the river shot their cannon and four hundred pieces of ordinance were fired from the Tower of London. The tower walls all along the waterside were colourful, with great streamers and banners. The following day, the queen waved the king farewell from the gatehouse as he rode to Westminster with all his lords, including Northumberland, for the opening of Parliament. The earl is listed as attending every session until Parliament closed in mid-July, lodging at Newington Green. Among those things discussed at Parliament, a second Act of Succession barred Anne's daughter, Elizabeth, from the succession; the Bishop of Rome's authority was entirely extinguished; and a subsidy was granted to the king, with Northumberland making the first payment of £25.

During these weeks, Northumberland was kept constantly abreast of occurrences by Sir Cuthbert Ratcliff, who informed him, 'There will not have been better redress since your grandfather was warden.' By return he had ordered him to appoint a day of redress in Liddesdale for 10 July. Northumberland was therefore in London when, on 10 June, Sir Nicholas Carew was appointed steward, receiver and surveyor of the king's manors of Perchnge, Preston, Poynings, Pengeden, Ashcombe, Waldren, Duncton, Sutton, and Chinting in Sussex at an annual rent of £6 13*s* 4*d*, and on 18 June when Thomas, Earl of Wiltshire 'delivered the King's Privy Seal, whereof he was custodian, into the king's hands'. On 29 June Thomas Cromwell was appointed Lord Privy Seal in his place. On 18 July, the newly knighted Sir Thomas Cromwell was appointed High Vicar over the Spirituality under the king and head of all bishops. Three days later, Henry's illegitimate son the Duke of Richmond died at St James's Palace after a long illness. Wriothesley wrote that the duke had never lain with his wife, Mary Howard, and so 'she is maid, wife and now widow'. He was buried at Thetford in Norfolk.

Around this time, John Widdrington wrote to Cromwell complaining Northumberland had appointed his brother Sir Ingram as Constable of Alnwick in place of him 'upon light information' and felt he ought to be reinstated. His request was apparently ignored but it shows Henry had not reinstalled his brother as vice-warden. Northumberland gave out a warrant on 23 July to Hugh Gallond and William Clenell, keepers of College Park in Northumberland, to deliver a buck to Lady Ogle.

On 13 September the earl informed the king that, although he had kindly granted Hexham Abbey to Sir Reynold Carnaby and Newminster Abbey to William Grene (one of the officers of his Court of Augmentations, so the king could have a strong house to safeguard his money), the two men, despite holding the king's letters, had been refused entrance by Sir Oswald Wolsthrope. He requested 'a letter in his favour to the chancellor of the Augmentations' so it could be seen he was not out of the king's favour. At the end of October, a warrant awaiting the king's signature shows an item: 'To the Earl of Northumberland for his costs in coming to London to make assurance of his lands to the king's use £1,000.' No record shows whether this was ever signed or paid.

On 3 October Northumberland wrote to thank Cromwell for his kindness and especially for 'getting the king to give the writer certain gorgeous and sumptuous apparel of his own wearing'. He brought up the abbeys again (which he was to purchase by valuation of the king's officers). As before, one concerned Sir Reynold and Hexham (favoured by Cromwell, as he knew), one concerned Newminster for the royal officer William Grene, and the third concerned Iklington for his physician Dr Wendy. He again mentioned Grene had letters of entry before Wolsthrope, 'whom I never took as my friend', had any interest in Newminster or Shether in Iklington. He trusted Cromwell to provide them with other places, especially as it is openly reported he has them of the king: 'It will be a great discomfort to be disappointed.' Another letter of the same day shows that gaining an audience with Cromwell was now much harder. Northumberland had to write to Wriothesley asking him to aid his servant in gaining access to Cromwell, for once his causes were finished he intended to repair northwards.

After a messenger came to him on 4 October, Northumberland wrote to Cromwell informing him of 'the obstinate and traitorous demeanour of the canons of Hexham'. Commissioners riding towards Hexham Abbey on 28 September received news the monks, barricading themselves in the abbey, were threatening to fire guns and cannon upon them. When they entered the agitated town the common bell had been rung, immediately followed by the monastery bell and the sound of gates being slammed shut. A canon, appearing on the roof, shouted, 'We are all prepared to die before you seize the abbey.' A sub-prior appeared and displayed a writing with the king's Great Seal and said the house, having 'the king's confirmation under his Great Seal, God save his Grace, we think it not to his honour to give forth one seal contrary to another. Afore any of our lands, goods or house be taken from us, we shall all die, and that is our full answer.' The commissioners retired to Corbridge.

A few days earlier, Louth townsfolk had also reacted upon hearing commissioners were heading towards them, having heard rumours church buildings, lands, plate, ornaments, crosses and bells were being seized, many such things having been given by local families. On 1 October, Nicholas Melton, nicknamed Captain Cobbler as he was a shoemaker, seized the keys to the church to stop its ornaments being taken. Indignant citizens banded together and seized lords and gentlemen of the country, forcing them to 'swear upon certain articles'. The day before the Hexham standoff, three thousand men had marched from Louth to Caistor in an attempt to seize the commissioners. Finding they had already fled, Lord Borough's servant was beaten to death, accused of warning his master, and the following day Dr John Raynes, chancellor to the Bishop of Lincoln, lying sick at Bolingbroke, was dragged from his bed and killed.

Chapuys was well informed. He wrote to the emperor on 7 October that the numbers rebelling in the north must be great and increasing, 'for there is not a gentleman of influence whom the king has not ordered to be ready with his power. He has sent for the Duke of Norfolk ... He came hither the day before yesterday from his home to go to Court and today he has dined with the Bishop of Carlisle.' The bishop told Chapuys that he thought Norfolk was happy that Cromwell might be ruined 'and whose head the rebels demand'. Shrewsbury, although lying 'sore crazed' with sickness, managed to rise from his sickbed on 6 October at the king's summons and rode by moonlight to his lodge in Sherwood, sending out summons for gentlemen to muster at Nottingham on 9 October.

In the meantime Robert Aske, a fellow of Grey's Inn, according to his own account, was captured while travelling south for 'the term' in London and in the ensuing days had been appointed the chief captain of the rebels. On the morning of Sunday, 8 October, the alarm bells rang at Beverley. A letter arrived from Robert Aske calling on every loyal man to repair to Westwood Green under the walls of the Grey Friars, a spot of common pasture just outside the walls.

William Stapleton was staying at Beverley, attending his sick brother Christopher, who moved there every summer for the change of air. He had got ready to leave for London when news came 'all Lincolnshire was up from Barton to Lincoln, and the way by Grantham was stopped'. Hearing the tumult outside, Christopher Stapleton insisted on locking and bolting all the doors of his lodging and ordered his household not to stir outside. His wife refused to obey him and mingled with the excitable crowds. Asked the whereabouts of her husband and his brother, she replied, 'They're in the Friars, go pull them out by the heads.' At her return her husband shouted, 'Would you have me, my son and heir and my brother cast away?' She yelled back, 'You should rise for God's quarrel.' When the crowd headed for the green the next day, they gathered outside the Stapleton lodgings, crying out, 'Burn the

Friars, burn them within it,' before breaking in and making them all swear the oath. They took William and his nephew Brian with them when someone shouted that they should let William be their captain. Stapleton attested later that, 'seeing worse would follow if he refused', he consented, thinking he could perhaps help stay the worst of the evil humour abroad.

On 11 October Northumberland sent a letter to Hull from Wressle Castle requesting men to come to his aid for on that day the commons had congregated around the castle and shouted at the gates, 'Thousands for a Percy.' Archbishop Lee, taking his guests with him, fled Cawood Castle to take refuge at Pontefract Castle with Thomas, Lord Darcy.

While William Stapleton with his Lincolnshire host set off for Hull, Aske with his company set off for York. On Saturday 14 October Sir George Lawson (sick in bed) and William Harington, Mayor of York, wrote to King Henry for aid as the rebels were coming towards them. Further north, Kateryn Clifford, Lady Scrope wrote from Bolton Castle to her father informing him rebels were forcing gentlemen to join them and that one band had been ordered to seize her husband and little boy, but her husband was making his way as fast as he could to join the earl at Skipton while she had sent 'her little boy with his nurse unto one poor man's house, to be kept privy there'.

At York, Aske's host mustered outside the city gates on Sunday, risen to twenty thousand strong and all arrayed in good order; four thousand or five thousand were horsemen, the rest servants and well-to-do yeomen and burgesses. Aske requested 'a free passage through the city at their peril'. Negotiations for a peaceful entry were conducted and, by proclamation, the 'army of pilgrims', as Aske had relabelled them, were told to pay for everything honestly. Only horsemen were allowed entrance, and they were to pay 2*d* a meal; no despoiling nor injury of any kind would be allowed. The prices of food and horsemeat had been set and declared to both army and citizens.

At five o'clock in the afternoon of 16 October Aske, at the head of the horsemen, entered the city in state. He dismounted at the Minster for Evensong, and before entering he posted an order on its doors instructing religious persons to re-enter their houses and do divine service. After the service, he went to lodge with Lawson. Some of those in York threatened to burn down the treasurer's house as it bore Cromwell's arms. Meanwhile Thomas Maunsell, captain of the commons of Selby, given news his brother was in peril for refusing to take the oath in York, hastened to the city. Having told Aske he would get his brother to swear, he was kicked out of his brother's house but nevertheless told Aske his brother had sworn. In his later deposition, Maunsell recounted the Earl of Northumberland had sent for him to 'take him because he would be taken with no villains' and, more credibly at Doncaster, one William Dale had come to him to obtain safe-conduct for the sick earl to pass through the Commons to reach Topcliffe. He said he had granted permission but this was unlikely as Northumberland remained under watch at Wressle.

Aske left with a small party on 18 October for Pontefract. The main body started shortly afterwards for it reached Pontefract three days later. Sir Thomas Percy and Sir Oswald Wolsthrope passed through York on 20 October, people greeting him affectionately and remarking on 'how gorgeously he rode through York with feathers trimmed'. According to his vague account, Sir Thomas Percy was at Seamer visiting his mother and had heard rumours they were up in Lincolnshire, which was confirmed within three days when Stringer brought a female deer from the earl to his mother. Stringer told him Aske had stirred up the commons at Wressle. He waited a day or two and then, dressing in a servant's coat and leading his horse, he tried to steal away. On his way towards Pickering he met William Percey of Ryton, who asked him if he knew the whereabouts of Sir Thomas Percy, who was being watched for; if not found, his mother would be left without a penny. He then returned to Seamer where men came to swear to him. He was first ordered to York, but it was taken; then to Hull, which was taken. He was then instructed to go to Pontefract, where he arrived with four thousand or five thousand men.

At Pontefract, Lord Darcy received two letters on 16 or 17 October: one from King Henry expressing his surprise at Lord Darcy shutting himself up in the castle rather than raising a force to deal with the situation; the other from Shrewsbury to tell him he was at Newark. On 18 October Shrewsbury wrote from Southwell to Suffolk at Lincoln with the news Yorkshire rebels had arrived in Doncaster the previous day and sworn mayor and citizens. He had been unable to deliver the king's letters to Lord Darcy as such a close watch was kept about Pontefract Castle, and the Earl of Northumberland was taken. On the afternoon of Thursday 19 October, Aske sent a message to Lord Darcy asking him to deliver the castle. Parley agreed upon, Darcy, Archbishop Lee and others came out before the gate, where Aske lectured them: the spiritual lords for not doing their duty and allowing abuses to occur and the temporal lords for not informing the king of the poverty in the north parts of his realm and how the abbeys offered relief to the commons.

At Hull on Friday, the gates were opened after the citizens were threatened with their windmills being burnt down and flaming tar barrels being sailed down the river to set the shipping on fire. As Stapleton was in the midst of drawing up articles of their grievances to be sent to Suffolk (with a request he be a petitioner for them), to be taken to him by William Worme and another, there arrived 'a post from Aske from Pontefract, saying my Lord Steward was about to give him battle. We were amazed…' On Saturday, another letter informed them Pontefract Castle was taken and later they 'heard how Sir Thomas Percy and Sir Nicholas Fairfax, with the abbot of St Mary's, had gone towards Pontefract with a goodly band' of four thousand or five thousand men. Their company was ordered to be at Pontefract by nine o'clock in the morning.

Meanwhile, in Northumberland, Sir Ingram had instructed all loyal men to be present at Alnwick on Sunday, 22 October at eleven in the morning to do service to the king for the common weal and for the safeguarding of the Marches. He then convinced the Abbot of Alnwick and others to go to his brother at Wressle to tell him he was true to the king and, if restored to the office of vice-warden, was ready to repress any disturbance. The earl believed Sir Ingram's professions and said that if he came for the patents he would be made warden, sheriff and lieutenant. Unfortunately, it was all a ruse: Ingram had taken the pilgrims' oath.

As soon as the gentlemen assembled at Alnwick, Sir Ingram locked them inside and forced them to take the oath, electing Sir Humphrey Lisle as his deputy warden. Immediately, with a band of men, he attacked the lands of Sir Reynold Carnaby and the houses of anyone suspected of hiding him. At Adderstone he confronted Thomas Forster, brother of Dorothy, Sir Reynold's wife. Finding neither man nor goods he swore 'by God's heart he would be revenged on Sir Reynold'. Asked by Forster what offence he intended to revenge, he snarled, 'Sir Reynold hath been the destruction of all our blood for by his means the king shall be my brother's heir.'

Sir Ingram was prevented from attacking Sir Thomas Grey's house at Newstead but he took possession of North Charlton, for the use of his brother Sir Thomas. Edward Bradforth, Sir Reynold's steward, refused to give up his master's rents and he was captured by force by eighteen of Sir Ingram's servants as he walked between his church and his house. Taken to Alnwick, he was 'laid in the stocks two nights and a day' and imprisoned three days longer. Sir Reynold's father had gained safety in Langley Castle, held by Northumberland's own men.

In mid-October the capital buzzed with rumours. The main bruit was that Sir Thomas Percy's forces had grown six-fold to 'join the commons in revenge for the wrong the king had done in denying his right to be declared heir to the earldom'. The host did, in fact, number nigh-on thirty thousand men. It was divided into three wards: Sir Thomas Percy led the van; Darcy and Sir Richard

Tempest the middle; and Aske among others led the rearward. By 26 October the pilgrim army arrived at Scawsby Leys, near Doncaster, to meet with Norfolk as had been agreed. Two days of discussion led to the duke agreeing to give a safe-conduct for Sir Ralph Ellerker and Robert Bowes to take the rebels' petition personally to the king, upon which the 'pilgrims' agreed to return home, their leaders to reassemble at a later date at Doncaster after the petitioners had returned.

The Earls of Shrewsbury, Rutland and Huntingdon arrived at Doncaster and wrote to the Earl of Derby that they, with Norfolk, had 'stayed the commons of Yorkshire and every man is sparpled and retired home' – except at Craven, where Cumberland was still trapped in Skipton Castle. Finding the castle impregnable, the attackers threatened to go to Bolton Castle to capture Eleanor, Lady Clifford, then visiting with her young son, and Lady Kateryn, 'to violate and enforce them with knaves'. That night, Christopher Aske (brother of Robert), with the help of only a groom and a boy, crept over the moors to bring the ladies safely and secretly into Skipton Castle.

After staying overnight at York on Sunday 29 October, Aske rode next morning to Wressle Castle with the stated intention of seeing Northumberland 'to have agreed him and his brother Sir Thomas'. The sick earl resolutely refused to have anything to do with his brother. Aske offered to get the earl's two coffers from London, seized by the commons at Snaith, sent on. A bill listed the contents as 'a gown, a doublet of crimson satin and the rest of small value'. (Aske may have been told to keep them; he attested the earl had made a gift of them to him for saving him from the commons.) Stymied, Aske returned to York. On Tuesday, All Hallows' Eve, he dined with Sir Thomas Percy (no doubt reiterating his complaints against his brother) at St Mary's Abbey.

William Stapleton, hearing they were going to ride to Wressle, asked to accompany them as he was repairing to his master 'as was his duty'. They rode off without him. When Stapleton reached the castle, Aske was with the earl haranguing him to make Sir Thomas lieutenant of one march and Sir Ingram lieutenant of the other. Northumberland point-blank refused. While Aske departed to the bedchamber he was sharing with Sir Thomas, the earl had William admitted into his bedchamber, and at sight of him the earl fell weeping, 'wishing himself out of the world', which William found 'sore to see'. Upon returning the following morning after Mass, Stapleton found Aske at 'his labours again' but found the earl in the same mind.

'Seeing what danger' the earl was in, William reported he was half-angry with him, 'for it was openly said in the field, "Strike off the head of the earl, and make Sir Thomas earl."' He told Henry that Sir Thomas Hilton, asking where he was, had said insultingly, 'He is now crept into a corner and dare not show himself, he hath made many knaves gentlemen to whom he had disposed much of his living and all now to nought himself.' William said he asked him to make a public appearance, after which he could 'sit still without further danger', but the earl was firm against the commons and for the king. Every time, over the next few days, William warned the earl of the danger he was in, he would simply reply that he did not care: 'I should die but once; let them strike off my head and rid me of much pain.'

On Sunday 5 November, Shrewsbury sent his chaplain John Moreton from Wingfield to Wressle. He told King Henry later that, hearing Northumberland was sick and in danger, he had sent a letter to the earl to learn the state of the country. It was not the friendliest of letters: 'I trust you do not forget your promise to my son Francis and Mr. Holmes that I should have 200 marks a year for my lady your wife ... She has been with me two years past on Our Lady Day the Nativity last and I have received nothing but the stuff your Lordship sent her.' He further demanded that 300 marks be immediately given to the bearer. The chaplain almost reached Wressle, but Aske's men intercepted him and took him to Templehurst, where Aske was visiting with Lord Darcy.

Aske arranged for Northumberland to be moved to York, possibly so he could be attended to by his physician, Stephen Thomason, one of the loyal royalists in York. It appears Northumberland and Aske lodged first at Selby Abbey where the earl, importuned by Aske, eventually signed a bill allowing Aske to lie at Wressle in his absence. Another bill would have made Sir Thomas lieutenant of one of the marches, but he did not sign it. Aske wrote from Selby to Watton Abbey for a spice plate of the earl's they held as pledge. At the prior's refusal, he wrote again on 10 November saying he 'had the Earl of Northumberland's writing under sign manual' and if they have the spice plate they should send it to him by the bearer – if they did not want their house spoiled. (It appears from Aske's interrogation in 1537 that the spice plate gift, which he said was given at the earl's desire, appeared on the bill Aske had got the earl to sign regarding Wressle.)

Aske then retired to Hull while Sir Thomas returned first to Seamer (and then north) and William Stapleton returned home to Wighill. Northumberland was at the Walmgate manor in York, still kept under watch. On 1 December, Suffolk wrote from Lincoln to the king that a messenger had arrived from the Earl of Northumberland with the 'enclosed ring as a token. The earl is kept so that he cannot write,' he said, but he added he did not 'put much faith in his message'. On 4 December, the Privy Council wrote to Norfolk in reply to his letters from Welbeck that the king would write as he advised to summon the Earl of Northumberland, 'if nothing chance to him in the mean season, and Norfolk will doubtless see that his brethren do no displeasure'.

Sometime in November, Sir Ingram visited his brother at York. He told him he would only take up the office of vice-warden if he was paid 700 marks and would only take up the lieutenancy in exchange for 100 marks. Quite possibly the earl had by now been given word of recent events, and he promptly discharged his brother of all offices held of him now and in the future. In front of the earl's servants, Sir Ingram 'spoke to his brother such malicious words as were abominable to any true man to hear, and specially touching my Lord Cromwell', wishing he could be hanged high and that he was present so he could put 'his sword in his belly'. Northumberland appointed Robert, Lord Ogle vice warden, and Sir Roger Grey and Sir John Widdrington lieutenants – all three were friends of Carnaby.

On 5 December, three hundred pilgrims rode to Doncaster, forty of them designated to meet with Norfolk on the following day. Norfolk told them the king agreed to give them a general pardon, the abbeys would be allowed to stand (at least until a parliament was convened at York), and their articles would be reviewed by him. The general pardon was proclaimed on 9 December, applying to all offences made before 10 December. Aske was given an invite to court for Christmas at Greenwich and issued with a safe-conduct valid until 5 January. On 13 December, Darcy wrote from Templehurst to Shrewsbury that open forays were being made by Sir Ingram Percy against the Greys and their friends and that Northumberland intended to go thither. In his next letter, five days later, he wrote asking him to give credence to his son Dawnay regarding news of Northumberland and his son Sir George Darcy. On Christmas Day, Northumberland wrote from Topcliffe to Cromwell of the 'love he had among his own tenants' and that his cousin Darcy was going to the king for they had so 'confettered together that if there had been a foughten field, the king would have proved their true hearts'. Northumberland, looking after his Yorkshire tenants, offered them twenty-one-year leases without raising them, the effect of which would be to stop them paying any 'gressums'* until their lease end (which also later deprived the king of any entry fines).

* A gressum is a fee paid upon the beginning of a new lease.

17

'FINALLY TO RESIGN AND SURRENDER'

During January 1537, Aske returned to Yorkshire and proudly declared to all and sundry that the king intended to hold a parliament at York and a convocation for 'ordering of the faith', with the Duke of Norfolk soon to bring up the orders under the king's Great Seal. Sir Francis Bigod told him he was deceived 'by a colour of a pardon' which was merely a proclamation; Norfolk, he warned, was coming to destroy them all.

Planning to provoke the commons into further rebellion, Bigod plotted with John Hallam. The latter was to enter Hull on 16 January on market day, and with him small groups of men hiding their weapons under farmers' smocks. But the people of Hull were on the alert. Realising his men were exposed, Hallam attempted to escape but turned back to assist one of his companions and was dragged through the gates by his horse bridle just before they were shut. Alderman John Elland smote him with his dagger but could not pierce his 'coat of fence' (rosined folds of linen cloth); then his horse, having its rein cut, ran into the ditch. Hallam and Elland fought, wounding each other, and finally Hallam was taken prisoner.

At Beverley, on the same day, eight hundred men were rounded up as they entered at dawn. Sir Francis, however, managed to escape. Henry VIII wrote to the Mayor of Hull, his letter arriving on 23 January, that in their examinations they should use 'all kinds of torture to get at the truth' and he 'was sending the Duke of Norfolk ... to administer justice and to reside amongst you'. Once they had obtained all the names and information they could, they were to execute and hang those guilty of rebellion 'in chains in open places near the town for example'.

Northumberland appointed Lord Ogle to hold a Warden Court at Morpeth in January but his letters were intercepted by Sir Ingram. Sir Thomas issued a proclamation promising redress for grievances 'so that poor men could not tell to whom to sue for justice'. Fearing trouble, Lord Ogle deferred the court and on 18 January he and Sir John Widdrington sent out counter-proclamations forbidding any assemblies and complained to Sir Reynold. King Henry ordered Sir Anthony Browne to travel to the Marches, ostensibly to oversee justice on the borders but secretly to fathom men's minds and seek out the authors of the late rebellion – with especial regard to the Percy brothers. The king had sent Ingram and Thomas Percy summons to come to his presence and issued orders to arrest them and ship them to Grimsby if they refused. Norfolk wrote to the Privy Council on 2 February from Doncaster that they had come to him that night and thought 'they will be found of better sort than the council has been informed by my lord their brother'.

On 3 February, Shrewsbury wrote to Cromwell thanking him for getting the king to send Dr Buttes to him in his illness and said he heard the Earl of Northumberland was in London and desired him be a good lord to his daughter (the earl's wife), 'who has been with her father two years from Christmas last and has received nothing of the 200 marks promised yearly by her husband for her maintenance ... and asks that he help the lady to obtain a reasonable living from her husband'.

In London Northumberland was stripped of his office of warden, although at the end of the month he might have been pleased by the news the king intended to elect his brother-in-law Cumberland a Knight of the Garter 'for his many glorious and loyal actions ...

very lately at the breaking out of the tumult of rebellion in the quarters where he lived' (although he was no longer to be Warden of the West Marches).

On 6 February, John Hussey reported to Lord Lisle that 'George, Lord Lumley's son and heir and Sir Thomas Percy are in the Tower'. Two days later, George Lumley confessed he had heard Bigod say 'Sir Thomas Percy was the lock, key and wards of this matter'; that the commons would not have risen for any but him and he had twice been proclaimed 'Lord Percy' during the first insurrection, and they showed 'more affection for him than for any other'. The subprior of Watton confessed that in order to save their goods they had sent horses to Sir Thomas Percy, William Hotham, John Hallam and William Courser, and that Robert Aske 'had of them by threats a spice plate of silver which was a pledge of the earl of Northumberland's'.

Bigod was captured by Sir John Lamplugh in Cumberland on 11 February, escorted to Carlisle Castle and warded. On 24 February, Norfolk wrote that since he had arrived at Carlisle six thousand offenders had submitted 'as humbly as could be, and if ropes enough had been found would have come with the same about their necks'. With the council and gentlemen of those parts he chose 'seventy-four as principal offenders' and sentenced them to suffer death by martial law; 'had he proceeded by jury, [he] thinks not the fifth man of them would have suffered; for they say I came out for fear of my life, or for fear of burning of my houses and destroying of my wife and children, etc'. On the following day he suppressed Hexham Abbey while the people quietly watched.

Bigod had written to Countess Katheryne asking her to send her son, Sir Thomas, to him and he would put him in possession of Northumberland's lands. As a consequence, she was moved into the custody of Sir Brian Hastings at his house near Doncaster, and on 27 February he sent an inventory of her goods to Cromwell which comprised 'very little, victuals for her household, plate to the value of £100 or more ... few jewels and clothes as any woman of honour can have'. On 5 March Norfolk wrote to Cromwell that he had put

Sir Reynold Carnaby in possession of Prudhoe and Lady Percy, on her way to Cromwell, was bringing the inventory of her husband's goods, which by indenture had been returned to her. He wrote she was a good woman and had obeyed Norfolk in all things.

Norfolk, continuing to interfere in Percy matters, wrote to Cromwell in the letter he sent asking how many people the king wished executed at York: 'The Earl of Northumberland has sent down to sell as much wood in Yorkshire as may,' he wrote, and being that it was 'as good to pull down the houses as destroy the woods', he was putting a stay to it. He wrote to the earl's servants William Tomson and Henry Smythe, forbidding them in the king's name to meddle with the earl's woods.

On 22 March, Norfolk wrote from York to Cromwell that he had invited Aske to ride with him: 'The man is marvellous glorious, often time boasting to me that he has such sure espial that nothing can be done nor imagined against the king', but he found most people abhor him and 'impute to him the whole beginning of the mischief'. Regarding Sir Thomas Percy, he appears to have had a change of heart for he writes that if he and Aske never returned to Yorkshire, 'I think neither true nor honest men will be sorry thereof, nor in likewise for my lord Darcy nor Sir Robert Constable ... nevertheless he cannot find that the said lord or Sir Robert had stirred any new business, but that they did their best to stay the last commotion.' (As had Robert Aske.) By 7 April, Darcy, Constable and Aske had been committed to the Tower, and arrest warrants were on the way for Sir Stephen Hamerton and Nicholas Tempest.

Northumberland wrote to Cromwell 'in great perplexity' on 30 March from Newington Green, desiring his intercession to obtain his arrears of salary for the wardenry, amounting to £300, so he could pay his deputies their fees and 'although he is discharged of the office he trusts the king will remember his poor service'. (And this is probably why he was trying to sell his wood.) He wrote again to Cromwell on 28 April regarding Dr Wendy's promised compensation of demesnes of Royston in place of Iklington which had not yet been executed.

There is a note in the interrogation of Aske, which took place during April, that because the Earl of Northumberland had granted 'Robert Aske, captain', his castle of Wressle with the rule of his tenants 'during such time as the said Aske shall lie therein garrison', and as he also gave him by 'the same bill' his spice plate at Watton Abbey, 'the earl committed high treason'. This did not take into account that Aske may have bent the truth, as he had in other instances.

On 29 April, Northumberland wrote he was 'grieved' at hearing from Dr Wendy via Cromwell that it could be thought he 'should in the time of rebellion lend Robert Aske my house of Wressle and recognise him captain of the baronage. He came to the earl, at Selby, who put his hand to a bill drawn up by him granting him his house of Wressle to lie in ... so he might be safely conveyed from the danger of the commons, and especially, to get his evidences out of Wressle Castle for the King's use.' He had, he said, been afraid Aske and his brother would take those evidences. He had caused servants Henry Smythe and William Key to convey them out of the castle at midnight, and 'they are now here ready for delivery to the king'. He further protested that although Aske pressed him to make his brother lieutenant of one of the marches under his rule and left a bill for his signature, he had 'refused and had never named him captain in any bill but Cousin Aske. He caused Aske to void the castle at Christmas and sent Henry Smyth and others to destroy his victuals there.'

On receiving a message via Wriothesley, Northumberland wrote to Cromwell on 2 May that he was 'content to go through with the king for possession of all his lands' and begged him 'to secure him such recompense as may be to his comfort'. Norfolk, at Sheriff Hutton, wrote a postscript in his letter to Cromwell of 10 May that he had heard a rumour that 'Northumberland daily gives away houses and the brick of Wressle and other things, so that unless remedy be applied it will be greatly decayed when it comes to the King's hands.' On 11 May Northumberland thanked Cromwell for his comfortable letters, enclosing a bill of articles by his kinsman Dr Cave and his attorney 'of which he desires good expedition'.

Northumberland did not see his brother-in-law installed at the Windsor Garter feast held on 13 May, presumably because he was too ill to travel. And he was in some agitation that Dr Wendy still had no access to the demesne lands of Royston in place of Iklington, writing on 16 May to Cromwell that despite 'labours made to the officers of the Court of Augmentations he cannot have his lease and further suits are expected to be made to the king to his hindrance'. He thinks the king 'is not so good lord to him as he trusted, if his servant is thus treated'. And although he would have allowed the doctor to attend on Cromwell, he himself is 'so diseased he cannot forbear him' and requested Cromwell 'to help him to the king's house of Hackney whereby he may the sooner recover his health'.

On the same day, Sir Thomas Percy and others were arraigned at Westminster, indicted of high treason and sentenced to be hanged drawn and quartered by a jury of knights.

> On 25 May, Friday in Whitsun week, Sir John Bulmer and Sir Stephen Hamerton were hanged and headed; Nicholas Tempest, Dr Cockerell, Abbot of Fountains and Dr Pickering were drawn from the Tower of London to Tyburn and hanged, bowelled and quartered with the heads set on London Bridge and several London gates. Margaret Cheney, Bulmer's wife so-called, was drawn after them from the Tower into Smithfield and burned. Being 'a very fair creature, and beautiful' as was remarked by the crowds.

On 30 May, Northumberland, allowed to move to Hackney Manor but worn down by king and Cromwell, wrote he 'regrets he is accused of delaying to go through with the king for possession of his lands in the North, which he has always been ready to do and has articled petitions in that behalf to the king' and had asked Dr Cave to attend daily on Cromwell to learn the king's pleasure. The Wriothesley Chronicle recorded: 'The second day of June, being Saturday after Trinity Sunday, Sir Thomas Percy, knight and brother to the Earl of

Northumberland, was drawn from the Tower of London to Tyburn and there hanged and beheaded.' His head was set on London Bridge and his body was buried at the Crutched Friars beside the Tower.

Next day, Northumberland, world-weary and grieving (for disliking a brother does not preclude loving him), wrote to Cromwell on 3 June that

> ... where before this time of mine own free will, I have offered to the king to surrender and yield up into his hands all my poor inheritance upon the performance of diverse articles signed with my hand ... and where also I have not so frankly and freely resigned the same unto his Majesty, ... I thought good therefore most heartily to desire your lordship to be mean unto his Majesty for me in that behalf; ... that I, relinquishing all my said requests contained in the said articles, do and am content finally to resign and surrender, yield up, and give unto his Majesty all mine estate, possibility and interest of and in all my said inheritance ... And that it may please his Majesty to consider the service of my poor servants, that they may enjoy such fees, annuities and leases as I have given unto them, in part of recompense of the diligent service done unto me. Trusting and so desiring your lordship to make relation unto the king of this mine humble submission.

The letter was taken by Dr Legh with a 'declaration of my lord's lands with rents, profits of courts wards etc' which totalled £3,876.

It can be hoped the earl gained some pleasure from the knowledge that Sir Thomas Wharton, whose career he had encouraged, was appointed the king's deputy warden of the West Marches at this time.

On 29 June, Richard Layton wrote to Cromwell of Northumberland's plight:

> It may please your Lordship to be advertised that this St Peter's Day at four of the clock at afternoon I went to see the Earl of

> Northumberland, being sent for five days past to have come unto him, and supposing to have found him sick, as I was wont, I found him *languens in extremis*, very desirous to have spoken to me, but it would not be. His sight begun to fail, proffer he could not one perfect word, his stomach swollen so great as I never see none, his face, breast, stomach, all his body as yellow as saffron; his memory as yet good and understanding whatever is said unto him, but speak he cannot. I told him for his comfort that you sent me to see him, and that ... your lordship willed him to be of good comfort, and that you would help to speed all his affairs with the king, now at your going to the court: And I comforted him before his servants in your lordship's name the best I could: But the truth is, I suppose, he cannot live fourteen hours. This three weeks he had no money but by borrowing, as his servants declared to me. He has made your lordship and [Edward Foxe, secretary to Cardinal Wolsey 1520–27] the Bishop of Hereford his executors, and the king his supervisor. I read his Will which meseemeth is of small treasure. I thought it to be my duty to advertise your lordship of the premises, supposing that he will be dead before this letter comes unto your hands. From London This Saint Peter's Day, at night, by your lordship's most bounden to command. Richard Layton, priest.

Henry lingered until between two and three in the morning of 30 June 1537, when he breathed his last. As he was buried on the day he died, the arrangements must already have been in place, only waiting for the sick man to die. With little space between his dying and interment, the king did not allow him the usual aristocratic funeral. His body was bowelled, tramelled (packed with herbs and spices), cered (wrapped in waxcloth) and leaded (placed in a lead-lined coffin). His corpse then remained in the house at Hackney. At the appointed time he was to be carried to the parish church, his coffin preceded by two ushers in black coats and staves, then the cross with four orders of friars.

In pairs, clerks and priests followed the friars. Only twenty poor men in black gowns and hoods followed, each bearing a torch in single rank. The earl's standard was carried by his officer, the elderly William Dale, wearing his long gown and hood. He was followed by eight gentlemen on foot, two by two, wearing black, hoods on their shoulders; among them were his auditor Thomas Edgore, Henry Sadler and London merchant Richard Gresham, who possessed two of the earl's manors. His two chaplains, Errington and Cuthbert Ogle, followed in the procession and in place of all the household officers were four overseers: Dr Thomas Legh, Dr Francis Cave, the earl's friend William Stapleton and Cromwell's receiver Henry Polstead. William Fawcett, who had fought alongside Henry on the borders just as an ancestor of his had once fought with the first earl, followed them bearing the banner of the Percy arms.

Northumberland's helm and crest was carried by Bluemantle Pursuivant; Lancaster Herald bore the earl's shield (and perhaps his sword) and Carlisle Herald the earl's coat of arms. Garter King of Arms gave order. (All four wore the king's coat of arms and not the earl's.) They preceded the hearse, which was garnished with bannerolls, sixty escutcheons and around seventy inescutcheons; the coffin was covered in black velvet with a white satin cross, carried by four yeomen with four gentlemen assistants. There does not appear to have been a cloth of estate. Surrounding them were twelve yeomen in black coats (one of them William Carnaby), each bearing a staff torch. At each corner of the hearse a banner was borne by a gentleman, two of whom were Cuthbert and Lionel Carnaby. Three banners were of the Trinity, Our Lady and St George; in the place of any saint favoured by the earl (perhaps St Blaise), the fourth represented the king.

Next, walking alone, was the chief mourner: Lord James Butler, son of the Earl of Ossory, who happened to be in London. He was followed by six 'day' mourners: Thomas, Lord Borough (who was distantly related to the Percy family as his great-grandmother was Elizabeth Percy, a great-granddaughter to the first Earl of

Northumberland); Ralph Sadler (clerk to Cromwell and son of Henry, living in Hackney); Sir Anthony Wingfield (a member of the Privy Council); John Gostwick (treasurer of first fruits and tenths); Richard Grenewaye (keeper and bailiff of Hackney manor for the king); and Cromwell's nephew Richard. All worked for Cromwell. After them came the yeomen grooms and other servants, dressed in black, followed by twenty torches singly, and in this order they proceeded to the church.

At the church, the dirge was done and the overseers saw the corpse buried. The drinking of the void took place in a convenient spot outside the church and afterwards all departed for the night. The next morning they reassembled and repaired in order to the church. Between seven and eight in the morning the Mass of Our Lady was performed, and then certain mourners offered the Mass penny. This was followed by the Mass of the Trinity and then the Requiem Mass, with other divine services executed by the Bishop of St Asaph, supported by two abbots. Next came the offering where the earl's sword, shield, coat, helmet, crest, standard and banner were offered, set up by the officers of arms in the church after dinner. The sermon and dole followed. After the ceremony, the chief mourner and the others, in degree, went to dinner.

Afterwards...

Just before he died, Northumberland's debts (annotated by himself and Stapleton) had been compiled, some of the items dating from the previous summer. It was calculated that he owed £1,689 5*s* 5½*d*. A simple breakdown shows the household food bill, including butter, spices (excluding some sent to Topcliffe at a cost of £16 10*s*) and flour came to £185 9*d*; beer and ale cost £29 6*s*; charcoal from Roger Whitereason 6*s* 8*d*; tallow £7 7*s* 10*d*; and wax £1 5*s* 8*d*. He paid 14*s* to David Capper's wife for washing. The apothecary costs came to £6 5*s* 4*d*. For lodging his and his servant's horses he paid £39 11*s* 11*d*; hire of beds and kitchen stuff cost £8 3*s* 6*d*; arrears of wages was £130 for northern officers. There was a £40 debt of his father's; silks for £72 (part of which was 'sent to my lady'); £34 9¾*d* to the skinner for fur of black jennet laid in purple (an old debt), and £13 14*s* 6*d* for shoes, slippers and buskins – these last three items were said to be spoiled by Aske. There were other oddments: to Skut, the queen's tailor, £5 7*s* 4*d*; to goldsmith Lawrence Warren for a flower of diamonds, £20; the last debt listed was 'to my lady his wife for her living, behind two and a half years at Easter last 500 marks'. Loans came to just above £600.

As for the other major players in Percy's world, seventy-year-old Lord Darcy was beheaded at Tower Hill on 30 June. Robert Aske was hanged in chains at York, where the king said 'he was in his greatest and most frantic glory'. Norfolk, still in the north, wrote to Cromwell on 3 July from the earl's house at Leconfield that he was arranging for Sir Thomas Percy's children to be removed from Prudhoe and confirmed on 8 July that the children were in Sir Thomas Tempest's custody. In a letter dated 20 July, Norfolk reported he had had 'sent for such goods as remained at Topcliffe, but they are of little value and not one good cartload'; the rest, going towards London, had been 'arrested by Sir William Fairfax for the earl's debt to the king [of £82], Sir William being so charged when he was sheriff'. How much more could the king wrest from the deceased earl?

On 5 August at Windsor, according to the Anstis Register, a chapter of the Order of the Garter was held in the king's closet. In Lord Darcy's stead, Sir Thomas Cromwell was chosen, but on the death of Northumberland there is no mention except 'that the other stall, then also vacant, should be reserved for the prince they then seasonable hoped for'.

Either at the end of 1537 or beginning of 1538, Sir Ingram Percy was released from the Beauchamp Tower (a carving he made can still be seen: '*Saro Fideli* (I will be faithful), Inggram Percy 1537'). He remained in London, possibly ill from his incarceration, for his will was dated 7 June 1538 in which he identifies his host as David Capper's wife, to whom he left 20*s*. He bequeathed £20 to his natural daughter Isabel, with the use thereof by his mother until she was of lawful age, while Isabel's mother received 20 nobles. He desired his servants to have their wages and one-quarter wages on top if his goods would extend so far, leaving a list of his servants and bequests. Lastly, to the Lord Mayor of London, he left instructions he was to 'have a bonnet of velvet with aglets of gold, and my lady my mother a tablet of gold'. He was buried in St Anne and St Agnes Churchyard in Gresham Street.

In the autumn of 1537, Shrewsbury had pestered Cromwell with regard to 'Mary's living' and begged him to intercede 'for his daughter, the widow of the late Earl of Northumberland, who is entitled to the third part of his lands, that she may have licence to sue for her dower'. She was granted an audience with the king at Greenwich on Monday 15 May 1538, which was described by an eyewitness. My Lady of Northumberland exhibited her bill unto the king with the words, 'I beseech your Majesty be good and gracious lord unto me, being a poor widow and wife to the late Earl of Northumberland, which has not had, nor yet has, any living of such lands as were my late husband's; wherefore I beseech your Majesty, of your most abundant goodness to tender this my humble suit.'

After listening courteously to her, his Grace bowed down upon his staff unto her and said, 'Madam, how can your ladyship desire any living of your husband's lands, seeing your father gave no money to your husband in marriage with your ladyship, or what think you that I should do herein?'

She answered, 'What shall please your Grace.'

He replied, 'Madame, I marvel greatly that my lord your father, being so great wise a man as he was, would see no direction taken in this matter in his time; howbeit Madam we will be contented to refer the matter unto our council.'

Mary did later receive a grant of abbey lands for her maintenance, upon which she lived until she died on 16 April 1572. He father died on 26 July 1538 at Wingfield Manor, aged seventy, and was laid to rest in the Shrewsbury Chapel in Sheffield Church (now cathedral), as was Mary when she died.

The earl's sister Margaret, Countess of Cumberland died in 1540, so his mother Countess Katheryne, who died in 1542, outlived all her children. She was buried – as she wished – without pomp on 9 November at the side of her husband in Beverley Minster. In her will she bequeathed to her chaplain, Robert Gell, for singing and saying Mass yearly for her soul, her husband's and all her friends' souls, her 'farmholde of Wilberfosse (lately purchased from Whitereason)' to go to her granddaughter Isabel after he died, who also was gifted, towards her marriage, a plain double-gilt standing cup with cover, goblet with cover, two silver pots, the best gilt salt gilt with cover, a gold spoon, another featuring St Katheryne, a silver basin with cover, a cup of assay with a crescent, a long silver spoon for sucket,* a long silver fork for sucket, a silver chalice, two silver cruets, a silver sacring bell gilt, a silver pyx and other church ornaments, vestments and psalter, three pieces of new arras with the Story of Venus, three piece of Alexander's story, a painted red-and-yellow hanging with a border of the Passion, a bed of down with a bolster, two feather beds with bolsters, a bedcovering of taffeta with 'tapis of gold and a tester of the same', four curtains of tawny sarcenet, a bed covering with birds and beasts on it, a pair of fustian blankets, a russet velvet cushion, a long carpet for a long bed, and other carpets and cloths.

To her other granddaughter, Mary (daughter of Sir Thomas), who had married Sir Francis Slingsby, she left all her other plate and household stuff: a standing cup, goblets, a cup of assay with a crescent on the bottom, her second salt gilt with cover, a spoon with an acorn and silver spoons, her great silver cross with Our Lady and St John with a foot of silver and gilt to set the cross in over the altar, a silver sacring bell with other church ornaments and vestments, a hanging of red and green say painted with a border of the Birth of Christ, a plain green hanging with a border of antique work, two feather beds with bolsters, a pair of fustian blankets, two velvet cushions (one blue and one black), two carpets, two cushions with pomegranates and two cushions with flower on them.

* A popular confectionery made of dried fruit in thick, spiced syrup.

She bequeathed to Lady Elizabeth Clifford and Lady Conyers, her sister, a ring of gold each by which to remember and pray for her; as for her grandsons, she left two silver candlesticks to Thomas and 'a standing cup gilt, with a cover, and graven' to his brother Henry. Her gentlewomen were bequeathed the horses they rode, with saddles and trappers and various clothes and wages. Anything left over was to be given to her granddaughter Isabel, whom she made her full executrix, instructing, for the 'confidence and trust' she put in them, Stephen Tempest of Broughton and his wife Anne to look after Isabel, especially as she was to marry their son, Henry (which she did in 1544). The countess had also outlived Henry Clifford, Earl of Cumberland, who had died in April 1542. His son was made the countess's executor for 'the confidence she had in him' in aiding Isabel, 'being but young and ignorant of knowledge', and for his pains she left him a 'silver cross all gilt, to set on an altar'.

The earldom of Northumberland was granted by Queen Mary in 1557 to Sir Thomas Percy's eldest son, Thomas. Queen Elizabeth, when she succeeded Mary, distrusted the seventh earl. He was encouraged to live at Petworth enjoying his 'hawks, hounds and horses'. Becoming resentful, Thomas espoused the cause of the imprisoned Mary Queen of Scots and fomented an unsuccessful rebellion in the north, for which he was executed on 22 August 1572 in York marketplace, where he declared, 'I am a Percy in life and death.' As his only son and heir, Thomas, had predeceased him, the title devolved onto his brother Henry.

Despite his conspicuous loyalty in the northern rebellion, the eighth earl was twice accused of being complicit in escape plots to free Queen Mary during 1572 and 1582, spending time imprisoned in the Tower of London. He was again arrested and lodged in the Tower in December 1584 after inviting Charles Paget, a known agent of Queen Mary, to Petworth. He protested his innocence, saying he merely wished to personally thank Paget for his kindness to his eldest son, Henry, when he lay desperately ill in Paris. On 21 June 1585 he was found dead in his cell, apparently shot through the heart. The official verdict was suicide; rumour that it was murder.

Henry, the ninth earl, was interested in history and sciences including alchemy and astrology. He purchased a crystal globe and amused his friends by casting their horoscopes, earning the nickname 'the Wizard Earl'. In 1595, he married Dorothy Devereux. The marriage was punctuated by bitter quarrels and periods of separation. Although a Protestant who had fought with Leicester in the Low Country Wars and had supported the accession of James I, he numbered many Catholics among his friends. His tolerant outlook found him accused in 1605 of being complicit in the 5 November Gunpowder Plot. One of the plotters was his kinsman, Thomas Percy, grandson of Joscelin (younger brother of the fifth earl).

After committal to the Tower on 27 November the earl was tried in June 1606 and found guilty of 'serious offences' against the king. Given in evidence were two letters he had written to tenants not to pay their rents to Thomas Percy but not ordering his apprehension. He was sentenced to life imprisonment in the Tower, and did not regain his liberty until July 1621. He retired to Petworth with his books and scientific apparatus and died there of smallpox on 5 November 1632.

His eldest son, Algernon, became the tenth earl. Having served at sea with distinction, in 1636 King Charles appointed him Admiral of the Fleet. He informed the king the navy was ill equipped and the sailors unskilled, and advised that sick bays should be provided on warships for the ill and wounded, which was dismissed as a 'new-fangled idea'. For his open opposition to the king's policies, he was removed from office in June 1642. Two years later his son and heir, Josceline, was born. Publicly opposing the king's execution in 1649, the tenth earl retired from public life. He saw the birth of his grandson Henry just before he died in October 1668, but Henry lived only a few months and died in 1669.

The following year, on 31 May 1670, Josceline, the eleventh earl, died of fever in Turin. He was twenty-five. When news of his death reached his pregnant wife, she miscarried. The earldom was extinct.

BIBLIOGRAPHY

Alexander, J. J., *Early Owners of Torbryan Manor* (The Devonshire Association, 1936)

Anstis, J., *The Register of the Most Noble Order of the Garter* (London: John Barber, 1724)

Arnold, Revd F. H., *Notes from Petworth: A Sketch of Its History and Antiquities* (Petworth: A. J. Bryant, 1864)

Bates, C. J., *The History of Northumberland* (London: Elliot Stock, 1895)

Bean, J. M. W., *The Estates of the Percy Family 1416–1537* (Oxford University Press, 1958)

Beauvois, M. E., *Un Agent Politique de Charles-Quint le Bourguignon Claude Bouton Seigneur de Corberon* (Paris: Ernest Leroux, 1882)

Bergenroth, G. A. (ed.), *Calendar of State Papers, Spain* (London, 1862)

van den Bergh, L. P. C., *Correspondance de Marguerite d'Autriche* (Leiden, 1845)

Bernard, G. W. (ed.), *The Tudor Nobility: Henry Percy, sixth earl of Northumberland, and the fall of the House of Percy, 1527-1537 by R. W. Hoyle* (Manchester University Press, 1992)

Bernard, G. W., *The Power of the Early Tudor Nobility: A Study of the Fourth and Fifth Earls of Shrewsbury* (Sussex: The Harvester Press, 1985)

Bourdeille, P. de, *The Book of the Ladies* (New York: P F Collier & Son, 1899)

Brears, P., *Cooking and Dining in Medieval England* (Devon: Prospect Books, 2008)

Brenan, G., *A History of the House of Percy* (London: Freemantle & Co, 1902)

Breverton, T., *Henry VII: The Maligned Tudor King* (Stroud: Amberley Publishing, 2019)

Brewer, J. S., and W. Bullen (eds), *Calendar of the Carew Manuscripts: preserved in the Archiepiscopal Library at Lambeth 1515-1574, Volume I* (London, 1867)

Broce, G., and R. M. Wunderli, 'The Funeral of Henry Percy, Sixth Earl of Northumberland', *Albion: A Quarterly Journal Concerned with British Studies*, vol. 22, no. 2 (1990)

Brockbank, J. L., *The East Riding of Yorkshire* (Oxford: Clarendon Press, 1913)

Brown, R. (ed.), *Calendar of State Papers Relating to English Affairs in the Archives of Venice* (London, 1873–1890)

Bush, M., *The Pilgrimage of Grace* (Manchester University Press, 1996)

Cavendish, G., *The Life and Death of Cardinal Wolsey* (Boston and New York: Houghton Mifflin and Company, 1905)

Clay, Sir C. T. (ed.), *Early Yorkshire Charters Vol XI: The Percy Fee* (Wakefield, 1963)

Cox, J. D., and D. S. Kastan, *A New History of Early English Drama* (Columbia University Press, 1997)

Davies, R., *York Records of the Fifteenth Century* (Gloucester, 1976)

Dawes, M. C. B., and J. B. W. Chapman, *Inquisitions Post Mortem: Volume 12, Edward III* (London, 1938) [accessed online: www.british-history.ac.uk/inquis-post-mortem/vol12/pp221-232, 21 October 2024]

Dickens, A. G. (ed.), *Clifford Letters of the Sixteenth Century* (London and Durham: Bernard Quaritch and Andrews & Co., 1962)

Dodds, M. H., and R. Dodds, *The Pilgrimage of Grace 1536–1537* (Cambridge University Press, 1915)

Dodieu, C., *Relation de ce qui fut negotié, en l'au 1525, avec Henri VIII, roy d'Angleterre, et le cardinal d'York...* (Misdated and should read 1527) [accessed online: https://gallica.bnf.fr/ark:/12148/btv1b54100543m, April 2025]

Drake, F., *Eboracum: Or the History and Antiquities of the City of York* (London, 1736)

Dyce, Revd A., *The Poetical Works of John Skelton* (Boston: Little Brown and Company, 1856)

Eden, W. A., M. P. G. Draper, W. F. Grimes, and A. Williams, *Survey of London Volume 28* (London, 1960) [accessed online: https://www.british-history.ac.uk/survey-london/vol28, May 2025]

Edwards, A. S. G., 'A Verse Chronicle of the House of Percy', *Studies in Philology*, vol. 105, no. 2 (2008) pp. 226–244 [accessed online: www.jstor.org/stable/20454317, 17 August 2024]

Ellis, Sir H., *Original Letters Illustrative of English History, Third Series Vol. III* (London: Richard Bentley, 1846)

Ellis, H. (ed.), *The New Chronicles of England and France by Robert Fabyan* (London: 1811)

Ellis, Sir H., *Three Books of Polydore Vergil's English History* (London: John Bowyer Nichols and Son, 1844)

Fisher, E., *The Lordship of Leconfield: Some Yorkshire Estates of the Percies 1450-1650 vol. 1* (unpublished PhD thesis, University of Leeds, 1954)

Fisher, E., *The Lordship of Wressel: Some Yorkshire Estates of the Percies 1450-1650 vol.* 2 (unpublished PhD thesis, University of Leeds, 1954)

Fonblanque, E. B. de, *Annals of the House of Percy* (London: Richard Clay & Sons, 1887)

Friedmann, P., *Anne Boleyn: A Chapter of English History 1527-1535, Volume I* (London: MacMillan and Co, 1884; reprint ed. J. Wilkinson, Stroud: Amberley Publishing, 2013)

Gairdner, J. (ed.), *Letters and Papers Illustrative of the Reigns of Richard III and Henry VII* (London: Longman, Green, Longman and Roberts, 1861–3)

Gairdner, J. (ed.), *The Paston Letters, Volumes I-VI* (London: Chatto & Windus, 1904)

Galt, J., *The Life and Administration of Cardinal Wolsey* (Edinburgh: Oliver & Boyd, 1824)

Gillespie, A., '"These proverbs yet do last": Lydgate, the Fifth Earl of Northumberland, and Tudor Miscellanies from Print to Manuscript', *Yearbook of English Studies*, vol. 33 (2003)

Glay, M. le, *Correspondance de l'Empereur Maximilien Ier et de Marguerite d'Autriche* (Paris, 1839)

Goldsmid, E. (ed.), *The Maner of the Tryumphe of Caleys and Bulleyn and the Noble Triumphaunt Coronacyon of Quene Anne printed by Wynkyn de Worde 1532-1533* (Edinburgh, 1884)

Grafton, R., *Grafton's Chronicle: History of England 1189 to 1558, Vol II* (London, 1809)

Grose, F., and T. Astle, *The Antiquarian Repertory Vol. IV* (London: Edward Jeffery, 1809)

Hamilton, W. D. (ed.), *A Chronicle of England during the Reigns of the Tudors from 1485 to 1559 by Charles Wriothesley, Windsor Herald* (London: J. B. Nichols and Sons for Camden Society, 1875)

Harris, B. J., *Edward Stafford, third duke of Buckingham, 1478-1521* (Redwood City: Stanford University Press, 1986)

Hartshorne, Revd C. H., *Feudal and Military Antiquities of Northumberland and the Scottish Borders* (London: Bell and Daldy, 1858)

Harvey, N. L., *Thomas, Cardinal Wolsey* (London: Collier Macmillan, 1980)

Hay, D. (ed.), *The Anglica Historia of Polydore Vergil* (London, 1950)

H. M. Commission, *State Papers Volume I: King Henry the Eighth Parts I and II* (London, 1831)

H. M. Commission, *State Papers Volumes IV and V: King Henry the Eighth Part IV* (London: George Eyre and Andrew Spottiswoode, 1836)

H. M. S. O., *Calendar of the Close Rolls of Edward II 1307-1318* (London: Eyre and Spottiswoode, 1892/3)

H. M. S. O., *Calendar of the Patent Rolls of Edward I 1281-1292* (London: Eyre and Spottiswoode, 1893)

H. M. S. O., *Calendar of the Patent Rolls of Edward II 1307-1313* (London: Eyre and Spottiswoode, 1894)

H. M. S. O., *Calendar of the Close Rolls of Edward III 1374-1377* (London, 1913)

H. M. S. O., *Calendar of the Close Rolls of Richard II 1377 to 1392* (London, 1914–1922)

H. M. S. O., *Calendar of the Close Rolls of Edward IV 1461 to 1468* (London, 1949)

H. M. S. O., *Calendar of the Close Rolls of Henry VII, vols 1 and 2 1485-1509* (London, 1955 and 1963)

Historical Manuscripts Commission, *Report on the Manuscripts of the Corporation of Beverley* (London, 1900)

Historical Manuscripts Commission, *The Manuscripts of his Grace the Duke of Rutland* (London, 1911)

Howard, G., *Wolsey the Cardinal and His Times* (London, 1824)

Hoyle, R. W. (ed.), *Camden Miscellany XXXI* (Camden Fourth Series, vol. 44) (London: Royal Historical Society, 1992)

Institute of Historical Research, *Victoria County History: A History of the County of York – the City of York* (London, 1961–1974)

James, M. E., *A Tudor Magnate and the Tudor State: Henry Fifth Earl of Northumberland* (York: St Anthony's Press, 1966)

Jerdan, W. (ed.), *Rutland Papers: Original Documents Illustrative of the Courts and Times of Henry VII and Henry VIII* (London: John Bowyer Nichols and Son, 1842)

Jones, M. D., *The Paston Letters* (Cambridge University Press, 1922)
Kirby, J. (ed.), *The Plumpton Letters and Papers* (Cambridge University Press, 1996)
Knights, J.-M., *The Plantagenet Socialite* (Stroud: Amberley Publishing, 2023)
Lancashire, I., *Orders for Twelfth Day and Night* circa *1515 in the Second Northumberland Household Book* (University of Chicago Press, 1980)
Leland, J., *De Rebus Britannicis Collectanea, Volume* 4 (London, 1770)
Lewycky, N., *Serving God and King: Cardinal Thomas Wolsey's Patronage Networks and Early Tudor Government 1514–1529* (York University of York, 2008)
Lodge, E., *Illustrations of British History, volume I* (second edn; London: John Chidley, 1838)
Luders, A., *et al.* (eds), *The Statues of the Realm, Volume the Third* (London: Dawsons of Pall Mall, 1817, reprinted 1963)
Lysons, D., *The Environs of London, Volume the Second* (London, 1795)
Matusiak, K., *Wolsey: The Life of King Henry VIII's Cardinal* (Gloucester: The History Press, 2016)
Maxwell, Sir H., *The Chronicle of Lanercost 1272-1346* (Glasgow: James Maclehose and Sons, 1913)
Merriman, R. B., *Life and Letters of Thomas Cromwell, Volume I* (Oxford: Clarendon Press, 1902, reprinted 1968)
Mertes, K., *The English Noble Household 1250-1600* (Oxford: Basil Blackwell Ltd, 1988)
Miller, H., *Henry VIII and the English Nobility* (Oxford: Basil Blackwell Ltd, 1989)
Nichols, J. G., *The Chronicle of Calais in the Reigns of Henry VII and Henry VIII to the Year 1540* (London: J. B. Nichols and Son, 1846)
Nichols, J. G. (ed.), *Narratives of the Days of the Reformation from the MS of John Foxe* (London, 1859)
Norton, E., *Margaret Beaufort: Mother of the Tudor Dynasty* (Stroud: Amberley Publishing, 2010)
Northumberland County History Committee, *A History of Northumberland Volumes I-XI* (Newcastle-upon-Tyne: Andrew Reid & Co. Ltd, 1893–1922)
Oliver, G., *The History and Antiquities of the Town and Minster of Beverley* (Beverley, 1829)
Percy, T. (ed.), *The Regulations and Establishment of the Household of Henry Algernon Percy, the fifth Earl of Northumberland, at his castles*

of Wresill and Lekinfield in Yorkshire, begun Anno Domini MCXII (London, 1770)

Poulson, G., *Beverlac: The Antiquities and History of the Town of Beverley* (London, 1829)

Raine, A. (ed.), *York Civic Records 1475 to 1548* (York: The Yorkshire Archaeological Society, 1939–1945)

Raphael, B., *A Time of Transition from Wolsey to Cromwell* (University of Central Florida, 2011)

Rawlinson, K., *The English Household Chapel,* c. *1100–*c. *1500: an institutional study* (E-theses online, Durham University, 2008)

Richardson, S., and E. Dennison, *Garden and other Earthworks, South of Wressle Castle, Wressle, East Yorkshire* (Castle Studies Trust, 2019)

Richardson, W. C., *History of the Court of Augmentations 1536-1554* (Louisiana State University Press, 1961)

Ross, J., 'Alienated Outsider or Integrated Courtier? Edward Stafford, Third Duke of Buckingham, 1498-1521 and the Royal Court', *History*, vol. 108 (London, 2023)

Russell, J. G., *The Field of Cloth of Gold: Men and Manners in 1520* (London: Routledge & Kegan Paul, 1969)

Selden Society, *Select Cases before the King's Council in the Star Chamber* (London: Barnard Quaritch, 1903)

Singer, S. W., *The Life of Cardinal Wolsey by George Cavendish* (London, 1827)

Society of Antiquaries, *Archaeologia: or Miscellaneous Tracts relating to Antiquity Volume VI* (London, 1779)

Society of Antiquaries, *Archaeologia Aeliana: or Miscellaneous Tracts relating to Antiquity volumes 4 and 6* (Newcastle-upon Tyne: Emerson Charnley, 1860 and 1861)

Society of Antiquaries of London, *Archaeologia: or Miscellaneous Tracts Relating to Antiquity volume XX: including an Account of the First Battle of St Albans from a contemporary Manuscript* (London, 1824)

Society of Antiquaries of London, *Archaeologia: or Miscellaneous Tracts Relating to Antiquity volume XXVI: including Remembrances for the Apparel, Accoutrements and Necessaries of Henry Algernon Percy, Earl of Northumberland and his Retinue... 1513* (London: J B Nichols and Son, 1836)

Society of Antiquaries of London, *Archaeologia: or Miscellaneous Tracts Relating to Antiquity volume XXXIII* (London, 1849)

Steele, R. (ed.), *Kings' Letters* (London: Alexander Moring Limited, 1904)

Stevenson, Revd J., *Church Historians of England Vol IV Part 1 containing various chronicles including those of John and Richard of Hexham, Holyrood and Melrose* (London: Seeleys, 1856)

Stevenson, Revd J., *The Life of Jane Dormer, Duchess of Feria by Henry Clifford* (London: Burns and Oates, 1887)

Surtees Society, *Testamenta Eboracensia or Wills Registered at York... from the Year 1300 downwards, Part I* (London: J. B. Nichols and Son, 1836)

Surtees Society, *Testamenta Eboracensia: A Selection of Wills from the Registry at York, Volumes III and VI* (Durham: Andrews & Co., 1865 and 1902)

Surtees, W. E., *A Sketch of the Male Descendants of Josceline de Louvaine, the Second House of Percy, Earls of Northumberland, Barons Percy, etc* (Newcastle-upon-Tyne: M. A. Richardson 1844)

Tate, G., *The History of the Borough, Castle and Barony of Alnwick* (Alnwick: Henry Hunter Blair, 1868–1869)

Thorstad, A. M., *Living in an Early Tudor Castle: Households, Display and Space 1485–1547* (Yorkshire: University of Leeds, 2015)

Tyrrell, J., *The General History of England* (London, 1704)

Westfall, S. R., *Patrons and Performance: Early Tudor Household Revels* (Oxford: Clarendon Press, 1990)

Whibley, C. (ed.), *The Triumphant Reigne of Kyng Henry the VIII by Edward Hall* (London: T. C. & E. C. Jack, 1904)

Williams, Dr A., and Prof. G. H. Martin (eds), *Domesday Book* (London: Penguin, 2002)

Woolgar, C. M., *The Great Household in Late Medieval England* (London: Yale University Press, 1999)

Yorkshire Archaeological and Topographical Association, *The Yorkshire Journal Volumes III and XI* (London: Bradbury, Agnew and Co., 1882 and 1891)

Yorkshire Archaeological Society, *Yorkshire Archaeological Journal Vol. XXXIII* (Leeds: John Whitehead and Son Ltd, 1938)